THE OHNO BOOK

a SERIOUS GUIDE *to* IRREVERENT TYPE DESIGN

JAMES EDMONDSON

PA PRESS

PRINCETON ARCHITECTURAL PRESS · NEW YORK

Published by
Princeton Architectural Press
A division of Chronicle Books LLC
70 West 36th Street
New York, NY 10018
papress.com

Printed and bound in China
28 27 26 25 4 3 2 1 First edition

Library of Congress Cataloging-in-Publication Data
Names: Edmondson, James (Type designer), author.
Title: The Ohno book : a serious guide to irreverent type design / James Edmondson. Description: New York : Princeton Architectural Press, 2025.
Summary: "James Edmondson of OH no Type Co. provides type specimens, process sketches, and advice in an exuberant memoir and handbook for graphic designers and typographers" -Provided by publisher.
Identifiers: LCCN 2024056456 | ISBN 9781797234199 (hardcover) | ISBN 9781797234205 (ebook)
Subjects: LCSH: Edmondson, James (Type designer) | Type designers-United States-Biography. | Type and type-founding. | Graphic design (Typography) | LCGFT: Autobiographies.
Classification: LCC Z250.A2 E36 2025 | DDC 744.4/5092 [B]-dc23/eng/20250120 LC record available at https://lccn.loc.gov/2024056456

Editor: Allison Serrell
Design: James Edmondson and PA Press
Layout and typesetting: Natalie Snodgrass

Most body text set in Degular Text
Many headlines set in Forevs

additional text set in Polymath, Forevs, Olde, Usj, Ohno Backslant, Gantry, Done, Degular Mono, Regrets, Casserole, Ohno Casual, Ohno Softie, Retail, Irregardless, Swear, Digestive, Degular , Cheee, Ohno Fatface, Obviously, Vulf Sans, Covik Sans Mono, Ohno Blazeface Italic, Coniferous, Eckmannpsych, Beastly, Covik Sans, Ohno Blazeface, Vulf Mono, Hobeaux Rococeaux, and Hobeaux.

OH NO TYPE COMPANY
DEATH TO WEAK FONTS
Ohno

Dear Loretta and PJ,

I don't want you to save any of my stuff when I'm dead. If you want to, go ahead, but I put this book together so you could have one thing that encapsulates my career. I don't want to burden you with possessions, or anything else.

By the time you're old enough to read and understand this dedication, the typefaces we've made at Ohno will have paid for countless meals you've eaten, trips you've taken, and any number of LEGO sets, craft supplies, princess dresses, and cracked iPad screens. I'm proud of the work we've made, but giving me the time to witness you grow up has been the best thing Ohno has ever done.

You had a tremendous effect on this business and my creative output. Before you were born, I thought being a parent would mean getting interrupted, losing focus, and spreading myself too thin among my responsibilities. And I was right! But eventually it led to me asking for help, getting support, and entering a new era. You've made me grow up, get better, and become less selfish and more patient.

It would be amazing if you went to art school. I would love for you to have an interest in design, making things with your hands, and creating beauty in the world. I get so excited when I think about having things in common with the adult versions of you. But the truth is, I just want you to enjoy life. I don't care about your résumé or your profession or how traditionally educated you want to be. I care most about how you treat others and how you treat yourself.

Forever grateful to be your father, and forever holding you in my heart,

Papa

FOREWORD

by Rob Stenson

It's hard to believe this foreword begins on a narrow street in Singapore in 2016, but that's precisely when and where—on our honeymoon—my wife and I were walking among the low-rise shophouses of Ann Siang Road when we came across a gigantic sign printed on an awning.

It read, simply, "CHICKEN," in a font I identified as Hobo.

I stopped to take a photo of the sign with my phone (probably something you've done if you've picked up this book), and then I paused for a moment to appreciate the huge letters. My wife paused too, to find out if the chicken was good. A few months earlier I might not have stopped, but recently—while looking for fonts to use for table numbers at our wedding reception—I'd come across a bizarre font called Hobeaux Rococeaux by a foundry I'd never heard of, OH no Type Co. The shapes had stopped me in my tracks. *Could letters really be so full of life? Was that legal?*

Like many others at the time, my typographic vision had narrowed to rectilinear grotesques and geometrics, the kinds of characters that sat in Barcelona chairs in well-tailored suits. But this font and its close relation—a slightly more conventional Hobo revival named Hobeaux—seemed more like the kinds of characters who reclined in Pratone grass chairs and danced in Nudie suits. Completely themselves. Completely alive. The kinds of fonts that make you think, *Less is a bore*.

I had to know more.

Then I saw that the foundry had a YouTube channel. I went to watch the videos.

The second one I clicked on was a time lapse of the type designer drawing a script face in RoboFont. The soundtrack was a song by my friend's band, Vulfpeck. I thought that was funny, so I sent a link to my friend to see if he also thought it was funny, but I don't think he clicked the link. A few weeks later, at my bachelor party, I made it a point to show him the video, and yes, Jack did think it was very funny. Also, he thought the font was very cool.

"Who is this guy?" he asked me.

"I have no idea," I replied.

In the years since first finding out about Ohno, I've had the great fortune of getting to know its founder, James Edmondson, as a friend and collaborator. True, I think anyone who's ever selected an Ohno font from a drop-down menu has felt—at least for a moment, at least on some level—that OH no Type Co. was their close personal friend and collaborator. The fonts are just that nice. That inviting. That fun.

Every time I get an email from Ohno announcing a new release, it's like a bolt of lightning—a new font that I could never have expected, drawn with Ohno's unmistakable wit and undeniable technique. A font that's happy to see me. Happy to be here. Ready to go.

As an untrained designer who first absorbed Gary Hustwit's documentary film *Helvetica* as an impressionable eighteen-year-old, for a long time I was under the impression that type designers were deadly serious people who sat motionless in front of large computer displays in rooms full of type catalogs on shelves that stretched to the vanishing point.

Now that I've met a number of type designers, I know they're not—for the most part—quite like that.

But James *really* isn't like that. While he has spent at least ten thousand hours in front of a monitor at a desk, I know he'd be much happier building the shelves rather than filling them with books.

After all, his influences aren't in the library. They're on the street: vinyl letters peeling off glass; single-brushstroke capitals fading on stucco walls; horizontally compressed headlines on neon flyers tacked to telephone poles. But he and the Ohno team don't just take from the world. They distill what they see. They reimagine those analog inventions as digital jumping-off points. A painted sign on a wall is a done deal, but a font is never an end in itself. It's clothing on a hanger. And when you try on an Ohno font in front of a mirror, you and your text feel instantly transformed.

↑
Author's note: Among the many collaborations I've had with Rob over the years, I always enjoy the opportunity to hand-letter a new Goodhertz logo. Art direction by Rob Stenson.

That's something my friend Jack Stratton understands: the power of a good font when you've got something to say. He was the guy at the bachelor party that I forced to watch the Ohno video. He leads a band called Vulfpeck.

A few days after seeing the video, Jack sent an email to James with a laconic opening sentence—*i've been thinking about a vulf font*—that has led to a years long, totally unprecedented collaboration between type foundry and musical outfit. They bonded quickly over their mutual appreciation of funky music and 12-point Light Italic (a font for the IBM Selectric typewriter).

I was still on my honeymoon when James replied to Jack with the first sketches of what would become Vulf Mono. Jack then forwarded me the sketches. He said he didn't want to interrupt my trip, but he couldn't believe how good they were. I had to see them, he insisted. I was floored.

And then I was out walking in Singapore, looking up at all the signs on Ann Siang Road. It's an incredible place to look at signage. Sleek skyscrapers tower above the pastel shophouses, and the shophouse tenants are always changing, unless they aren't. The old and the new are in constant conversation, and they converse in many languages. Writing systems from all over the world elbow each other for space on the same signs.

But sometimes the signs are in just one language, or just one font. Sometimes the signs are just a single English word.

CHICKEN.

If you go looking for that sign, I'm afraid you'll be disappointed. I've consulted Google Street View, and the sign is now gone. In fact, it was there for only a little while. In 2015, the first floor of that shophouse was a French restaurant with a neon sign. In 2018, it was an Indonesian restaurant with a sign set in Arial. But in 2016—there it is! A Thai restaurant called Bird Bird. A glorious sign with big, bold, yellow letters.

Had I not stumbled upon Hobeaux and its Rococeaux a few weeks earlier, I might never have stopped there on the sidewalk to take a picture. I've always been more of a person influenced by the indoors, someone more likely to fill the shelves with books rather than build them. A deadly serious person, at least according to some.

But something changed in me when I first met those Ohno fonts. My vision had been recalibrated by the immense joy of Ohno's happy-to-be-here letterforms. And they weren't just happy. They were as crisp as the canon.

When I got back from my honeymoon, I sent James a picture of the chicken sign, thinking he might get a kick out of it, that it might be something he'd add to his Hobo Tumblr (theywentwithhobo.tumblr.com). But what he wrote back knocked me off my feet: The font on that sign wasn't Hobo at all.

The font on the sign was Hobeaux.

And it turned out that James's type design grad school friend Mark De Winne designed that sign above the chicken shop. Which means that, halfway around the world, only one year into Ohno's existence, I'd happened upon an Ohno-in-the-wild. I don't think there's all that much meaning in that coincidence, not really. But there is something funny about it. Ohno's work had inspired me to take a closer look at the world, and then when I went to take a closer look, I found more Ohno.

It's an increasingly common feeling. Isn't that Obviously on this box of cereal? Isn't that Cheee on this sticker on the lamppost? Isn't that Eckmannpsych on that orange camouflage hat?

Just last weekend I stopped into Vroman's in Pasadena to look at the architecture books, and there was Covik Sans, lovely in a small setting on the cover of a book about tropical modernism. This morning my daughter flipped over *The New Yorker*, and there was Hobeaux.

The fonts smile at me. I always smile back.

Rob Stenson
Monrovia, California
August 2024

INTRODUCTION

Who Am I?

The majority of my life has been juxtaposed against the heartbreaking backdrop of my brother George's failing mental health. At twenty, he had his first psychotic episode and dropped out of college. Our family watched his bipolar disorder keep an unrelentingly cruel grip over every aspect of his life. Over time, his addictions got the best of him, and his erratic behavior consistently landed him in the county jail. On September 27, 2022, just three days out of jail, he overdosed on fentanyl and passed away. This is the great tragedy of my life.

Seeing my brother's downward spiral had me looking for something I could control. Luckily type design was there when I needed it—and has been ever since. It has paired well with my proclivity toward working alone, a fondness for selling things on the internet, and a desire to provide for my family through an infinite creative practice.

↑
James and Loretta Edmondson, 2020.

My innate attraction to letters is hard to explain. When I was about eight, my family lived by two grocery stores: Lucky and Vons. Lucky's logotype had a beautiful, upright script, while that of Vons featured plain capitals in slightly tracked-out Univers Bold Condensed. Lucky was the obvious winner here (duh!), and I vividly remember preferring it as a tiny kid. In my mind, certain logotypes signified a good vibe and a mark of higher quality. Whether it was Fender guitars, Coca-Cola, or LEGO, all my preferences had a basis in typography. I thought only the best companies were allowed to have the best logos. I was certain some government agency was in charge.

↑ My childhood in a nutshell: calligraphy pens, a Fun Meter, construction paper lettering, and wine tasting on the Central Coast.

As a kid, I spent most of my free time playing with LEGO, skateboarding, and building miniature skate ramps out of cereal boxes for Tech Decks. Classic little kid stuff! Lettering came into play in middle school when I just wanted to doodle my name in wannabe graffiti styles. In an effort to earn some money for a Squier P Bass, I designed an order form where customers could fill in their name, select the graffiti style they wanted it rendered in, choose colors, lighting, and dimensional effects, and pay me to hand-letter it for them. I had absolutely zero clients, and that was the beginning of disappointing sales for my expressive typography!

My father taught high school English and was extremely indulgent with school supplies. One day at OfficeMax, I picked up a pack of Sanford felt-tipped calligraphy pens that came with an instruction sheet. This was an absolute marvel to me. Watching contrast flow out of the pen was mesmerizing. I couldn't understand why no one had told me about the wonders of calligraphy.

Initially, I was not interested in design because it could be a job—I just intrinsically liked it the way kids like anything. My first real paycheck came from scooping ice cream. I absolutely hated it and hated my boss. (You suck, Greg!) After a while, I became so annoyed by customers that I asked to stay in the back washing dishes. I saved up enough money, bought a computer from Costco, and taught myself Photoshop.

I tended to scoop really big for the kids that looked like they'd enjoy it. My boss called me out one day and sternly warned, "You're scooping really big right now, James." It was then that I realized my days in the ice cream business had come to an end.

Twenties

Luckily, my pirated copy of Adobe Photoshop ushered in my next gig. My brother Paul had started an early web business that helped real estate agents show up in Google searches, and he hired me to make little graphics with their headshot and contact information. He paid me twenty dollars for each graphic, which was more money than I could wrap my head around. I was rich! I continued working for Paul well into my twenties; through those jobs, I cut my teeth as a graphic designer, learned HTML and CSS, and spent more time than any designer ever should in Microsoft PowerPoint.

Fontstruct, a popular website around that time, allowed you to build simple fonts using modular tiles. I made a couple but got frustrated with the limited shapes. I was comfortable with the pen tool, but font software at that time wasn't super accessible.

I had dropped out of my first college and was living in San Francisco when a friend of a friend saw that I was getting more interested in graphic design and suggested that I apply to California College of the Arts (CCA), where she was studying. Sight unseen, I applied, got accepted with a "portfolio" of undercooked Fontstruct fonts, and showed up for class. On the first day of school, I spotted a kid wearing a fake fur coat and smoking a cigarette from a long, old-fashioned cigarette holder. He looked exactly like Cruella de Vil! Despite having a disturbing bout with nervous diarrhea that day, I knew I was in the right place.

My first typography teacher was Angie Wang, and she was absolutely perfect. Angie was stylish, professional, kind, and genuinely passionate about typography and craft. We made type specimens, created our own analog typefaces, wrote about design every week, and learned how to set a paragraph. I would leave her class unable to keep from smiling. I was learning exactly the stuff I'd hoped to learn from the best possible person. (Years later, Angie encouraged me to write a book.)

I had many other wonderful teachers at CCA, including Bob Aufuldish, Backwards Man, Barron Storey, Christopher Simmons, Eric Heiman, Brett MacFadden, Scott Thorpe, David Asari, Michael Vanderbyl, and Dennis Crowe. Not only were they excellent at covering concepts but they were people I wanted to be around as well as great designers. I tried to follow Corita Kent's advice of going to absolutely every event, lecture, and field trip I could.

During my undergrad years, a new pay-what-you-want type distributor launched called Lost Type. Riley Cran was at the helm, and he generously hosted my first attempts at type design. These fonts helped a great deal with my tuition, so the mistakes in them are just barely palatable.

Through reading the design blogs that were extremely popular at the time, I learned about TypeMedia, a one-year graduate program in type design at the Royal Academy of Art in The Hague. Essentially

↑ (top)
The first typefaces I released between 2011 and 2012.

↑ (bottom)
Early sketches for my first released typeface, Wisdom Script. This project, despite being completely amateur hour in every way, taught me that type design could be a viable career.

↑
The Ohno launch party, August 28, 2015. Even my folks were there.

Hogwarts for type designers, this school combined foundational calligraphy, stone carving, creating revival and original typefaces, and coding in a way that seemed tailored to exactly my interests. From the moment I discovered that the school, I wanted to be there.

I was coming out of screen-printing class in Oakland when I read the email that I'd been accepted. That drive over the Bay Bridge was euphoric! I called my family to let them know I'd be moving to the Netherlands for a year.

My time in The Hague was tough. Culturally, the Netherlands wasn't so different from San Francisco, but being away from my family and friends turned out to be harder than I expected. School was challenging, and our little cohort of about eight students was giving it absolutely everything we had. Grad school was a great time for me to look around the room and realize I was far from the best student, but I was interested in stuff that no one else seemed to care about, like the typeface Hobo.

Graduating was absolute bliss. No more school forever! Unfortunately, there aren't too many jobs in type design, so coming back to San Francisco with nothing to my name except an esoteric art degree meant I had only one option: go my own way.

The History of Ohno

In between occasional lettering commissions, I began developing my vision for my very own type foundry. At this point I'd seen enough historical material to understand the vast possibilities in type, but the type landscape at that point felt very restricted, professional, and sterile compared to the things I was interested in. The point of a new foundry would be to celebrate everything I loved about type and wasn't seeing on MyFonts.com.

I set up a desk in the back of a T-shirt shop in San Francisco's Outer Sunset neighborhood. It was there that I started cooking up new versions of Hobo and exploring what my brand could look and feel like.

Ohno launched on August 24, 2015. I printed posters, made shirts, and threw a party at the Aesthetic Union, a letterpress print shop. My dad sewed a flag, and even legendary type designer and lettering artist Jim Parkinson showed up. Friends and type designers

Frank Grießhammer and Nick Sherman sold merch. It was outrageously fun, but then I had to confront an unfortunate reality.

No one wanted to buy my fonts! After the excitement of the launch wore off, I had to face the fact that my current library of Hobeaux and Viktor Script (a collaboration with lettering artist and friend Erik Marinovich) wasn't selling as much as I'd hoped. But I had a plan: to make the most absurd typeface ever drawn, so that people would just have to buy it. The plan was foolproof, and the resulting project was Hobeaux Rococeaux.

Shocker—no one bought it. It was back to square one.

Over the next few years, I kept making new typefaces that provided immense amounts of creative satisfaction while generating meager amounts of revenue. Yes, the foundry could sustain me in the room I sublet for seven hundred dollars a month, but could it sustain anyone else? In the most expensive place to live in California? For how long? My emphasis was on creating interesting work that was often somewhat experimental, but was that business model actually working?

Things were getting more serious with my girlfriend, Sadie, and I told her she'd make an amazing mom. She said, "Don't say that unless you mean it."

I replied poetically and articulately, "OK."

Sadie got pregnant around the time we were asked to leave our rent-controlled apartment. The building had changed owners, and in a classic San Francisco chain of events, they wanted the current tenants gone. With the help of some lawyers, the Housing Rights Committee, and the San Francisco Tenants Union, we arrived at a settlement and left. Sadie was three months pregnant, and we had a lot to figure out before the baby came.

Even though the gravity of our situation weighed heavily on me, I still found plenty of time to work on some truly esoteric typefaces. Cheee, Eckmannpsych, and Beastly were mostly drawn during that time. All my nervous energy was getting channeled into type design. It's a coping mechanism that has done more for my business than anything else.

Sadie and I found a charming two-bedroom, put the settlement and loans from our family into our down payment, subsidized the mortgage with a roommate, and began the humbling experience of paying everyone back.

Our baby, Loretta, came at the end of May, and I faced the reality that I was still treating Ohno like an unsuccessful art project. It was tremendously fun for me to work on the fonts, and we were gaining recognition as a source of interesting work, but the business was nowhere near a home run.

I met up with my good friend and mentor Marty Grasser. I was lamenting my sleeplessness and financial stress, when Marty's words of advice hit me like a ton of bricks: "You gotta come back to Earth!"

"Marty, what are you talking about?"

"Your type, dude. You gotta come back to Earth." It took a while for his words to sink in, but then I finally thought I understood. I texted Marty a screenshot of Obviously, a new grotesque I had started working on. Marty was encouraging, but I knew I still hadn't convinced him yet. I did eventually release Obviously, and it has turned out to be a decent seller, but things didn't click until I made something even more regular.

Degular came like a bolt of lightning to the Ohno library, and immediately the foundry became sustainable. I no longer needed to supplement my income with contract lettering work, and sales of all of the other typefaces picked up as well. Conceptually, it wasn't the most impressive project, and I began to understand the difference between type for type users, and type for type designers! By listening to Marty, I stumbled into something that actually sold. It was my seventeenth family for Ohno. As my father says, "I might not be that good, but at least I'm a slow learner!"

The pandemic gave me everything I'm grateful for: a space to work from home, family living nearby, and a completely clear calendar. It reminded me so much of growing up: no extracurricular activities and plenty of time. But the pandemic also meant that people in our community were struggling in many ways. I began to meet with students once a week through Type Crit Crew, offering free critiques and listening to students describe their struggles in design.

Our second girl, PJ, entered the world in February. My growing email fatigue was exacerbated by a lack of sleep, and I was losing enthusiasm quickly. For six years, I had run the business alone, designing nearly all the type and responding to every customer support request and Instagram DM. I had shipped every merch item and written every thank-you note, blog post, and typeface description. I threw my hands up, took another page out of Marty's book, and posted a help-wanted ad for a studio admin. The gods of typographic entrepreneurship sent me Jamie Otelsberg to handle customer service and Lynn Barber to take on licensing correspondence. Releasing control over every aspect of the foundry was tough at first, but

Jamie and Lynn quickly began taking a lot of work off my plate. In just a few months, I couldn't imagine how I ever lived without them.

Asking for—and Getting—Help

Then I went on a family vacation and was able to leave my computer at home. It was like a refrigerator turning off that you didn't realize was on. Our customers were getting better service, and I was getting lots more free time. Jamie and Lynn turned out to be wonderful people who truly understood what I was trying to do with Ohno.

One day I woke up with an idea that I wasn't sure Ohno could afford. Colin Ford was on my radar as a great potential hire, but the fear of paying a salary, providing health care and a 401(k), and doing that every month scared the life out of me. But I kept on coming back to the idea, and I eventually reached out to Colin to see if that would be something he was even interested in. It was a good sign that he was wearing an Ohno shirt in the meeting, and a few months later, on June 1, 2022, after we figured out the paperwork and business filings, he started. It's an awesome feeling to see the company grow and to gradually bring in more people who are kind, supportive, and care a lot about what we do. I can't say I'm eager to take on more staff, but at the same time, I never would have expected Ohno would get to this point.

That brings us to the present day, and we are still figuring out the balance between type that works and type that inspires us. We have tried many, many things that didn't really work, and we will definitely try some more. I'll never be able to pay back all the people who helped me on this journey. That's why I'm committed to making Ohno a positive force in the graphic and type design community. We talk to students, do lectures, offer occasional free critiques, and put out free educational content. In the future, I hope to strengthen all of those things and one day create a maker space combining everything I love about crafts and typography. This is still just the beginning of Ohno, and I am so grateful to every single customer who has licensed fonts, followed us on social media, subscribed to our newsletter, mentioned us to a friend, or just read this story. Without you, I might still be working in PowerPoint.

Why Are We Here?

At its best, our hobbies bring us peace, satisfy our curiosity, and give us unlimited space to explore and improve. They answer the question "What if we did it this way?" or "Am I capable of this?" They are not a distraction from what we should be doing—it's the other way around! In type design, I found a hobby first, then a job, and more recently, a sort of spiritual practice. This might sound insane to people with actual spiritual practices, but it's true. The feeling of getting in the zone has always steered the ship.

We are here because it is hard. And because it's hard, it's fun.

Type design provides unlimited opportunities to exercise control. I was always a fan of that, but after having kids, it became even more emotionally beneficial. I think that's why dads typically love to get up early and pack the car for a trip, for example. Everyone likes something they can control. This can feel exhilarating, overwhelming, or some combination of those two things.

I was not born a visual person, and I needed to understand how certain tools worked for me before I could begin drawing my own letters. I was not gifted from a young age. I was never the design student who brought in homework miles ahead of everyone else. (I think my only gift is my ice-skating ability; I've never trained, but when I hit the ice, it's like poetry in motion.)

This book will show you some rules, explain how typographic systems work, and demonstrate how modular pieces come together to make an alphabet, a font, a typeface. By learning this myself, I have enjoyed thousands of hours of work and had the pleasure of creating many, many things. I would bet that not everyone reading this will become a type designer, but my hope is that by learning a little about this mysterious design niche, you'll have a bit of fun, get in the zone, and enjoy some moments on this planet while you're still here!

A Note on Craft

Not everything in this book is my own knowledge. It is the knowledge that's come from my teachers and from every piece of type or lettering that I have looked at and gained something from. If there is anything you take from this book, it's from them and not me.

This book is not about software. It's about the thinking behind the choices you'll eventually make in software.

Legendary Dutch type designer and instructor Gerrit Noordzij described typography as "writing with prefabricated letters." Type design is drawing and spacing those letters so they can exist in any order and speak with the same voice no matter the words or languages used. But it's not just letters! Figures, punctuation, symbols, dingbats, and emojis all could be considered a part of type design.

Does it end there? Not really! Open to the back of any old specimen and you'll see borders, containers, ornaments, all sorts of clip art, logos, and any graphic object you can think of. Historically, we've seen those things as separate from typefaces, but I've always loved the challenge of incorporating them into the typefaces to give designers more to play with. Beastly has a set of ornamental borders, Ohno Casual has a set of tiles for creating patterns, and Regrets has a set of art nouveau–influenced illustrations.

The tricky part is not designing a single, fabulous glyph—but rather an entire system. Letters are hard, words are harder, and sentences are trickier than that. Then paragraphs, pages, and books. I've seen students become quite overwhelmed when starting to study type design seriously. I've overheard some say things like "I thought I knew about this stuff, and I had no clue!"

Understanding both the fundamentals and the order in which they're employed can lead to a smoother process that's fun and rewarding. And conversely, being oblivious to the importance of creating a system can make the whole thing a huge pain in the ass.

The purpose of this book is to make type design fun. For me, it's been a refuge, an infinite playground where I'm constantly excited to explore something new. It's a place where I can exercise my need for control in a productive way that doesn't piss off my wife or kids! It's one of the single best tools I have for my mental health, in addition to my SSRIs, of course!

In Jeff Tweedy's book *How to Write One Song*, he writes about learning to play guitar:

> I have sort of a survivor's guilt about it that makes me want it for everyone. Not the "guitar" exactly, but something like it for everybody. Something that would love them back the more they love it. Something that would remind them of how far they've come and provide clear evidence that the future is always unfolding toward some small treasure worth waiting for. At the very least, I wish everyone had a way to kill time without hurting anyone, including themselves. That's what I wish. That's what the guitar became for me that summer and is to me still.

That's exactly how I feel. Type design has always loved me back. I don't know why or how. It's not always easy, and occasionally frustration gets the best of me after I've been banging my head against the same problem for a while. But there's always something for me to sink my teeth into. It's not for everyone. I get that. But if you've read this far, it could very well be for you.

CHAPTER ONE

THE TOOLS

In the most rudimentary sense, all you really need to design type is a sheet of paper, a pen, and some scissors. Of course, this can be a slow way of working, and it doesn't do much to accommodate modern publication practices, but I said we were talking rudimentary here!

The first couple of questions I get from *designers* (rather than normal people) about type design are about software.

"Hey, that's interesting. What software do you use?"

"Oh, it's RoboFont."

"Huh. Never heard of it. Does Adobe make it?"

"Uh, no. It's made by this one guy in Belgium named Frederik!"

"Oh. OK."

"Frederik's great—he and I went to the same school in the Neth—hey, where are you going?!"

I always do my best to answer in a way that *doesn't* make people scared and run away. But they do. Every. Single. Time.

But software is far from the most important tool we use. At the core, we are using our eyes to evaluate positive and negative space. So software isn't nearly as important as what you see and how you see it.

There's No Wrong Way to Eat a Reese's

Before we worry about the perfect paper and the perfect pen, I want to remind you that there is no magic bullet better than your own enthusiasm and curiosity. Feeling energetic about practicing, reading, or otherwise learning is the single greatest factor in determining how far you will go. Talent is completely overrated, but what is consistently undervalued is the curiosity that drives exploration and experimentation. Wondering what will happen if you do something a particular way is much more powerful than thinking, *I'm awesome at this!* The former leads to an action, and the latter leads nowhere.

For that reason, one should be thankful simply to be in a position to want to learn about something. Curiosity is a gift from the heavens and should be treated as such.

When Enthusiasm and Curiosity Run Out

Unfortunately, we can't always count on our natural inclination to motivate us—in fact, enthusiasm is as fleeting as the carbonation in that tangerine LaCroix you're drinking. When our enthusiasm runs low, we must lean on a little discipline to get us through. I love the sort of work I am lucky enough to call a profession, but admittedly there are days when I lack any semblance of mojo. That's natural, and it's a good opportunity to steer your willpower in the direction of more work. Without a doubt, renewed enthusiasm and curiosity are waiting on the other side. Type design as a job is about 5 percent creativity and 95 percent production work. Both can be enjoyable, but finishing something is infinitely more difficult than starting.

Community College

The best way to stay motivated and make progress is to have a community. This can be in the form of meetups, conferences, or even just a weekly accountability meeting with a buddy. I can't say enough about how finding a community of like-minded folks has led to good things in my creative life. These people have inspired and educated me in innumerable ways, and occasionally they've put me in my place!

Once at a type meetup in Oakland, I showed some proofs of an in-progress typeface to Jim Parkinson. Jim has an absolutely righteous tattoo on his arm that says, "BORN TO LETTER," which tells you everything you need to know about this legend. He looked at my proof and said, "Yeah, man, you got too many ideas." It stung at the time, to hear my hero criticizing my work, but after a while I realized just how right he was! Another time Jim saw some of my lettering work, and all he said was, "Well, keep practicing!" That was probably the most productive thing he could have said.

↑
A visual depiction of translation and expansion is probably a lot easier to understand than pages and pages of text talking about them.

When I was an undergrad, I emailed my work to type and lettering heavyweight Michael Doret, and he said not to try and draw like other people. At the time I was a little hurt and confused, but eventually I understood what he meant.

The type community—an informal network of thousands of generous enthusiasts (and maybe one or two assholes)—has done maybe the most productive thing of all: offer an inflated sense of just how important this job is. At the end of the day, it's the administrators and trash collectors who keep the world turning, and type designers are extremely far down the list of necessary occupations. So we need a group of delusional aficionados to keep us on track.

The Tools (Nah for Real Tho)

This must be so frustrating for you, dear reader. I keep talking about abstract tools like enthusiasm, curiosity, and community and only mentioning a few real ones.

> And where are your tools, man?
> These are my tools.
> They're crappy student model tools, and I play better than you.
> James Jamerson used one finger.
> —Vulfmon

Here are a couple of tools you should know.

The Broad Nib Pen

The first important tool of the type designer is a pen with a broad nib. A broad nib pen is absolutely worth the eight dollars the cheap refillable ones cost. I've bought many over the years, and I've lost many more. Using the broad nib will teach you so much about how type conventions work. Why is the left side of a capital *A* thin, and the right side thick? Why is that reversed on the *V*? Why is the *O* drawn as two downstrokes instead of a single loop? It's hard to gain an understanding of that without the tactile sense of feeling how the pen wants to move on the page.

In short, the answer comes down to the human hand and the fact that most people are right-handed. Holding the broad nib pen in a natural way will put the angle somewhere around 30°.

This changes depending on the shape you're drawing (diagonal letters like *v* and *z* will work better with something around 45°), but it's usually around 30°.

With that as a constraint, one can imagine how diagonal strokes moving from the top right to bottom left would create a thin stroke, and moving from the top left to the bottom right would create a thick one. That's it! The entirety of the pen's logic is right there! It's not complicated.

Noordzij called the model of contrast that the broad nib creates *translation*. In other words, the pen creates a fixed shape, and the thicks and thins only appear because of how the pen is moved, or *translated*, around the page. Typefaces like Jenson, Lydian, and blackletter typefaces employ translation.

The Pointed Pen

The second important tool of the type designer is the pointed pen. It features a split tip and is engineered to open up with a little pressure and create a thicker stroke.

Unfortunately, I've always found using these things to be a bit of a pain! I haven't found a great refillable one, the nibs wear out, and then I'll spill ink on my desk and shout obscenities as it dribbles off my work surface and down the front of my pants.

Both the broad and the pointed nib tend to want to move downward. Trying to move upward (especially with the pointed pen) will make the tip of the nib get stuck on the fibers of the paper and splatter more ink.

With the pointed pen, modulation in stroke is created by *pressure*. Extremely light pressure creates a hairline, and heavy pressure creates a thicker stroke. An expert hand can accurately and consistently control everything in between. Noordzij called this model of contrast *expansion*. Typefaces that exemplify expansion include Bodoni, Didot, and Clarendon.

Translation and Expansion

Great. Is that it? Not even close. There are hybrids of those two models. There are different models based on the brush that incorporate expansion, translation, and even rotation all in the same glyph. You can even invent your own! But translation and expansion serve as the basis of so much of type history that they deserve special attention. Everything always comes back to the fundamentals.

It took me an embarrassing amount of time to thoroughly understand what these two models do and how they do it. I was in

Olde Fatface
Regrets Blazeface
Retail Beastly
Swear Polymath
Forevs Degular

↑ (left)
Olde, Regrets, Retail, Swear, and Forevs are firmly translation-based designs.

↑ (right)
Ohno Fatface, Ohno Blazeface, Beastly, Polymath, and Degular are more in the expansion camp.

grad school then, long after I had heard the terms and explanations many times. I don't know why, but something clicked. It was like the keys to the kingdom were handed to me! Suddenly I felt like I had a basis for a more holistic understanding of type design, and I wouldn't be limited by genre.

Years later, I can look at the Ohno library and classify much of it into one of the two camps.

Point of View

The first graphic designer I was ever aware of was my older brother Cameron's best friend, Ian Coates. He was majoring in graphic design in a real college! I asked him for a little guidance, and his advice was simple: Just save everything you like.

As an undergrad at California College of the Arts, I would take the 22 bus down Sixteenth Street from the Mission District to Potrero Hill. Every day I'd stare out the window and think about what storefronts moved me. Stagi's Liquors, Casa Latina Super Market, and J. Georgie's Donuts come to mind. Some featured deftly executed sign painter scripts; others were charming for their eccentricities. My typography teacher Angie Wang advised students to always keep a camera ready to capture what we liked. Later, designer Tim Belonax* impressed on me the importance of keeping a sketchbook to record ideas—no matter how rough or loose.

Eventually these ideas of saving everything, taking my own photos, and doodling even just a few letters every day on whatever paper I had nearby became a natural part of my creative process, and they continue to pay dividends to this day.

At some point I had the idea to catalog this combination of photos and random inspiration into a searchable database that could be tagged with things like "script," "2-color," or "Rudolf Koch" so I could easily find them later. In the end, I didn't use that database as much as I thought because I began to love the shift that would happen when I drew things from memory. This is a trick I learned from Christian Schwartz, who redrew Antique Olive from memory

** A side note about Tim Belonax: I was presenting my final project in Christopher Simmons's Graphic Design 2 class at CCA when Tim was a guest critic. I perfect-bound my book for that project, and when I went to present, every single page fell right out. My heart sunk, and honestly I wanted to burst into tears! One guest critic really laid into me. But Tim's response was really kind. I don't remember exactly what he said, but I remember how he put me at ease, made me feel as if those sorts of things happen to us all, assured me that I'd do a better job next time—and suggested that I might just avoid perfect binding altogether.*

→ (overleaf)
I wanted to include some examples in this book, but I didn't want to go through the trouble of getting signed releases for their use, so I drew some. It took a while, but it was definitely more fun than email.

ABCDEFGHI
JKLMNOPQR
STUVWXYZ
abcdefghijklm
nopqrstuvwxyz

Ohno Expansion

ABCDEFGHI
JKLMNOPQR
STUVWXYZ
abcdefghijklm
nopqrstuvwxyz

Ohno Expansion Italic

ABCDEFGHI
JKLMNOPQR
STUVWXVZ
abcdefghijklm
nopqrstuvwxyz

Ohno Translation

ABCDEFGHI
JKLMNOPQR
STUVWXYZ
abcdefghijklm
nopqrstuvwxyz

Ohno Translation Italic

to arrive at his typeface Duplicate. Referencing source material is always a helpful strategy, especially for newcomers. But as I got more comfortable building up my internal shape library in my head, it became more thrilling to work from that.

Opening my eyes to the world around me was illuminating, and San Francisco felt like the perfect place to do it thanks to the plethora of handmade signage by folks from all walks of life. At first, I scoffed at all the typographic blunders I came across. Things like an upside-down *N* or *S*, or an *M* or *A* with inverted stroke contrast. All the uses of Brush Script and Impact just seemed lazy and pedestrian. But as time went on, I grew to appreciate these accidents and obvious choices. My taste became an equal mix of obscure exotica, working-class stalwarts, and naivete.

There is a section of Valencia between Twenty-Second and Twenty-First that had several of my favorites: Lucca Delicatessen, We Be Sushi, Valencia Cyclery, and finally Thomas D. Harvey Realty. If there was anyone who understood the power of graphic design, it was Thomas D. Harvey. The guy had no less than five signs on his store, and they were all bangers.

As graphic designers, we're often guilty of looking only online for our first point of inspiration for new projects. Combine that with the fact that most of us use the same software, and it's not a real stretch to say that similar inspiration + similar tools = similar results. I've found that having my own libraries to look through when starting on something new can be really fun and helpful.

To sum it all up:

- Photograph everything you like.
- Save everything you like (extra points for a searchable database).
- Draw in a sketchbook every day (more on this in the next section).

→
A selection of works in progress. In isolation these don't tell anyone much, but by looking at the broader collection of things that captivate my attention, we can see a common thread. Maybe.

Amply
Zombi
Refute
Unites

Encompassing
Unworthiness
Discretionary
Crossexamine
Tyrannically
Equivocations

Packaging
Necessary
Spaceship
Adjectives
Modulates

Mechanistic
Postmortem
Showground
Legitimising

Underwear
Quantifiers
Meditating
Burgeoned
Personable
Drumbeats

finals
silent
yawn
quasi

Fidget
Gating
Infant
Melon
Zealot

Sanforizes
Forcipated
Buckthorns
Chalkstone
Supervisal

ADULTERY
Wanderland
BRACKETS
Humanistic

Rolfer
Stenos
Dories
Crated

Documentation
Submissiveness
Inappropriately
Responsiveness
Censoriousness
Accelerometers
Earthshattering

PROTESTANTISM
SUBCOMMITTEES
TRANSISTORISED
RECONSTITUTED
CRIMINOLOGISTS
MEGALOMANIA

GLOW
INSET
DISCO
IDIOM

Taschenlampe
Romantischer
Schwertkampf
Demokratisch

Predating
Falconers
Jubilancy
Glaireous
Terminals

CLINGER
DICKENS
TRUCKIE
ETCHING
GYNECIA

SMEAR
MACRO
VAMPS

Enlarge
Alcoran
Lacking

Fulltone
Devilcat
Hombre

Moulinet
Underwit
Defrauds

Remark
Hibachis
Whipster
Neckline

FINALES
OPTICAL
COPITAS
ISOLATE
GITANES

AVIATOR
Exclusory
HONORS

PERCEPTIVE
SHARPENED
ELIMINATES
CAPTIVATED
HEXAGONAL
TELEPATHIC

JAUNDICE
EMBARKS
PIGTAILED
AUREVOIR

ADVOCATED
POSTPONED
OBJECTORS

INCAPABILITY
TACHOGRAPH
DOWNLANDS

HAIRCUTS
FABRIKEN
MISTANKE

NUDITY
FILTER
AZYGOS
MOISER
LUCERN

ROTTEN
MEANIE
FALSITY

CULTIVATES
UNFURLING
KNOCKOUT

Twister
Locknut
Pinfold
Conduit

Rotulas
Coldest
Studios
Gruntle
Hearing

LAWS
Angle
WHIM
Silver
PROP

FLATIRON
TRENAILS
OLEFIANT

Letrastica
Inevitably
Decalogist
Unluckiest
Spraklings

Recline
Gesture
Lineout
Endless

styles
rouge
prowl
ashen

Dolce
Tracy
Eight

Amply
Zombi
Refute
Unites

ALPINO
CURVES
Mai Tai
Bonsoir

Factoid
Elusion
Buckets
Ludovic

Angina
LEPTON
Fringes
IMBUED
AIRMEN

PULSED
WIDELY
SUNDRI
ORIGEN

GOLDEST
DOLPHIN
FELTPEN
OUTSETS
SALUTED

PIVOTED
VENTURI
OCTUPLE
YOLKIER

CHAPTER TWO

SKETCHING

In undergrad at CCA, my Typography 1 teacher, Angie Wang, told me I really had to take Rod Cavazos's type design elective. She was so right. Rod is disarmingly kind and lends a completely Zen vibe to the classroom. He's exactly the sort of guy you want to have on your side for your first foray into making fonts, and I'm deeply sorry that he didn't write this book. We started the first couple of studios of his class by drawing with a Sharpie on paper towels. At first I was totally confused! Then it became really liberating to get some rough drawings down quickly and keep moving.

In grad school, I got to study under Erik van Blokland. In my mind, Erik reigns supreme as the heavyweight type design champion of the world and the teacher who continues to voice opinions in my head about everything I draw on a daily basis. I remember him cracking me up in class by saying stuff like, "Why are all these people posting their sketches on Instagram?! You should hate your sketch! Not show it off!"

I've continued to regurgitate Erik's advice about sketching more than any of my other stolen teaching material. "You should hate your sketch!" is a classic. I usually add that the only real reason your sketch exists is to expose all the flaws in your system. Erik also continually stressed the importance of "exploring the designspace."

It's not really fair to just throw that out there, because I think *designspace* is a word he invented. Let's try to break it down.

What the Heck Is a Designspace?

There are two ways of looking at it.

1. On one hand, *designspace* is a literal, technical term for the abstract space where sources of a font can blend together, interpolating instances between each other to generate the different styles of a type family. I just reread that, and I'm still confused! A literal designspace can be one-dimensional (like going from light to bold, creating a weight axis), two-dimensional (weight axis and width axis), three-dimensional, and so on.
2. On the other hand, *designspace* is a figurative term for the possibilities that can be explored when prototyping ideas for a new typeface. This is the one that's most important for sketching.

While our new baby typeface is in its infancy, we are desperately searching for the sweet spot: a part of the designspace where each parameter is perfectly dialed in to emphasize and underpin the typeface's concept. Unfortunately, there are no shortcuts to finding the sweet spot, so we must use a leave-no-stone-unturned method of sketching. But fortunately, sketching can be loose, and when things are loose, they go quick.

We have to push everything to its breaking point, so we can walk it back. What does too bold look like? How high can an x-height go before it doesn't serve its purpose anymore? How short or long should descenders be? How condensed is "Condensed," and what the heck is "Normal"? Would script capitals work here? How about a blackletter version? Can I do a reverse-contrast connected script with an extreme back slant and ultrahigh contrast?

Type design is delightful in part because the answers can't be looked up in the back of a book. The only way we can answer these questions is by drawing them, looking at it, and making a decision.

Not Too Pretty

It's important to note that sketches for type design are not drawings. Lots of times when I'm teaching I see students bust out their lead holders and fine Japanese erasers ready to create the most perfect sketches the world has ever seen. While it's impressive and always fun to nerd out on gear, it misses the point of sketching.

(p.40-41)
Examples of sketches for lettering. Lettering usually answers the question "What can't fonts do?" That's why we have free rein to play with composition, effects, swashes, underlines, and all kinds of bonus elements.

(p.42-43)
Examples of sketches for typefaces usually stick to a flat baseline and cover a diverse range of characters.

(p.44-45)
Digging around in my sketchbooks reveals many things that are and aren't concerning the project at hand. Every mark drawn is counted as a win.

Burlingame
SOCCER
CLUB

Burlingame
S

DALLAS

DALLAS

DALLASS

Jet-Puffed

La Tortilla Factory

MEXIC
OCOITY

Mexico City MM

The Joy of Music
The Job of Real Estate

I HÄHV A SEESTEM, AND IT'S WÜRKING PÜHFECTLY!
ABCDEFGHI
JKLMNOPQR
STUVWXYZ&
$57 29
YOURS WELD
Raleigh
Hampton
CHECK PLAESE
uh dude
uh dude
uh dude
Frang
it's obvious
Ferrari fund
1234567890

EVONUST
ELONUS
ELONUST
ELONUST
45676
Paulista
Saved!
Holiday
Open-House
OH NO PRESENTS
VOHAR
40 YEARS OF
DISSAPPOINTMENT

heirloom

Often2 Saturn
Alhars Fleisa
Henyxi Fdvöfi
B Bpz! Něze A
Cuwkw

246 247
246 246

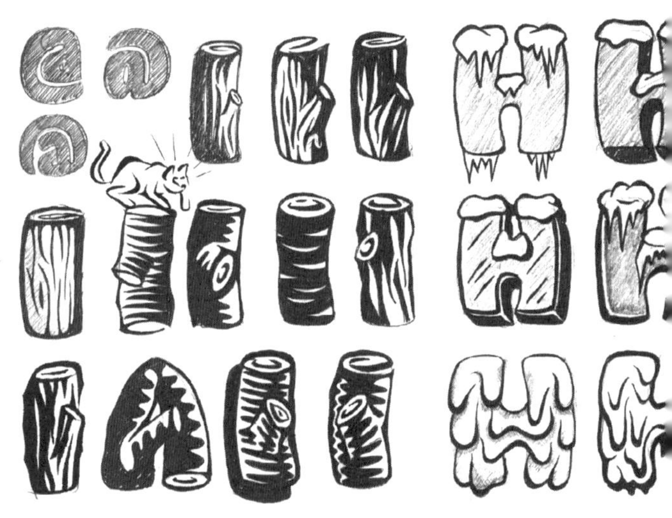

YCEPO
MACE

atlassian
atlassian
atlasin

3574218980√
32176
65712 dB/Oct
128 128 667853
1613458
111677256

EVONUST
EVONUST
EVONUST
achieving
Robothon ROBOTHON
ROBOTHON ROBOTHON
ROBOTHON ROBOTHON
ROBOTHON ROBOTHON
ROBOTHON Robothon
Paulista Paulista
OAKLAND
Paulista PAULISTA
OAKLAND
PAULSTA PAULIST
PAULSTA! PAULISTA

↑ Even challenging yourself to draw smaller and smaller can lead to surprises that become evident when you blow the drawings back up again.

We're trying to cover *ground*. We want our name to be Philip dePage. We want to explore as much of the designspace as possible with the time we have. To do this, we employ a few strategies.

→ Use Sharpie or other low-res tools.
→ Work at a size of about a 1" to 2" cap-height, which usually gives enough detail while not taking too much time to draw.
→ Trace as much as possible. If a sketch looks OK, but you want to explore different details, just draw on top of it!
→ Use negative-space tools as much as positive-space tools. Did your Sharpie slip? Don't throw the baby out with the bathwater. Just bring in the Wite-Out.
→ Cut and paste. Tape and scissors are go-to sketching tools for their immediacy. They can be really helpful for *respacing* everything so you don't have to *redraw*.

In the end, a good sketch looks less like a beautiful drawing and more like a jacked-up ransom note—except the only person you owe money to is me for all the value I'm providing in this book!

The Classic Mistakes

Beyond being too delicate, students often fall into these traps.

Staying zoomed in. Every few minutes, it's helpful to stand up and increase the distance between you and your sketch. This exposes unforeseen issues (and usually spacing problems) every single time. If you suffer from magnet-ass syndrome, you can take a pic with your phone or use a reducing glass.

Drawing only outlined shapes. It's hard to evaluate spacing when you're looking at outlines only. Drawing the "meat" of your sketch with a dark enough color to assess the positive/negative space relationship leaves your mistakes no place to hide.

Sketching in the order of the alphabet. We're prototyping fonts, not alphabet posters! I find myself drawing nonsense words like *CRANEW* and *BYIVQNSH* simply to give myself a random mix of shapes I'm curious about seeing. *Hamburgefonstiv* is another classic for the mix of straight, round, and diagonal strokes, combined with ascenders and descenders. Really, anything is fine, but the idea is to create word-like sketches that are spaced the way you're intending.

Where Do Ideas Come From?

Another gem I picked up from my dawg Eric van Blokland is the world-famous TypeCooker, a prompt-generating tool intended for type designers looking for practice challenges that break you free of drawing habits. Anyone can go to Typecooker.com and get a random recipe for typeface creation. This is a great tool for folks starting out, and I always suggest to students who are interested in exploring type design to do a TypeCooker every day. How many days? A million billion!

In Scott Thorpe and Brett MacFadden's Typography 4 class at CCA, we explored "hybrids." This is a pretty straightforward process that yields completely unexpected results. Just grabbing two typefaces (or two of anything) and smashing their properties together can be inspiring and fun. What would Times look like if drawn by Matisse? Or DIN combined with the Leica logo? No one knows, so go draw and find out!

Hypocritical Bullshit

I'll always advocate for starting the sketching process by hand, especially to students. But as I've gotten more comfortable in font editors, I have felt less and less friction between what I want to see and getting the pen tool to draw it. Because it's faster, sometimes I'll jump right to the computer. The temptation for blazing speed is sometimes too much to resist! But every time I feel like I'm doing myself a small disservice. There's often something unexpected that happens with drawing, and I don't see that as much with Beziers.

→ (p.48–49)
When you are working digitally, things look immediately cleaner, so you have to work extra hard to remind yourself you're still just sketching.

→ (p.50–51)
Working digitally has many benefits but comes at a cost. There is nothing as liberating as pencil and paper, so I try and reserve digital sketching for when I have a clear objective.

→ (p.52–53)
A selection of sketchbook spreads from my time in grad school.

ike Ike ike

ike Ike Ike

ike Ike Ike

Tokyo

TORONTO

Berlin

SAN FRANCISCO

I'm Not Telling You for You.

I'm Telling You for Me.

Goldie Goldie Goldie Goldie Goldie

Goldie Goldie goldie Goldie Goldie

Goldie Goldie

Goldie Goldie Goldie Goldie GOLDIE

goldie Goldie Goldie Goldie Goldie

Goldie Goldie

Chicago
FOSTERS
Benny's
Birds
Controversial Letters.
Words Upon Which
We Can All Agree!
Oakland, California
BIG KITTY
in the

nana
nnn ankle a e
N Frank ekam
sas Hem
mingw a rHem and
Modern Scie TH
Ernest POSITION
avid W AT NOON

Raa aWx ee & mox
n avids Sham&
NATANS
MORE CAPS
UPRIGHT ITALIC 2013
DESCENDERS N stem right heavy
phase is
David Grahae raf
ADVEN Victor af Pa
DEA san Canning fans
Cann sam rasm Co
Cann nnas co ksse
nva Draon
nass San Francisco Simple G
foramp pleasee CALIFORNIA
Death BECOME NEVADA POIN POINTD

as 75 na
MV OLDFILE.TXT NEWFILE.TXT
MV OLDFILE.TXT ~/DESKTOP
was nfnfg
naa n ebcal
califor
califo & IR e a
nn par
panch A pe

Landuke Evis
SanFrancisco Ca
Ranger Everlasting Quic
Fond Regard
Brush Upright Mi
Prickly Ass Quasar J
TEMPORARY SADNESS
12345667888912 3
Amerlieke Amst
SuperA

rangs CALIFORNIA Heming
Wangkatro scr
Adventure ADVENT
Jonathan Cape p.v
Dr Donald Knut
RIGHTranadesiw
Micare Sclsnhmre
francis aesthe IRS
FPESHGRLIOONARES
& theONEY BOATG
BEAT ictorialno
secret Partiess1678

Scafris
aenpks
cransy
MCHSR

ABCDE
FGHIJK
LMNOP
QRSTUV

LEXICON
CAECILIA
JOANNA
BEMBO
COURIER
OPTIMA

8 ARIAL
4 BEMBO
2 CAECILIA
7 COURIER
3 JOANNA
1 LEXICON
5 OPTIMA
6 UNIVERS

UNIVERS
ARIAL
Francis
Edmost
Favorite

RaeM
Sarchst
Fatfilsgh
afcoh

Hendrix
Southern
Fairbank R
ShitHead
Outkast attica
Confession
ta ke No
Queen St
IRIS
National
Swell Proffesso
FABR
IR
Past
67581
nf
ABC
DE
NI

IR
RRRRRRank
IR San Francisco
Guess Shar
Caratteri
PROFFESORin
Alhambbras
aeld
ABCDB
EFGHZ Assholes
KLMN
OPQR HELOSHIT

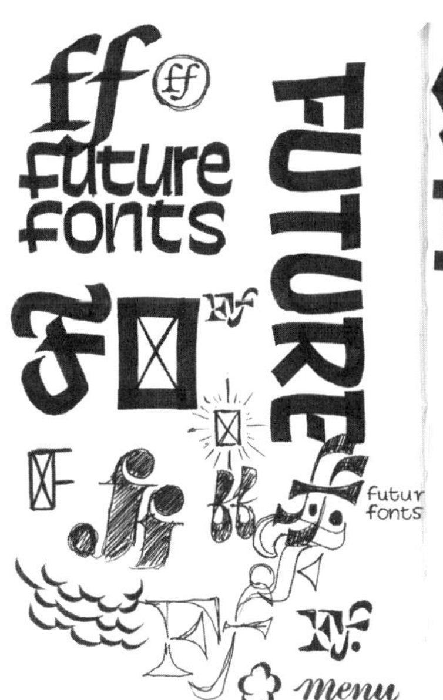
ff
future
fonts
FUTURE
futur
fonts
menu

Future
Fonts
Future
FONTS
Future

Berlin

Damen Damen

Zwicker

Darent

Lastig anfo

Wondr

Sonderfah

SLINKY SLINKY BURLY? ZAO

REGULAR TURBO MIGHTY PRIMO

SKINNY TOP NOT EVEN HEAVY &

HYBRID ULTRA BASS 12-STRING

EXTRA 34F 56 67J MEGA 89!

oagnbes

oaetwfs

oagnbe

oaetwfs

udian for

ngo Fairly

EEG Engs

GRAS

GOUSE

vivis

try

SGRA5

IS

CALIFORN

CCCC aiksé

SSSS aikse

ASJN

Rñitcsa Nanf

Rñitcs Nanf

Uni Vibe

BearDog

Viola origina

Animal & R

An Fetto C Ka

T H E

PARAM

ETER

CHAPTER THREE

THE PARAMETERS

If we can break down every bit of type or lettering into a recipe, we can analyze the ingredients, figure out how they work together, and apply them independently at will to our own inventions.

ee
ee

↑
For expansion (top) and translation (bottom), we see different constructions for both roman (left) and italic (right).

Put another way, imagine trying to construct a house with no knowledge of building materials. You might be confused to find that Home Depot doesn't have a "Walls" or "Ceilings" aisle. But what if you had a sophisticated understanding of every kind of concrete, wood, brick, stone, drywall, paint, shingle, tile, flooring, fastener, electrical component, and plumbing fitting? Then it wouldn't matter if someone asked you to build a tiny home or a mansion. You could build any kind of house that you wanted.

Studying type design has taught me exactly that. I've gotten an understanding of the building materials, and now I feel free to assemble them in any way that makes sense for the project at hand.

We can think of the parameters of type design as a Venn diagram with two circles. Some parameters belong in one circle, some in the other, while the remainder belong in the space where they overlap.

On one side, we have things that affect the *pen*, or the shape of the nib, and how it behaves when it follows along the path. The most obvious example of a pen parameter is weight, or how bold the type appears.

On the other side, we have things that affect the *path*, or the line that a pen would follow to draw the letters. The most obvious example of a path parameter would be width, or how wide or condensed the type appears.

There are a few parameters that affect both the pen and the path. For instance, we could look at *contrast type* (such as expansion or translation). Expansion and translation both come preloaded with traditional pen angles and constructions.

Pen Parameters

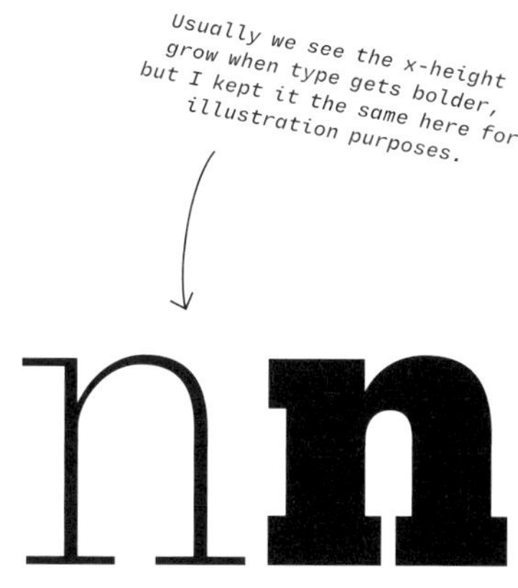

Weight

Simply adding a stroke to thin type will produce less than desirable results. Because our baseline is always fixed, weight can be first added on either side. Unfortunately, that can lead to the type looking wider in the bold, and narrower in the light. Because we need the ability to change one parameter while leaving the others static, weight is sometimes added on top as well, effectively changing the x-height. A slightly larger x-height is usually an almost imperceptible change, while having a bold look like it came from a wider font would be too jarring.

There are many names of weights, and there is no official standard in the order. Hairline, Thin, Light, Regular, Medium, Semi Bold, Bold, Extra Bold, Black, Super, and Ultra can all be used to describe weight. Sometimes designers throw Book in there, which I find super confusing. Is Book heavier than Regular? I'm sure you have an answer, and I'm sure that answer differs from someone else's. Thin is definitely lighter than Light, though. I know that.

Contrast

In a low-contrast typeface, the horizontal and vertical strokes are nearly equal in stroke width, but remember the word *nearly*. Among the distortion our eyes perform is adding weight to horizontal strokes. Does this have something to do with the wide aspect ratio of our field of vision? I'm not a scientist, but I do know this: Compensating for our ocular shortcomings is the name of the game in type design.

In high-contrast typefaces, we can take things to the extreme with razor-sharp thins and oppressive thicks that stomp all over the page with monster truck force.

Sometimes contrast is *inverted*, meaning that everything that was thick now becomes thin and vice versa. This is tricky to apply systematically, particularly on letters like *a*, *e*, and *s*, which have three horizontal (or horizontal-ish) strokes. We can simply run out of available real estate and be forced into some compromises.

ON
NARROW
WIDE
MONO
CLASSICAL
PROPOR.
COMPRESSOR
EXPANDER

Capitals
Ascenders
Descenders
x-height
Waist
Vertical Metrics

↑
Another way to think about type parameters is using the metaphor of guitar pedals.

Path Parameters

nn

Small caps need to be a little bit larger than the x-height, just so they don't feel too small. It's a weird problem that can only be solved by making a gut decision.

nnN1

Width

We all know that stretched type looks bad, but why? Changing the width of a typeface isn't quite as simple as stretching things out and calling it a day because stretching changes contrast. But maybe we could go a bit more sophisticated than that and delicately grab the points on the left, and bring them out, and get the points on the right, and bring them out in the other direction. Unfortunately, even that would be problematic because that would leave a higher ratio of negative space to positive space, effectively leaving the type much lighter than it was before.

When naming fonts with different widths, Compressed is used for the narrowest, then Condensed, Narrow, Wide, and Extended. This is another arbitrary sequence, and some type designers ditch it completely in favor of numerically based naming systems.

Construction

The most common choice of constructions is between roman and italic. Roman, or upright type, features an *interrupted* construction, meaning that the pen is lifted off the page at different times during the creation of a single letter. Italics use a *continuous* construction, meaning that the pen makes contact with the page for the entire letter. Of course, there are exceptions to this rule, like the crossbar on a *t* or *f*.

X-height

The x-height is the invisible line above the baseline that many of the lowercase letters hang from. But because *x* is most often the glyph that has no ascender or overshoot, we call it an x-height. I find it insane that we got all the way to x in the alphabet before we found a letter fitting for the term.

Elementary school students are often taught handwriting on an exemplar that places the x-height at exactly half the cap height. This is an insanely low x-height, and we are doing the children a huge disservice. A more "normal" x-height might be closer to two-thirds of the cap height.

Ascenders and Descenders

To differentiate between a capital *L*, a numeral *1*, and a lowercase *l*, ascenders are usually drawn a little higher than the cap-height. With regard to descenders, I'm often surprised at how compact they can be without impacting legibility.

Grouped together, these two terms are called *extenders*, but they don't have to be exactly the same length because they are doing two very different jobs. Often, their lengths are related but are not a geometric match.

It's interesting to see really condensed type and really wide type with the exact same extender length. In the condensed version, the extenders will look extremely long, and in the wide version, they'll be barely noticeable. Like all the other parameters, ascender and descender length must be evaluated in context.

Proportions

Classical and modern proportions refer to the width of uppercase letters. In a typeface with classical proportions, *C*, *G*, *O*, and *Q* look like circles, and *B*, *E*, *F*, and *L* have about a 1:2 width-to-height ratio. In a font with modern proportions, the capitals are all more similar in width.

These two terms are quite frustrating because they're not physical descriptions. I would argue that they should be called varied-width and even-width proportions. But no one seems to care about what I have to say!

Pen and Path Parameters

Contrast Type

We already discussed the differences between expansion and translation in the preceding chapter, but let's just put it simply: Expansion (left side of image) and translation (right side of image) feature stroke weights that are modulated by pressure and movement, respectively. Because of how the pointed pen and broad nib work on paper, these contrast types have big implications in construction as well. The gradual branching in a lowercase *n* in an expansion-based design is quite a bit different from the perpendicular meeting of these two strokes in a translation-based design. That simple move is echoed in dozens of other places in the lowercase letters.

Another interesting thing about contrast types is that a lot of what we see is a hybrid of both expansion and translation working together. A good example of this is the typeface Times, which has visible pen angles on some glyphs, but not all. Some things will never be understood!

Optical Size

It might not get the same attention as other parameters, but the optical size, or the physical size for which the type is intended, is a powerful factor in determining many features of the design. Often, as type gets smaller, contrast goes down, x-height goes up, spacing increases, and all minor details (like ink traps) are either made larger or omitted completely. Negative spaces that would be in danger of filling in—like the top counter of an *e* or the bottom counter of an *a*—are emphasized so the likelihood of their becoming a confusing blob of ink is minimized.

Common names of optical sizes are Text (usually designated as around 14 point and below) and Display (usually 72 point and above). Deck, Headline, Poster, and Banner are all used as well.

Stroke Endings

It's easy to think of the two biggest genres of type as serif and sans serif. But I'd argue that what we do with stroke endings is more incidental, and any time spent on categorization systems for type would be better spent pounding a rusty railroad tie into your eye socket.

Stroke endings can be round, straight, flared, serif, bifurcated, or even trifurcated!

Serifs can be drawn in a way that makes them a logical fit for their contrast model. Sometimes they are bracketed, or drawn so that they blend seamlessly into the main architecture of the letter. Sometimes they are drawn as triangles, which are often called *wedge serifs*. They might also be called *Latin serifs*, but I don't recommend language that describes type with abstract words that don't mean anything physical.

With this information, we can easily analyze existing typefaces to reverse-engineer their design decisions. For instance, if we look at Ohno Fatface, we could label it like this:

width

Fatface Fatface

Fatface Fatface

optical size

weight

Retail Retail

Retail Retail

optical size

- Weight: extra bold
- Width: compressed to normal
- Optical size: 12 point to 72 point
- Stroke endings: bracketed serif
- Contrast: high
- Contrast type: expansion

↑
When assigning attributes to entire typefaces, we must consider the entire designspace, not just a single style.

Looking at Retail, we could determine the following:

- Weight: thin to black
- Width: normal
- Optical size: text to display
- Stroke endings: straight, no serif
- Contrast: some visible contrast to inverted contrast
- Contrast type: translation
- Stem concavity: some concavity

If you noticed, we added an extra parameter there at the end. Stem concavity is something we see in many typefaces. I've become fond of it as a way to add a touch of the human element to stems that would otherwise be fairly static rectangles.

The interesting thing here is not the simple idea of adding a little curve to the stems, but the idea that we can make up as many extra parameters are we want.

Lettering Parameters

In the context of lettering, things can go completely wild:

- → **Baseline.** This parameter describes whether we're working on a flat, inclined, declined, bouncy, arched, or otherwise manipulated baseline.
- → **Bounce.** Bounce is how much letters vary in relation to one another. There can be proportional bounce, positional bounce, and even rotational bounce. The thing to keep in mind with bounce is that most of the time, less is more, and a little bounce goes a long way.
- → **Effects.** Effects are anything extra applied on top of an existing lettering foundation. They are truly limitless, and are often indulged in by airbrush artists, sign painters, graffiti writers, and calligraphers alike.
    - **Lighting.** If we are treating the lettering as a physical object, what sort of light is applied, and how much does it show up inside and outside the letters? Highlights and lowlights can exist inside the perimeter of any letter, but drop shades and sometimes sparkles can extend beyond.
    - **Dimension.** Again thinking of the type as an object, how much are letters extruded, in which direction, and with what sort of perspective? Much of the time, the dimension that's applied can have its own set of lighting effects.
    - **Material.** Are the letters made to look like they're carved in stone, made out of cheese, dripping in blood, or cut from logs? Material can be absolutely anything, but of course logs and blood are among my favorites.
    - **Stroke.** Sometimes effects just echo the architecture of the letters. An example of this would be inlines or stencils.

When we begin to think about our own parameters, and create new and interesting constraints, we can take our designs into completely new territory. It might seem as if learning the rules of how these parameters work together would stifle creativity, but in reality this knowledge will blow the doors off what's possible and give you the keys to the kingdom.

→ (overleaf)
It's easy to put your understanding of type parameters to the test. Look at absolutely anything, and see what you can describe. See if you can avoid language like "edgy" or "vibing."

The Aesthetic Union

PetHelpful

PairedLife

TurboFuture

AxleAddict

ReelRundown

Spinditty

Dark Ray

JoeDart

Lobdell

QUENCH

ToughNickel

SCOUT

FeltMagnet

HealDove

cum together

MASCULINITY

Paulista

OHno x Paulin

LevelSkip

Saved!

dengarden

Holidappy

WanderWisdom

Ex

Be

Ow

De

Kin

Si

Typ

Ty

MARK and MO'S

Gh

plove
ory
tion
ably
Bond
pore
phics
aki
o
ph
17
ghz

Goodhertz
Fontegné
RECORDS ARTWORK
heirloom
Fat Night Selects
La Tortilla Factory
Adapt
SIX
BaoBao
ROBOTHON
FUTURE FONTS

GORE
ELVIS
CHROM
STAN
BERK

10 11 12 1 2 3 4 5 6 7 8 9
Motown
zapier
Higlobe
VIDETTE
Soapboxie

Staying Connected
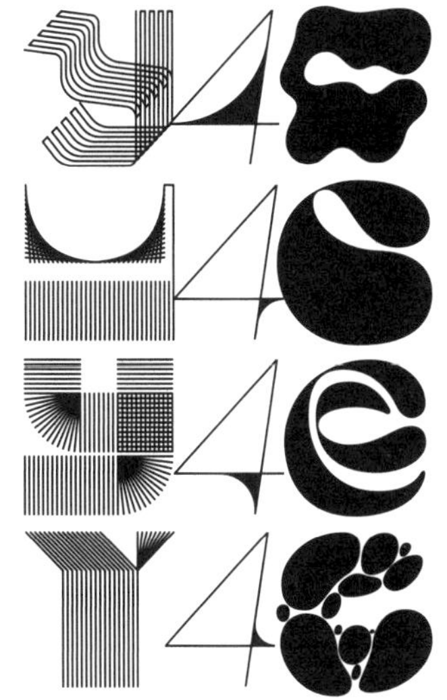
Whipeck
TURNER

Cory

Spacing

THE SPACING S

SPAC

Spacing, Spa

AND NOT TO M

Spacing

spacing

ACING SPACING

g & Spacing

TION SPACING

spacing

CHAPTER FOUR

SPACING

As an undergraduate design student, I spent more than a healthy amount of time in a state of confusion about the lettering I loved. I wondered why certain word shapes made my heart sing, while others commanded nothing more than a passing glance. For years I was clueless, desperately searching for the secret ingredient that was baked into the work of my favorite type designers and that I had yet to master. It wasn't until grad school that it was pounded into my brain by every one of my instructors.

It wasn't the smell of the paper, the opacity of the ink, or the fidelity of the impression that had the final say in the quality of a word (although those things can help). It was simply the negative space. The answer had been in front of my face the entire time, but I was too focused on the black shapes to recognize it. The more I questioned it, the truer it became: Divine spacing is perfect balance. The mind can rest, knowing that no possible improvement can be made to the shapes.

After many teaching experiences trying to explain this concept in the clearest way possible, I have broken the technique for achieving desirable spacing into a two-pronged approach.

under

under

There's way more space here in between letters than inside of letters. Haven't seen the rhythm jacked up this bad since I tried to nail the Electric Slide at my cousin's wedding. Just kidding, I'm great at the Electric Slide!

↑
To gain an understanding of rhythm, all you need to look at are examples of good (top) and bad (bottom) spacing.

Counterspace Equals Letterspace

When I was studying pointed pen calligraphy with Erik van Blokland at TypeMedia, he would glance over my practice sheets and simply draw a red dot within the counter of a letter, and another one beside it. "You should make those two equal," he'd say, and despite having no idea what he meant, I would nod furiously in agreement. Luckily, after seeing similar marks on everyone else's sheets, I slowly got the picture. There was supposed to be a relationship between the space inside an *n* and the space between two *n*'s.

When I started teaching, I thought I'd better name the thing I was referring to so much. I started calling it Rule 1 of Spacing, or the Counterspace Equals Letterspace technique. In some styles, it's incredibly obvious. Blackletter, for instance, thrives on Rule 1.

There is perhaps no lovelier example of Counterspace Equals Letterspace than in script. The rhythm of movement pounds the rule into your brain quite effectively, and your eyes are free to cascade along the measure with ease and delight.

The beauty of this technique is how all-encompassing it can be. Whether it's capitals or lowercase, roman or italic, the Counterspace Equals Letterspace strategy for achieving spacing enlightenment goes a remarkable distance.

This is simply a long way of saying, "Bold letters need tighter spacing" or "Don't track out lowercase." We hear many truisms like that during our typography education, but we rarely talk about why.

→
Both script and blackletter employ this rule to great effect. Trickier letters that involve a diagonal or otherwise break the rules can be handled on a case-by-case basis, but should not disrupt the rhythm.

minimum
minimum

Now we know! Bold letters need tighter spacing because the negative spaces inside them are smaller. We shouldn't track out lowercase because the grid upon which they are built is decided by both the letters and the spacing. You cannot change one without changing the other. You can often get away with increasing the spacing in capitals because the counters are larger, lending themselves to more generous spacing.

Three at a Time

You might be saying, "Don't try and sound like you know everything, Edmondson. I've seen some stuff that looks great and doesn't pay any attention to your rules." True. Let's examine one of the ways in which the Counterspace Equals Letterspace rule can fail.

I am not a dummy. I know that the tight spacing for which Herb Lubalin and his associated colleagues were famous creates a marvelous impact. But why? My guess is consistency.

To space anything, all one must do is group three letters at a time and judge whether the middle letter actually feels like it's in the middle. Not geometrically in the middle, or mathematically, but optically.

What I love about Three at a Time is that it works all the time. Script? Three at a Time. Hairline super extended non-lining figures? Three at a Time! In the Latin alphabet, there are almost no cases where it can't be used. Even with very informal or casual styles, Three at a Time lets the spacing be great while allowing the positive shapes to be as irregular as you like. No matter how bizarre the letters are, the spacing should always be consistent. Legibility is improved, and fewer pockets of illogical white space distract the eye.

← (top)
Manipulated spacing to reflect the Counterspace Equals Letterspace rule (top). The unedited original logotype drawn by John Pistilli, art direction by Herb Lubalin (bottom). Adding space here does nothing to improve the lettering. If anything, it takes away from the impact.

← (bottom)
The Avant Garde logotype, also by Herb Lubalin with Tom Carnase. The spacing of the *AVA* and the *VAN* is, of course, very logical; the same channel of white space is used for consistency. But how much should the *GA* overlap? What about the *RD*? The *DE*? These are all questions that can be answered by utilizing the Three at a Time technique.

If we were to add space here to reflect traditional rules around spacing, again, all impact would be lost.

Consider the Opposite

Sometimes I have said, "Spacing is the most important thing—in type, and in life in general." That might be overstating things, but I do believe it is paramount to consider. The English writer and speaker Alan Watts wanted us to think about death not to enjoy being dead, but to make the most of life. Musicians have often remarked that it is not the notes but the space between them that makes a successful melody. All cooking is based on the balance of opposing flavors. In countless disciplines, thoughtful consideration of the contrasting element informs its partner in a powerful way. For that reason, a design decision that improves spacing is a good one indeed.

CHAPTER FIVE

PROOFING

I often receive correspondence from students eager to show off their newest projects, and I usually welcome it. But often, the resulting email includes only a font file attachment and little information about the intentions of the typeface. As a critic of the work, I really have no interest in the actual font file. I need a proof. I don't want the recipe—I want to taste the food!

A proof is a document, usually in PDF form, that tests the typeface in question. A good proof answers the following questions:

- What problem is the typeface trying to solve?
- What are the problems with the typeface?
- What are possible solutions to those problems?

Like a sketch, a proof is simply a means to an end. It only exists to illustrate areas of improvement and to test ideas. A proof with no mistakes is a waste of paper.

Give a Man a Fish...

When I was teaching regularly in the classroom, every year we'd have some version of a discussion about whether we should provide students with a proofing template. Because the students weren't full-time, we'd usually give them something. And when we didn't, their proofs got crazy!

Sometimes students would print out a thirty-page proof. Were they thinking they were gonna get a thirty-page critique? Hope not.

Q Q Q Q

PIQUE PIQUE PIQUE PIQUE

physics physics physics physics physics physics

åçéü
åçéü
åçéü

"wait, don't."
"wait, don't."

carne
carne
carne
carne
carne
carne

Wow, I was really trying to get a capital **R** to work in lowercase. Young James was so naïve, but also tenacious.

Creating a proof is an important part of the design process. Being able to think critically about what to include or not increases a student's awareness of their project. Here's a basic checklist:

- Every drawn character, in a size large enough to make notes
- Paragraphs or headlines at the intended size(s)
- Spacing strings

Let's look at each of these in more detail.

Every Drawn Character
Proofs are printed or exported digitally so they can ultimately be marked up. This means we have to have a nice place with room to write notes. If you've already marked up something and it's finished, there's no reason to include it in your proof anymore.

Paragraphs or Headlines
The real meat of a proof is seeing the fonts in action. If the project is intended for small sizes, we'll need to see some paragraphs, and if it's more suited to large sizes, we'll need headlines.

Spacing Strings
"Strings" is the confusing part of this one. In this context, a "string" is a programming term that simply means a bit of text.

When spacing the lowercase, we always begin with *n* (the most logical letter with two vertical strokes) and *o* (the most logical

↑
Testing alternates in the context of an actual word is the only way to make an informed decision. And proofs are all about informed decisions!

→ (overleaf top)
We can diagnose some problems from just the alphabet, but it tells us nothing about spacing.

→ (overleaf middle)
Seeing actual text tells us much more about spacing, texture, and inconsistencies in weight. Dark or light spots will attract your eye and alert you to problematic glyphs. I always have to remind myself to read the text in a proof because I am often guilty of just looking at it.

→ (overleaf bottom)
Spacing can be evaluated by looking at every glyph between control characters. The trick (as covered earlier under "Spacing") is to look at three letters at a time.

Seeing each glyph large is helpful so we can make little notes about how individual glyphs are jacked up as hell.

ABCDEFGHIJKLM
NOPQRSTUVWXYZ
abcdefghijklm
nopqrstuvwxyz
1234567890
!?@&*()ß.,…“”‘’

ABCDEFGHIJKLM
NOPQRSTUVWXYZ
abcdefghijklm
nopqrstuvwxyz
1234567890
!?@&*()

I was born among palm trees at one end of Interstate 10. I currently live at the other end of the 10, where my kitchen has a great view of a palm tree.

Last summer my fiancee and I escaped Boston (no palm trees) on June 1st. The plan: a cross-country excursion, destined ultimately for Los Angeles, though the arrival date was fuzzy. July? We spiraled our way down to and across the deep south, relocating every few days. Durham, Charleston, Atlanta, Memphis. We drove the length of Mississippi along I-55 and ended up in New Orleans for a Sazerac. With beignet powder on our fingers, we entered "Houston, TX" in Google maps and chose the scenic route: Route 90, a solid line cut across the ragged bayous.

In Jeanerette, I did 78 in a 65. A lanky black cop unfolded from the driver's side of a hulking SUV. I told him I thought the speed limit was 75. He told me to visit jeanerettetx.com if I wanted to pay with a credit card. Thirty minutes later, after some fried okra and hushpuppies and a full tank for the Corolla, we merged onto Interstate 10 for the first time.

In those first few hours — crossing into Texas, seeing an alligator — I knew almost nothing about Interstate 10. I did not understand its length, that it connects Jacksonville and Los Angeles (birth and residence, respectively), or that this road would take us all the way to the Pacific. That is to say: we had not yet read its Wikipedia article.

Without the internet, a roadtrip is a series of unanswered questions. With the internet, a roadtrip is a series of weird facts. For example: Texas is full of F-150s pulling into and out a place called Buc-ee's. What is a Buc-ee's? Why do so many of the F-150s have "King Ranch" logos? Do all these Texans work at the King Ranch? Answers: (1) Buc-ee's is an excellent chain of beaver-themed gas stations common in Texas' southeast; (2) "King Ranch" is a luxury trim option for F-150s; (3) no, not all Texans work at King Ranch, though that it is a real ranch, larger than Rhode Island, founded by a former riverboat captain.

We moved westward, downloading obscure Wikipedia articles, consuming Buc-ee's beaver nuggets. San Antonio, Alpine, El Paso. Like the lip of a wine glass, America sung with trivia, and with reviews.

For my fiancee, Diana, a roadtrip hunger pang is a chance to Yelp something strange and wonderful. The hushpuppies we had in Lafayette didn't happen by accident; they came at the recommendation of a prolific Yelper whose reviews combine biography (she has family in Louisiana's bayou) with inventive vocab. "Got a smiggy-bit of each," she wrote of the fried food buffet in Lafayette. "And I do mean a smiggy-bit" (Googling "smiggy-bit" should lead you right to her reviews.)

A week later, on Interstate 10, we planned a one night stay in Las Cruces with Yelp's assistance. ⊗⊗⊗⊗⊗ Haunted. A old Union soldier apparition stood at the end of our bed. Did nothing. But was still creepy as all hell. Me, my, girlfriend, and dog all confirmed seeing him at the same time as our dog was the one waking us up barking at the tall, dark, uniformed apparition. The rooms are nice, as is the atmosphere.

Soon our tires hummed along a particularly dry and straight stretch of I-10. Hunger panged again, and another search loaded slowly. 15 minutes later, we ordered a torta Milanesa in Deming, New Mexico. Though we had never before tried this style (pounded, breaded pork), Diana ordered it with authority. I asked her if she'd ever had one. "No." She'd just read about it online. We sat in the window at Tacos Mirasol, eating tortas, looking at the little bit of Deming framed up before us. Dusty and hot. Only two bars of data, but we had lots of questions. "Deming"? The maiden name of a railroad magnate's wife. In 1881 the Silver Spike was driven here, completing America's second transcontinental railroad, the interstate 10 of its day. This earned Deming a weighty nickname: "New Chicago." Thousands and thousands of future Angelenos must've stopped here for lunch on their one-way journeys westward, though their breaded pork might not have been a la milanesa.

But their desert route was our route too, especially in Deming. There in the dust, Interstate 10 harmonizes with the Southern Pacific tracks for miles and miles. Train headlights ripple on the horizon and for a while the train lasts forever — fills the windshield and the rear view mirror — though eventually it rumbles past, eastward. We zipped westward. In two days, we were in Los Angeles.

~~~

Did you know that an unspooled human small intestine is, on average, 23 feet long? Our 3000-mile transcontinental drive has an inverse relationship with Los Angeles. Here, in the ragged desert, all that pavement tangles together; all

HHAHOHOAOO
HHBHOHOBOO
HHCHOHOCOO
HHDHOHODOO
HHEHOHOEOO
HHFHOHOFOO
HHGHOHOGOO
HHHHOHOHOO
HHIHOHOIOO
HHJHOHOJOO
HHKHOHOKOO
HHLHOHOLOO
HHMHOHOMOO
HHNHOHONOO
HHOHOHOOOO
HHPHOHOPOO
HHQHOHOQOO
HHRHOHOROO
HHSHOHOSOO
HHTHOHOTOO

HHUHOHOUOO
HHVHOHOVOO
HHWHOHOWOO
HHXHOHOXOO
HHYHOHOYOO
HHZHOHOZOO

nnanonoaoo
nnbnonoboo
nncnonocoo
nndnonodoo
nnenonoeoo
nnfnonofoo
nngnonogoo
nnhnonohoo
nninonoioo
nnjnonojoo
nnknonokoo
nnlnonoloo
nnmnonomoo

nnnnononoo
nnononoooo
nnpnonopoo
nnqnonoqoo
nnrnonoroo
nnsnonosoo
nntnonotoo
nnunonouoo
nnvnonovoo
nnwnonowoo
nnxnonoxoo
nnynonoyoo
nnznonozoo
nnßnonoßoo
nnfinonofioo
nnflnonofloo
nnðnonoðoo
nnþnonoþoo
nnłnonołoo
nnænonoæoo

nnœnonoœoo
nn@nono@oo

1101010000
1111010100
1121010200
1131010300
1141010400
1151010500
1161010600
1171010700
1181010800
1191010900
11$1010$00
11£1010£00
11€1010€00
11¥1010¥00
11⊖1010⊖00
11¢1010¢00
11<1010<00

11>1010>00
11=1010=00
11+1010+00

HH0HOHO0OO
HH1HOHO1OO
HH2HOHO2OO
HH3HOHO3OO
HH4HOHO4OO
HH5HOHO5OO
HH6HOHO6OO
HH7HOHO7OO
HH8HOHO8OO
HH9HOHO9OO
HH$HOHO$OO
HH£HOHO£OO
HH€HOHO€OO
HH¥HOHO¥OO
HH⊖HOHO⊖OO
HH¢HOHO¢OO

HH<HOHO<OO
HH>HOHO>OO
HH=HOHO=OO
HH+HOHO+OO
HH×HOHO×OO
HH÷HOHO÷OO
HH−HOHO−OO
HH&HOHO&OO
HH.HOHO.OO
HH,HOHO,OO
HH:HOHO:OO
HH;HOHO;OO
HH·HOHO·OO
HH…HOHO…OO
HH¿HOHO¿OO
HH?HOHO?OO
HH¡HOHO¡OO
HH!HOHO!OO
HH¶HOHO¶OO
HH§HOHO§OO

HH#HOHO#OO
HH†HOHO†OO
HH‡HOHO‡OO
HH'HOHO'OO
HH"HOHO"OO
HH°HOHO°OO
HH%HOHO%OO
HH‰HOHO‰OO
HH*HOHO*OO
HHªHOHOªOO
HHºHOHOºOO
HH™HOHO™OO
HH(HOHO(OO
HH)HOHO)OO
HH[HOHO[OO
HH]HOHO]OO
HH{HOHO{OO
HH}HOHO}OO
HH/HOHO/OO
HH|HOHO|OO

HH\HOHO\OO
HH^HOHO^OO
HH~HOHO~OO
HH‹HOHO‹OO
HH›HOHO›OO
HH«HOHO«OO
HH»HOHO»OO
HH_HOHO_OO
HH-HOHO-OO
HH–HOHO–OO
HH—HOHO—OO
HH‘HOHO‘OO
HH’HOHO’OO
HH“HOHO“OO
HH”HOHO”OO
HH‚HOHO‚OO
HH„HOHO„OO
~~~

ABCDEFGHIJKLM
NOPQRSTUVWXYZ
abcdefghijklm
nopqrstuvwxyz
1234567890
!?@&*()ß.,…“”‘’

ABCDEFGHIJKLM
NOPQRSTUVWXYZ
abcdefghijklm
nopqrstuvwxyz
1234567890
!?@&*()ß.,…“”‘’

I was born among palm trees at one end of Interstate 10. I currently live at the other end of the 10, where my kitchen has a great view of a palm tree.
Last summer my fiancee and I escaped Boston (no palm trees) on June 1st. The plan: a cross-country excursion, destined ultimately for Los Angeles, though the arrival date was fuzzy. July? We spiralled our way down to and across the deep south, relocating every few days. Durham, Charleston, Atlanta, Memphis. We drove the length of Mississippi along I-55 and ended up in New Orleans for a Sazerac. With beignet powder on our fingers, we entered "Houston, TX" in Google maps and chose the scenic route: Route 90, a solid line cut across the ragged bayous.
In Jeanerette, I did 76 in a 65. A lanky black cop unfolded from the driver's side of a hulking SUV. I told him I thought the speed limit was 75. He told me to visit jeanerettetix.com if I wanted to pay with a credit card. Thirty minutes later, after some fried okra and hushpuppies and a full tank for the Corolla, we merged onto Interstate 10 for the first time.
In those first few hours — crossing into Texas, seeing an alligator — I knew almost nothing about Interstate 10. I did not understand its length, that it connects Jacksonville and Los Angeles (birth and residence, respectively), or that this road would take us all the way to the Pacific. That is to say: we had not yet read its Wikipedia article.
Without the internet, a roadtrip is a series of unanswered questions. With the internet, a roadtrip is a series of weird facts. For example: Texas is full of F-150s pulling into and out a place called Buc-ee's. What is a Buc-ee's? Why do so many of the F-150s have "King Ranch" logos? Do all these Texans work at this King Ranch? Answers: (1) Buc-ee's is an excellent chain of beaver-themed gas stations common in Texas' southeast; (2) "King Ranch" is a luxury trim option for F-150s; (3) no, not all Texans work at King Ranch, though that it is a real ranch, larger than Rhode Island, founded by a former riverboat captain.
We moved westward, downloading obscure Wikipedia articles, consuming Buc-ee's beaver nuggets. San Antonio, Alpine, El Paso. Like the lip of a wine glass, America sung with trivia, and with reviews. For my fiancee, Diana, a roadtrip hunger pang is a chance to Yelp something strange and wonderful. The hushpuppies we had in Lafayette didn't happen

I was born among palm trees at one end of Interstate 10. I currently live at the other end of the 10, where my kitchen has a great view of a palm tree.
Last summer my fiancee and I escaped Boston (no palm trees) on June 1st. The plan: a cross-country excursion, destined ultimately for Los Angeles, though the arrival date was fuzzy. July? We spiralled our way down to and across the deep south, relocating every few days. Durham, Charleston, Atlanta, Memphis. We drove the length of Mississippi along I-55 and ended up in New Orleans for a Sazerac. With beignet powder on our fingers, we entered "Houston, TX" in Google maps and chose the scenic route: Route 90, a solid line cut across the ragged bayous.
In Jeanerette, I did 76 in a 65. A lanky black cop unfolded from the driver's side of a hulking SUV. I told him I thought the speed limit was 75. He told me to visit jeanerettetix.com if I wanted to pay with a credit card. Thirty minutes later, after some fried okra and hushpuppies and a full tank for the Corolla, we merged onto Interstate 10 for

HHAHOHOAOO
HHBHOHOBOO
HHCHOHOCOO
HHDHOHODOO
HHEHOHOEOO
HHFHOHOFOO
HHGHOHOGOO
HHHHOHOHOO
HHIHOHOIOO
HHJHOHOJOO
HHKHOHOKOO
HHLHOHOLOO
HHMHOHOMOO
HHNHOHONOO
HHOHOHOOOO
HHPHOHOPOO
HHQHOHOQOO
HHRHOHOROO
HHSHOHOSOO
HHTHOHOTOO

HHUHOHOUOO
HHVHOHOVOO
HHWHOHOWOO
HHXHOHOXOO
HHYHOHOYOO
HHZHOHOZOO

nnanonoaoo
nnbnonoboo
nncnonocoo
nndnonodoo
nnenonoeoo
nnfnonofoo
nngnonogoo
nnhnonohoo
nninonoioo
nnjnonojoo
nnknonokoo
nnlnonoloo
nnmnonomoo

nnnnononoo
nnononoooo
nnpnonopoo
nnqnonoqoo
nnrnonoroo
nnsnonosoo
nntnonotoo
nnunonouoo
nnvnonovoo
nnwnonowoo
nnxnonoxoo
nnynonoyoo
nnznonozoo
nnßnonoßoo
nnfinonofioo
nnflnonofloo
nnðnonoðoo
nnþnonoþoo
nnłnonołoo
nnænonoæoo

nnœnonoœoo
nn@nono@oo

1101010000
1111010100
1121010200
1131010300
1141010400
1151010500
1161010600
1171010700
1181010800
1191010900
11$1010$00
11£1010£00
11€1010€00
11¥1010¥00
11⊖1010⊖00
11¢1010¢00
11<1010<00

11>1010>00
11=1010=00
11+1010+00

HHOHOHOOOO
HH1HOHO100
HH2HOHO200
HH3HOHO300
HH4HOHO400
HH5HOHO500
HH6HOHO600
HH7HOHO700
HH8HOHO800
HH9HOHO900
HH$HOHO$OO
HH£HOHO£OO
HH€HOHO€OO
HH¥HOHO¥OO
HH⊖HOHO⊖OO
HH¢HOHO¢OO

HH<HOHO<OO
HH>HOHO>OO
HH=HOHO=OO
HH+HOHO+OO
HH×HOHO×OO
HH÷HOHO÷OO
HH−HOHO−OO
HH&HOHO&OO
HH.HOHO.OO
HH,HOHO,OO
HH:HOHO:OO
HH;HOHO;OO
HH·HOHO·OO
HH…HOHO…OO
HH¿HOHO¿OO
HH?HOHO?OO
HH¡HOHO¡OO
HH!HOHO!OO
HH¶HOHO¶OO
HH§HOHO§OO

HH#HOHO#OO
HH†HOHO†OO
HH‡HOHO‡OO
HH'HOHO'OO
HH"HOHO"OO
HH°HOHO°OO
HH%HOHO%OO

Italic tracking: 0
The United States of America USA or U.S.A., commonly called the United States US or U.S. and America, is a federal constitutional republic consisting of fifty states and a federal district. The country is situated mostly in central North America, where its forty-eight contiguous states and Washington, D.C., the capital district, lie between *The United States of America USA or U.S.A., commonly called the United States US or U.S. and America, is a federal constitutional republic consisting of fifty states and a federal district. The country is situated mostly in central North America, where its forty-eight contiguous states and Washington, D.C., the capital district, lie between the Pacific and Atlantic Oceans, bordered by Canada to the north and Mexico to the south. The state of Alaska is situated in* the Pacific and Atlantic Oceans, bordered by Canada to the north and Mexico to the south. The state of Alaska is situated in the northwest portion of the continent, with Canada to its east and Russia to its west across the Bering Strait. The state of Hawaii is an archipelago in the mid-Pacific. The country also possesses several territories in the

Italic tracking: 4
The United States of America USA or U.S.A., commonly called the United States US or U.S. and America, is a federal constitutional republic consisting of fifty states and a federal district. The country is situated mostly in central North America, where its forty-eight contiguous states and Washington, D.C., the capital district, lie between *The United States of America USA or U.S.A., commonly called the United States US or U.S. and America, is a federal constitutional republic consisting of fifty states and a federal district. The country is situated mostly in central North America, where its forty-eight contiguous states and Washington, D.C., the capital district, lie between the Pacific and Atlantic Oceans, bordered by Canada to the north and Mexico to the south. The state of Alaska is situated in* the Pacific and Atlantic Oceans, bordered by Canada to the north and Mexico to the south. The state of Alaska is situated in the northwest portion of the continent, with Canada to its east and Russia to its west across the Bering Strait. The state of Hawaii is an archipelago in the mid-Pacific. The country also possesses several territories in the

Italic tracking: 8
The United States of America USA or U.S.A., commonly called the United States US or U.S. and America, is a federal constitutional republic consisting of fifty states and a federal district. The country is situated mostly in central North America, where its forty-eight contiguous states and Washington, D.C., the capital district, lie between *The United States of America USA or U.S.A., commonly called the United States US or U.S. and America, is a federal constitutional republic consisting of fifty states and a federal district. The country is situated mostly in central North America, where its forty-eight contiguous states and Washington, D.C., the capital district, lie between the Pacific and Atlantic Oceans, bordered by Canada to the north and Mexico to the south. The state of Alaska* the Pacific and Atlantic Oceans, bordered by Canada to the north and Mexico to the south. The state of Alaska is situated in the northwest portion of the continent, with Canada to its east and Russia to its west across the Bering Strait. The state of Hawaii is an archipelago in the mid-Pacific. The country also possesses several territories in the

Italic tracking: 12
The United States of America USA or U.S.A., commonly called the United States US or U.S. and America, is a federal constitutional republic consisting of fifty states and a federal district. The country is situated mostly in central North America, where its forty-eight contiguous states and Washington, D.C., the capital district, lie between *The United States of America USA or U.S.A., commonly called the United States US or U.S. and America, is a federal constitutional republic consisting of fifty states and a federal district. The country is situated mostly in central North America, where its forty-eight contiguous states and Washington, D.C., the capital district, lie between the Pacific and Atlantic Oceans, bordered by Canada to the north and Mexico to the south. The state of Alaska* the Pacific and Atlantic Oceans, bordered by Canada to the north and Mexico to the south. The state of Alaska is situated in the northwest portion of the continent, with Canada to its east and Russia to its west across the Bering Strait. The state of Hawaii is an archipelago in the mid-Pa-

Italic tracking: 16
The United States of America USA or U.S.A., commonly called the United States US or U.S. and America, is a federal constitutional republic consisting of fifty states and a federal district. The country is situated mostly in central North America, where its forty-eight contiguous states and Washington, D.C., the capital district, lie between *The United States of America USA or U.S.A., commonly called the United States US or U.S. and America, is a federal constitutional republic consisting of fifty states and a federal district. The country is situated mostly in central North America, where its forty-eight contiguous states and Washington, D.C., the capital district, lie between the Pacific and Atlantic Oceans, bordered by Canada to the north and Mexico to the south. The state of Alaska* the Pacific and Atlantic Oceans, bordered by Canada to the north and Mexico to the south. The state of Alaska is situated in the northwest portion of the continent, with Canada to its east and Russia to its west across the Bering Strait. The state of Hawaii is an archipelago in the mid-Pa-

Italic tracking: 20
The United States of America USA or U.S.A., commonly called the United States US or U.S. and America, is a federal constitutional republic consisting of fifty states and a federal district. The country is situated mostly in central North America, where its forty-eight contiguous states and Washington, D.C., the capital district, lie between *The United States of America USA or U.S.A., commonly called the United States US or U.S. and America, is a federal constitutional republic consisting of fifty states and a federal district. The country is situated mostly in central North America, where its forty-eight contiguous states and Washington, D.C., the capital district, lie between the Pacific and Atlantic Oceans, bordered by Canada to the north and Mexico to the south. The state* the Pacific and Atlantic Oceans, bordered by Canada to the north and Mexico to the south. The state of Alaska is situated in the northwest portion of the continent, with Canada to its east and Russia to its west across the Bering Strait. The state of Hawaii is an archipelago in the mid-Pa-

↑
It's always important when testing an idea to take it too far in both directions. That way, you know exactly where you want to be.

letter with rounds). These two letters serve as the foundation of the house—everything else is built on top. In the uppercase, the normal straight letter is *H*, and the round letter is still *O*. Side note: When there is a spacing error on a control character, there is a crack in the foundation, and the whole house must be rebuilt.

For that reason, it's helpful to see every letter between these two. With that in place, it's easy to diagnose exactly where spacing problems occur and figure out how to fix them.

Going Goldilocks

I love a proof with a particular question in mind. For instance, "I was unsure about the spacing, so I made a proof with the tracking adjusted. Here are examples of six paragraphs showing the italic going between 0 and +20."

Testing spacing is just one example. You could just as easily test different weights, x-heights, extender lengths, or alternate forms, as I previously mentioned. The important thing to remember is Goldilocks. Looking at too hot and too cold can surprise you, as there is often interesting stuff at the extremes.

Beyond Boring

While nothing is as straightforward as a traditional proof, I do a lot of proofing in normal graphic design software. It's terrible for looking at spacing strings and the like, but it's great for getting a sense of what it feels like to *use* the typeface. This is particularly useful for display typefaces, but keeping things loose and chaotic is a great way to quickly test ideas and see if they're working.

Other Tips for Proofs

- **Define your .notdef.** The .notdef is the glyph that shows up when a user attempts to type a glyph absent from your character set. It commonly looks like a rectangle with a cross through it, and it can be very distracting in the early phases of your design. If you delete the outlines and set the width to zero, it won't be a bother in the proof.
- **Keep it short.** The best proof is no longer than necessary. If you notice yourself printing many pages that aren't covered in red pen, you might be wasting paper.
- **Date everything.** Keep the current output date in the header or footer of your proof. That way, every time you print something out, the proof is automatically dated. This can be very helpful when you put a process article together at the end of a project, or when historians discover your incredible proofs hundreds of years from now.

→ (overleaf)
While traditional proofs do a terrific job of stress testing fonts in a systematic way, I always find it helpful to do faux design work in a sprawling artboard that lets me be as loose as I want.

MEXICO

RUSSIAN RIVER BREWING

6.7% ABV 750 mL

DEATHLOVE

THE MISSION DISTRICT

SAN FRANCISCO

THE WEDDING SINGER

BLIMEYR

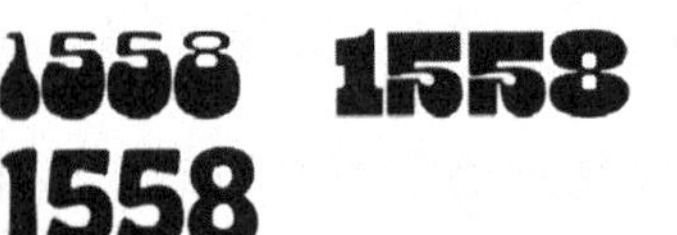

01

CZECH

La France, en forme longue la République française, est une république constitutionnelle unitaire ayant un régime parlementaire à tendance présidentielle dont la majeure partie du territoire et de la population sont situés en Europe occidentale, mais qui comprend également plusieurs régions et territoires répartis dans

02

SWEDISH

España o el Reino de España es un país soberano, miembro de la Unión Europea, constituido en Estado social y democrático de derecho y cuya forma de gobierno es la monarquía parlamentaria. Su territorio está organizado en 17 comunidades autónomas y dos ciudades autónomas. Su capital es la villa de Madrid.

03

CZECH

Česká republika, oficiálním jednoslovným názvem Česko, zkratkou ČR, je stát na území českých zemí ve střední Evropě. Vznikl 1. ledna 1969 jako formálně svrchovaný národní stát pod názvem Česká socialistická

04

SWEDISH

Sverige (officiellt Konungariket Sverige) är ett nordiskt land på Skandinaviska halvön i Nordeuropa. Sverige har landgräns i väst med Norge (svensk-norska gränsen) och i nordost med Finland, samt en fast

HAMBURG

800 CLEMENT ST SAN

Fat Night Selects

I HAVE

Russian River

PISMO BEACH

Guerneville

Arroyo Grande

LAKE LOPEZ

PASADENA

San Luis Obispo

Oceano

HASE

Quiet No Notes

KP Alleged TO

Albatross Suds

Frequent Open

omni Direction

VULF PEEK PORTLAND

DANG

PARANOIA BLUES

Paranoia Blues

Type Media

WEEKEND

I will go

I will st

The Bellweather

OBI

@1734

12345

67890

(NO, STOP.) #GOD

WAIT—STOP 194%

"SHOWN & TELLIN"

TERRIBLE*NOW?

HTTP://OBNO.COM

PHIL@SCHEMER

B-W $2.57—$9.39

ABOUT-CONTACT

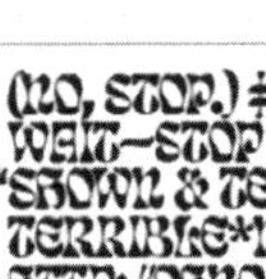

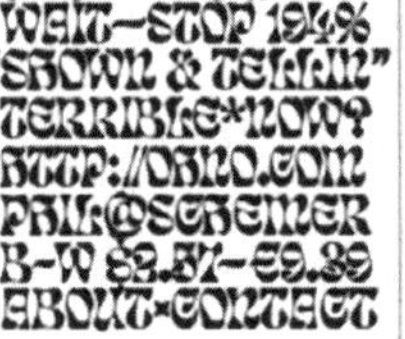

Idioplasms Ingrateful Tittlebats Insulated

Agilas Sumphs Ordinee Hamper Greeter Erodi

Idioplasms Ingrateful Tittlebats Insulated

Agilas Sumphs Ordinee Hamper Greeter Erodi

Idioplasms Ingrateful Tittlebats Insulated Agilas Sumphs Ordinee

Hamper Greeter Erodium Superadditions Volunteering Priorships

Idioplasms Ingrateful Tittlebats Insulated Agilas Sumphs Or

dinee Hamper Greeter Erodium Superadditions Volunteering Pri

SEROTINES CORDAGES CARCASED CAR

TOONED ROTATES NIPPINESS VIVAT TAIV

SEROTINES CORDAGES CARCASED CAR

TOONED ROTATES NIPPINESS VIVAT TAIVER

SEROTINES CORDAGES CARCASED CARTOONED ROTATES NIPPI

NESS VIVAT TAIVERING SHOTT VINTNER AESTIVATING DISPERSOID

Optical

OBNO COMPANY

CALIFORNIA

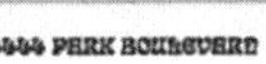

4444 PARK BOULEVARD

Dang

"LIFE'S A THRILL,

RAKSTANDE

ABERWIESEN

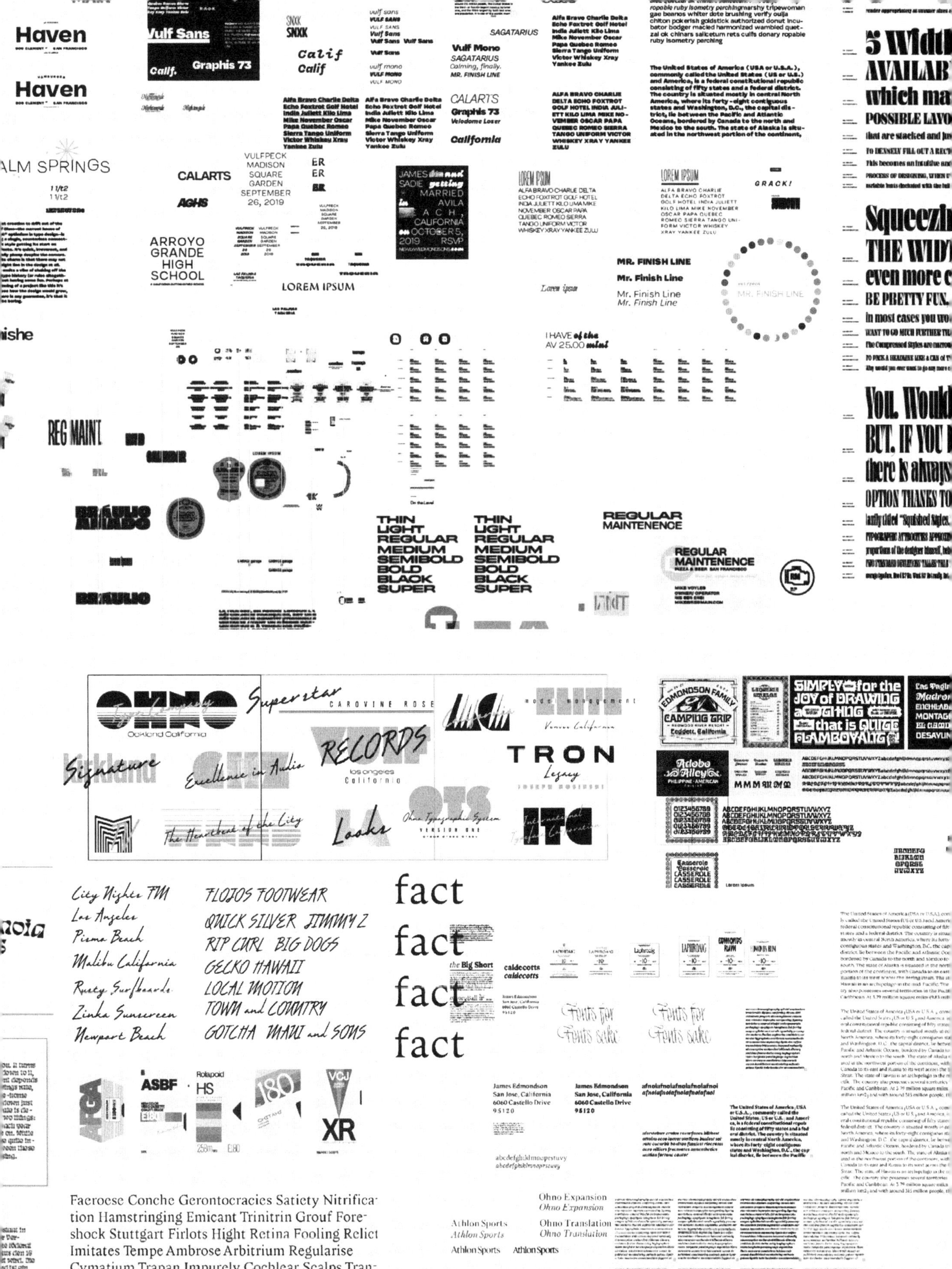

VECTO

RIZING

CHAPTER SIX

VECTORIZING

Pierre Bézier was a French engineer who came up with the idea of representing complex curves that couldn't otherwise be expressed in mathematical formulas by way of a start point, an end point, and a couple of control points that influence the curve along the way.

Decades later, we're still using good ol' Pierre's *Bezier curves* (pronounced Bezzy-EH) to draw type and graphics—and to design the hulls of commercial boats. But this book isn't about *that*.

Drawing with these sorts of curves on a computer, via the redundantly named Pen Tool, feels very unintuitive at first. I can't tell you how many times I opened up Adobe Illustrator as a kid, attempted to get the Pen Tool to do what I wanted, failed, curled up into fetal position, crapped my pants, and started to cry. One day, something clicked, and the Pen Tool and I have been quite close ever since.

I don't want to overstate the importance of good vectors. They're certainly necessary but perhaps less important than a clear concept and good spacing. I've seen students grasp the best practices for digital drawing much faster than spacing. I'm not sure why this is, but in type design education, it seems that good technical drawing isn't the most challenging hurdle.

The fine-tuning required for a decent end result means that the drawing should facilitate tinkering. If you can edit easily, quality is already in your crosshairs.

The Starting Line

The infinite potential for error is intimidating to many folks starting out. I've seen students afraid to make any changes on the computer because the fear of screwing it up paralyzes their progress. They come in with a chisel, carefully moving one or two units here or there, when in reality what they need is a wrecking ball.

The mental hurdle of making what feels like destructive edits to your work is terrifying. When progress is slow, you might hesitate to undo your hard work. Something as simple as a Save As can liberate you emotionally, allowing you to march forward fearlessly. Whenever I'm stuck, I reach for the Save As, and it often saves my As.

The Right Points

As a rule, it's a good idea to keep the number of points as small as you can. Extraneous points make editing laborious and awkward. As long as you're achieving the drawing you want, less is more.

The Right Places

Here's the first weird vocabulary term you might be unfamiliar with: *extrema* (the plural form of *extremum*). Math people will understand extremum to be the maximum or minimum value of a function. For our purposes, the extrema are the highest, lowest, farthest right, or farthest left points on a curve. That verbal definition probably doesn't help at all, so here's a graphic.

Having points on the extrema means you will have horizontal or vertical handles coming off your points. That makes it easy to edit, because you can hold-shift in most drawing applications to lock on to 90° angles.

The exception to this is where you have a point on the corner of a shape, and there is no way that you can achieve the desired shape with a handle shooting off at a 90° angle.

Another exception would be points at the inflection of a curve. Imagine you're driving in a car along an *S*, starting at the bottom. You immediately begin turning left, but at some point in the middle of the *spine*, your steering wheel will be at exactly twelve o'clock. This is known as the *inflection point*, and it often helps to put a point there to achieve the desired curve. (The inflection point isn't always necessary, of course. In really narrow shapes, you're less likely to need it.)

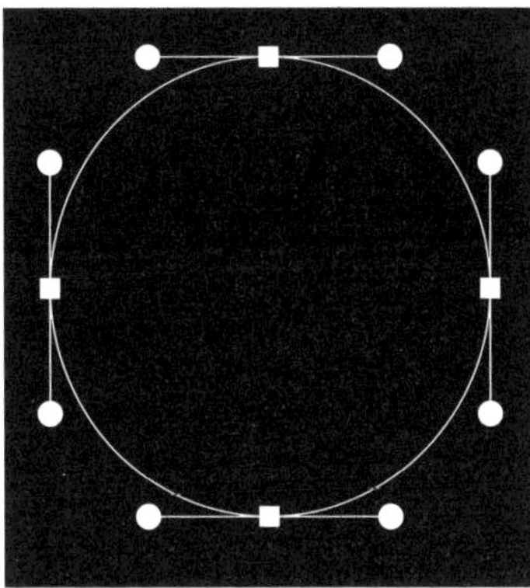

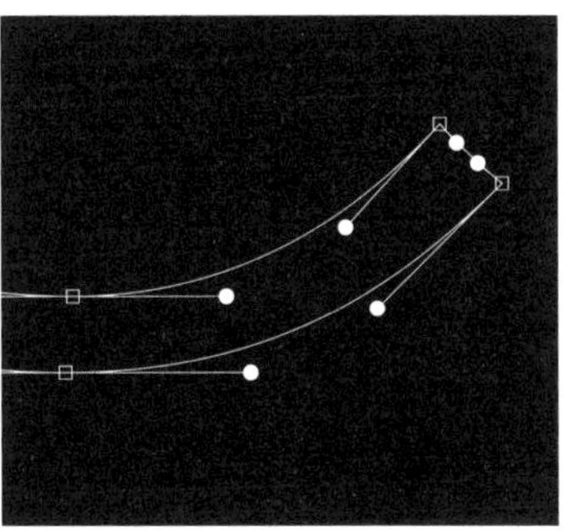

↑ (top)
Points at the extrema of a circle. Type design is extreme! The points located off the curve go by a lot of names, but are mostly called off-curve points or handles.

↑ (bottom)
The bottom half of the c in Vulf Mono Light Italic. On the terminal, we see a good example of handles coming off at weird angles because the points define a corner. Sometimes I hear a student say, "I can't keep my handles on 90° angles and get the shape I want!" That's when I say, "OK."

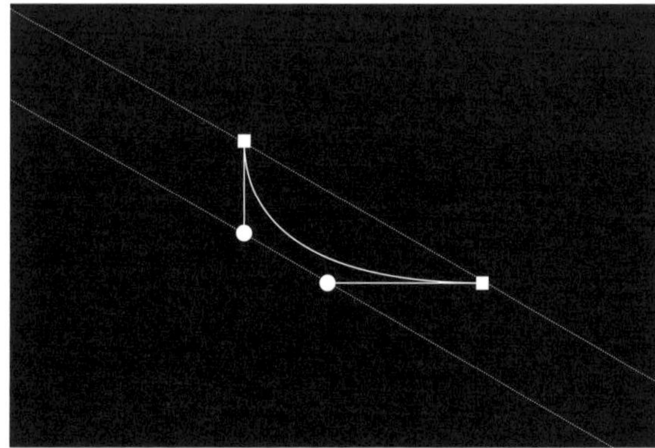

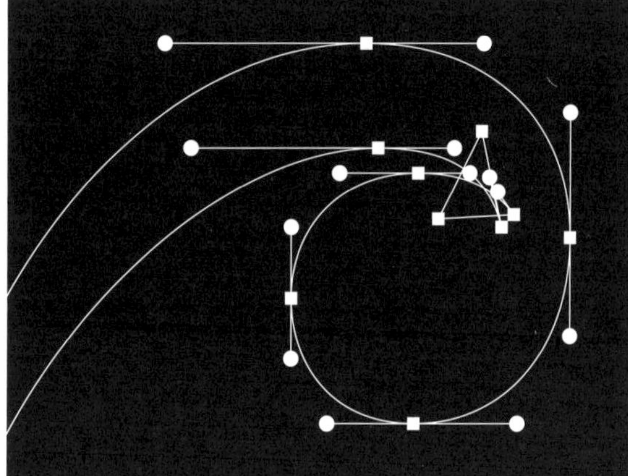

↑ (top)
If you draw a line connecting two points, and then a line connecting two handles, the two lines will often be parallel, or nearly parallel.

↑ (bottom)
Ball terminals can be the trickiest things to draw. By including a little triangle of overlap, you can change the shape of the ball without affecting the stroke leading into it, and vice versa. This idea is seriously powerful, and my typefaces are riddled with little triangles of overlap all over the place.

Vector Lessons from the Greats

My first type design instructor was Rod Cavazos, whom I mentioned in chapter 2. He was the first to teach me about sharing *curve tension*. To achieve a smooth shape, examine the relationship between the points and the handles.

A few years back, I saw Jesse Ragan speak about the process of digitizing Showcard Stunt. In his presentation, he showed that the way he vectorized was similar to how the strokes would have been painted. If a sign painter would complete a *T* in two strokes, Jesse would outline each stroke as a single shape. It's an excruciatingly simple idea, but still powerful: Trace the stroke, not the shape.

This helps with two things. First, it creates a more authentic digitization that is more closely related to the tool that the typeface references, be it a sign painter's brush, a broad nib pen, or anything else. Secondly, it lets you edit one shape without unintentionally messing with the other.

Years after I saw Jesse talk, I got to learn about proper drawing in grad school at TypeMedia. I got a couple of hot tips from my teachers over there.

Drawing for Interpolation

All of these techniques allow for easy editing, but the added benefit is that the shapes are already optimized for interpolation. That's a whole other can of worms, so I won't get into it for now.

Additional Killer Tips

To the beginner, it can feel impossible to get the curve you want while following the rules, so here's a couple of tricks I use.

- Forget the rules and draw the shape however you can. Then, add the extrema later. Once that's done, you can delete extraneous points and clean up your drawing.
- Move the point and keep the handles in the same place.
- Forget about curves; just click a bunch of straight lines to create a very rough drawing that can then be traced with curves. This is a sort of digital sketching, but any sort of sketching can help too.

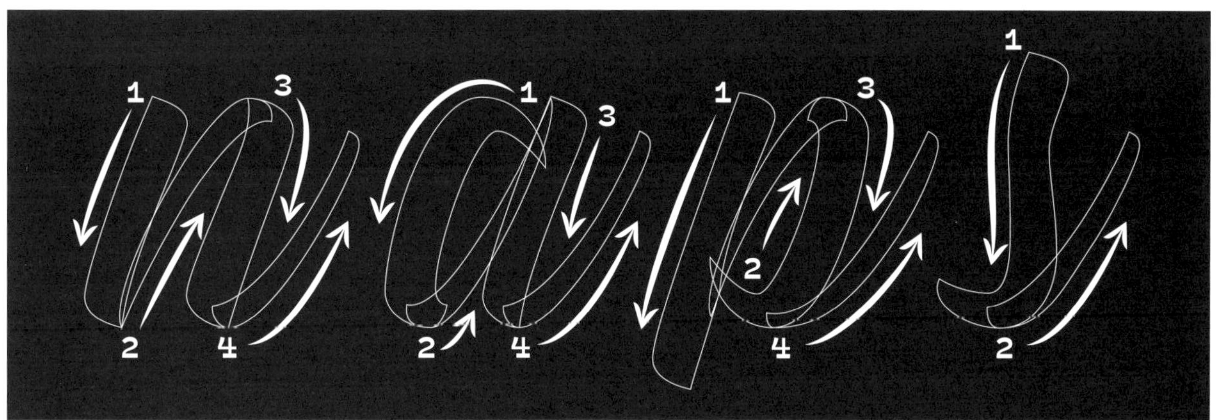

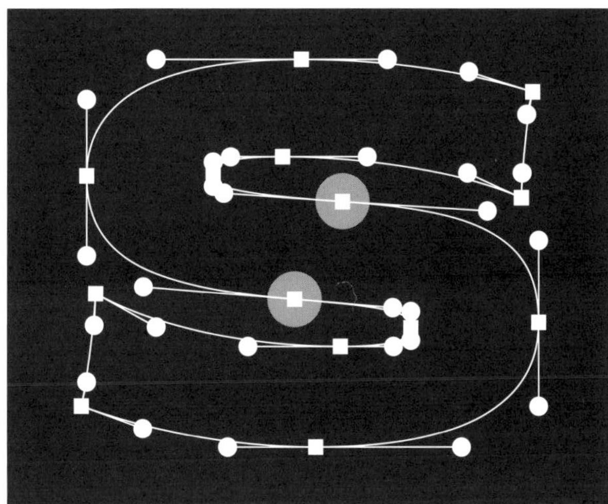

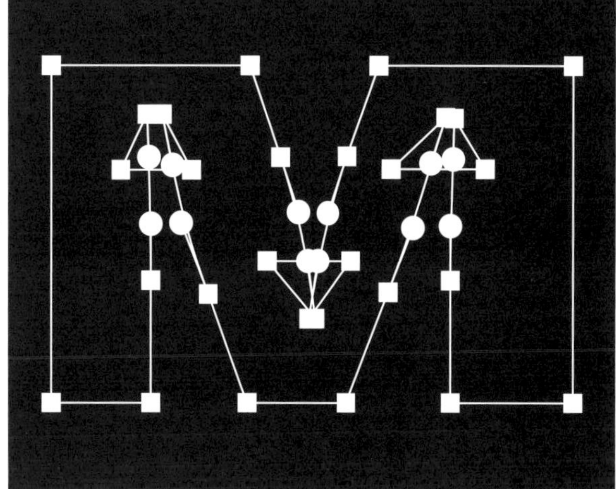

- Opening up other designers' fonts in font software can be illuminating for many reasons, but for the purpose of this section, just seeing how the curves are drawn is pretty helpful. In released fonts, the overlaps have usually been removed, but if you are sneaky, you can find some good-quality open-source projects and open the actual working files and see the real-deal drawings as they were created.

To reiterate:

- Place points on extrema.
- Share curve tension.
- Trace the strokes, not the perimeter.
- Overlap with triangles.
- Listen to the Steely Dan album *Aja* until you achieve enlightenment!

↑ (top)
When vectorizing, it's important to trace the stroke, rather than the perimeter of the shape. We can carry this idea to the logical extreme, but it might not be necessary to go that far.

↑ (bottom left)
The inflection points on the *S* are highlighted. Notice how the handles shoot off with one side inside the shape and one side outside the shape. Could you achieve this curve without the inflection points? Possibly, but I doubt it!

↑ (bottom right)
Here we see more triangular overlaps, which allow you to edit on one side of the stroke without affecting the other stroke.

PRO

CESS

CHAPTER SEVEN

PROCESS

As students, we had to include a process book for all of our big projects. Sharing early sketches and showing how projects evolved over time allowed us to present our work in a way that told the full story and showed the class where we were in our design journey. Since then, in all of our typeface releases, I've tried to do the same. These process notes are a few selections from our library that show how we approach familiar genres, explore options in the sketching phase, iterate, and ultimately make decisions that shape the work. I made these selections to show the full breadth of the Ohno library (and honestly, reading them again after all these years, some just made me laugh!).

→ (top)
The most important part of the type design process happens right at the beginning, when we are nailing down what part of the designspace will be home to our future typeface. Treat this phase with all the love and attention you'd give a newborn babe.

→ (bottom)
This diagram shows the order of how I often work through a lowercase. The basic idea is to define the basics early on, so they can be copy/pasted for maximum efficiency.

1 BEGIN w/ n & o
2
no
3
p
THE p CAN BE MADE FROM YOUR n & o.
7
d
*NO SERIF ON THE TOP RIGHT
16
17
ft
CROSSBAR OF t & f MATCH
21
JUST AN i ON TOP AND A DESCENDER.
j
THE DOT OVER-SHOOTS STEM WIDTH SLIGHTLY
8
FLIP p TO GET q & b
13
14
qb
18
a
STEAL FROM EVERYTHING!
JOINT FROM u.
THE i IS THE LEFT SIDE of n. w/ THE o ON TOP
USE i FOR THE STEM OF b & d
4
i l
STRETCH THE i OUT TO GET l.
5
THE o CAN TURN INTO YOUR c & e.
6
oec
15
r
r IS JUST AN i THAT'S DEPRESSED.
22
PUT A v ON TOP & SLANTED j ON BOTTOM
y
23
JUST l ON LEFT... h ... AND n ON RIGHT
c
MAYBE A DIFF. FORM?
10
v
TAKE UPSIDE DOWN n SERIFS & CONNECT w/ A DIAGONAL TO FORM v.
9
FLIP n TO GET u!
u
26
m
EASY!
19
s
PULL s OUT OF THIN AIR DRAW SERIFS FIRST. IF YOU GOT EM!
24
z
SAME THING HERE
11
w
LAYER TWO vs TO GET A w.
*THIS IS TRICKY
12
k
THE RIGHT OF k CAN BE STOLEN FROM v OR w.
20
g
s AND g BOTH HAVE A "SPINE"
25
x
x IS A STINKER! JUST GET THROUGH IT

OH NO

THE PROCESS OF OBVIOUSLY

YEAR	OPTICAL SIZE	STROKE ENDINGS	WEIGHTS	WIDTH	STRAIGHT LINES
2019	Large	Flat	Thin–Super	Compressed to Extended	Nah

In 2015, I was invited to speak at a conference in Chattanooga, Tennessee. I had the option to set up a little merch table at the side of the conference, but I had absolutely no merch to sell. Because Chattanooga is one of the best city names ever, I decided to do a play on vintage postcards.

The postcards posed an interesting typographic problem: how to get the letters super bold, with whatever distorted proportions are needed, to make as much room as possible for the contained illustrations. I knew the letters wouldn't be a problem, but I had no idea how I'd fill them up. Then I got around that idea by creating a die-cut, allowing folks to put whatever image they wanted behind the lettering.

As is often the case with these sorts of lettering projects, I couldn't help but begin working on the rest of the alphabet. There is something irresistible about the puzzle of super bold letters. Many parameters must be played with in an interesting way when you are prioritizing a match of negative space (counters and letter spaces) rather than the (typical) match of positive space (strokes, stems, etc.).

I continued working on a wider width of this same style and had a real bucket o' fun. This was back before a child and a mortgage had shifted my priorities. My rent was *cheap*, and there was no reason not to fiddle aimlessly with a bunch of half-baked ideas for silly display faces.

If a city can't fill each letter of its name with a tourist attraction, is it even worth going there?

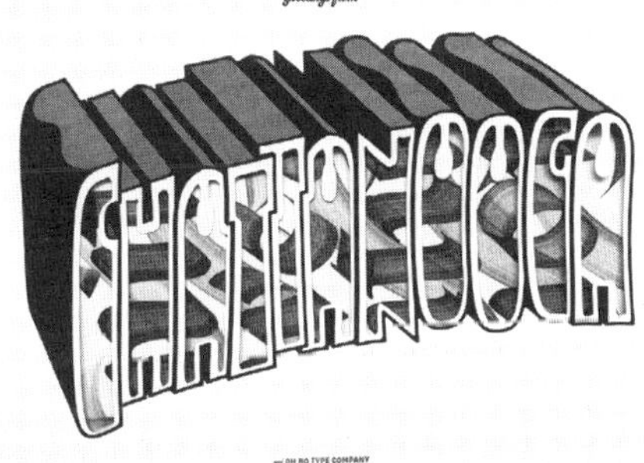

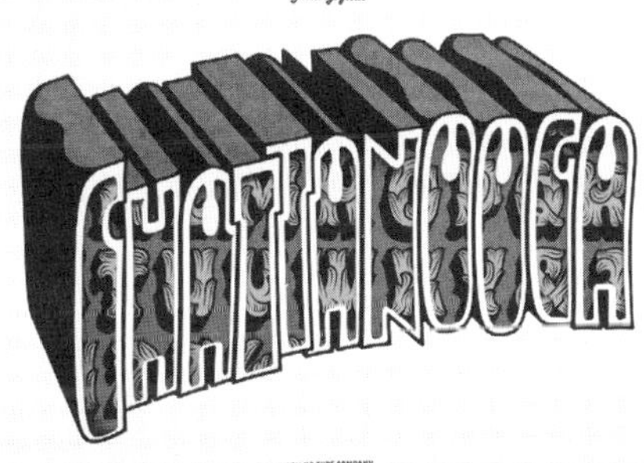

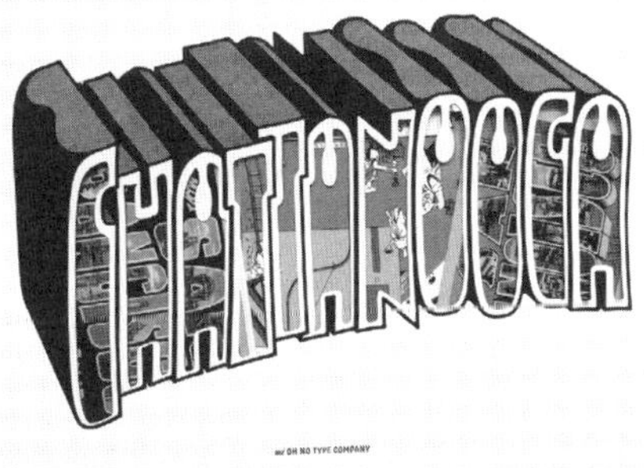

↑ (top)
I love these postcards, but who has the time to fill each letter with an illustration?

↑ (bottom)
I was hoping people would put maps, origami paper, or any cool patterns or textures behind the letterpressed and die-cut top layer I designed. But I have no idea if anyone actually did. These were printed by James Tucker at the Aesthetic Union.

ACE FGHIJ LNOP STU

ABCDEFGHJK
LMNOPRSTU
adefgilnorst

↑ (top)
The typeface at this time had the working title of Chattanooga. Unfortunately, there was already a typeface with this name.

↑ (bottom)
Soon after fleshing out some of the condensed alphabet uppercase letters, I came to the normal width and began playing with the lowercase.

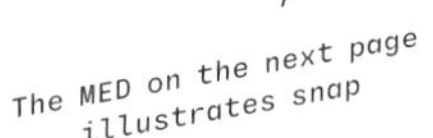

A Little Less Silly

Around this time, I went to TypeCon in Denver and took a preconference sign-painting workshop with John Downer. John introduced me to the idea of "snap," one of the coolest type terms I've ever heard. *Snap*, as I came to understand, referred to slightly flared terminals that imbued letters with a little extra warmth and clarity. Letters with snap were the subtle mark of a true master of the craft. I was drawn to this concept because it was the opposite of something you'd see in the typical geometric grotesque. Also, it seemed in line with some of the characteristics I was baking into Chattanooga. Finally, it is much easier to get some snap with Beziers than it is with a squirrel-hair lettering quill!

After the conference, I returned to my project and was struck with an overwhelming exhaustion with the extreme zaniness of the style. This can happen very quickly with a project. If I take a break and lose steam, all of a sudden the letters aren't getting me stoked anymore, and progress halts.

Aren't those terminals just terrific? Good from up close, and good from far away.

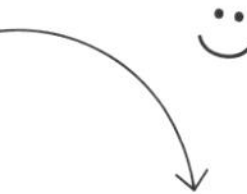

MED

ABCDEFGHJK
LMNOPRSTU
adefgilnorst

↑ (top)
My digitization of John Downer's brushwork. His original letters were 2½ inches tall. The brush lift at the terminals, creating those little corners, is a sight to behold.

↑ (middle)
This version is a bit less silly but still vibrant and warm—and had a greater potential for use. I started playing around with the lowercase.

↑ (bottom)
One of the sources of inspiration: stretched vinyl signage that is slowly distancing itself from its substrate.

CONGIUS CONGIUS
unceasing unceasing

cçćčĉċGĞĜĢĠSŚŠŞŜȘaàâá
ăāąåǻãäæǽcçćčĉċeéèêëĕ
ěėēęɑɑ̀ɑ̂ɑ̈ɑ́ɑ̆ɑ̄ɑ̨ɑ̊ɑ̊́ɑ̃œœ́gğ
ĝġģgğĝġģsśšşŝștţťţțŧŧţțy
ýŷÿyýŷÿ23569&?¿¿©$¢£€
§ªº23569$£€½¾ 23569 23569

↑ (top)
Unfortunately, terminals that worked in the bold didn't work as well in the light condensed styles. I had to find a solution to deal with this. I briefly considered switching the terminals depending on weight and width, but it was too dramatic a change. I posted this online looking for guidance. Type designer Jordan Bell chimed in with the helpful feedback of breaking these two options off into different stylistic sets.

↑ (bottom)
Alternates always seem like a good idea at the beginning of a project and a terrible idea at the end.

Still fond of the general idea, and desperate to push myself to create a larger-than-normal type family, I simplified the forms and expanded the designspace.

Even Less Silly—Chattanooga Is All Grow'd Up

The result was oddly satisfying. The designspace seemed limitless, and I thought it would be a handy font for designers. I knew it was going to be a heavy undertaking, so I braced myself for a tremendous workload.

I was working in the Mission at that time. To get to my studio, I had to walk past one of the print shops that advertises things like "BUSINESS CARDS, COPIES, FAX" in stretched vinyl lettering. I didn't realize it at the time, but I have a total soft spot for stretched Arial, Antique Olive Nord, Microgramma, Impact, and Gill Kayo. I love imagining a designer squishing those already bold letters and thinking,

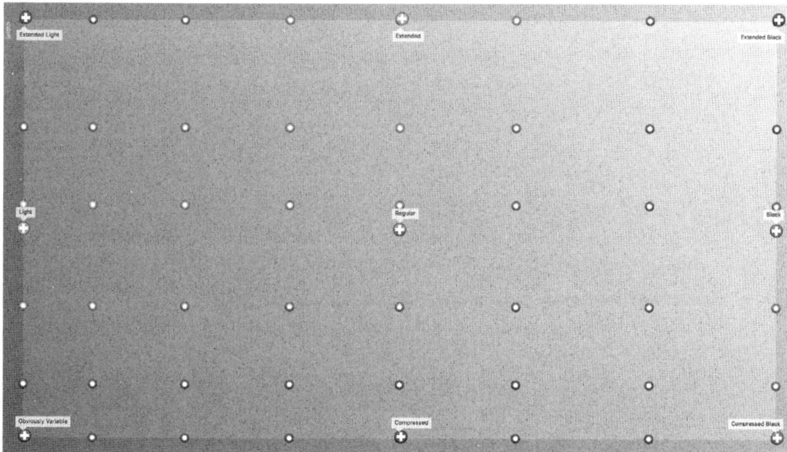

←
The pluses are sources: the actual drawings I have to create by hand. The dots are instances: computer-generated blends of the sources. Obviously had grown to a nine-source family, so any character that got added needed to be drawn nine times. What makes that difficult isn't the actual drawing but the consistency checks that get exponentially more difficult with each additional source.

"Yup, this is perfect." The best part is when the edges of those vinyl letters curl up from too much time in the sun, and a snap-like effect is briefly achieved before a corner gives way and the letter fully distorts.

The Terminal Dilemma

The first issue that really threw me for a loop had to do with the terminals. In the heavy weights, it made more sense to have vertical terminals on *C*, *G*, *S*, *a*, *c*, *e*, *g*, and *s*. However, in the lighter weights, those terminals created unsightly pockets of white space. The letters were fine in isolation, but words were bothering me.

I mostly avoid solving problems via stylistic sets. In most cases, they don't get used, and it becomes tricky to get everything working properly. It also creates more work in terms of kerning, specimen making, and customer support in the future. Even with all those strikes against it, I still liked Jordan Bells's suggestion. Also, at this point, I was oblivious to just how much work I was creating. Immediately I realized that *2*, *3*, *5*, *6*, *9*, *$*, *¢*, *£*, *€*, *&*, *§*, *©*, and *ª* all needed alternates as well. Then I realized that all the alternate figures needed old-style alternates, and later, I figured out that all fractions, superiors, and inferiors that had those figures in them needed still more alternates. I was exhausted, and I hadn't even started kerning yet.

Being Crushed Under the Weight of My Own Designspace

At this point, I had done typefaces with a weight axis, and I had done typefaces with a width axis. How hard could it be to put those things together?

Working Title Chattanooga ss01

Handglove Handglove Handglove Handglove
Handglove Handglove Handglove Handglove
Handglove Handglove Handglove Handglove
Handglove Handglove Handglove Handglove

Working Title Chattanooga ss02

Handglove Handglove Handglove Handglove
Handglove Handglove Handglove Handglove
Handglove Handglove Handglove Handglove
Handglove Handglove Handglove Handglove

OBVIOUSLY
color
television

Garages
Garages

OBVIOUSLY
VARIABLE
COMING
SOON!

↑ (top)
On September 5, 2018, I emailed Chattanooga, in its limited form, to Marty.

↑ (bottom and opposite)
I changed the name from Chattanooga to Obviously and put the first specimens on Future Fonts: a single condensed style with seriously limited punctuation and no accented characters. The license that Future Fonts gives type designers for releasing early and often is tremendously useful. My love for that platform and community can't be overstated.

HALF OFF
GOING OUT OF BUSINESS
CASH ONLY
FOUR FOR A DOLLAR
FLEA MARKET
NO SHIRT NO SHOES NO SERVICE
SALE!
CLEARANCE

HALF OFF
GOING OUT OF BUSINESS
CASH ONLY
FOUR FOR A DOLLAR
FLEA MARKET
NO SHIRT NO SHOES NO SERVICE
SALE!
CLEARANCE

Had my first sangria on a field trip with my Spanish class to Spain as a fifteen-year-old. I still love the stuff!

This genre of signs (often printed on a fluorescent green) has my heart for eternity.

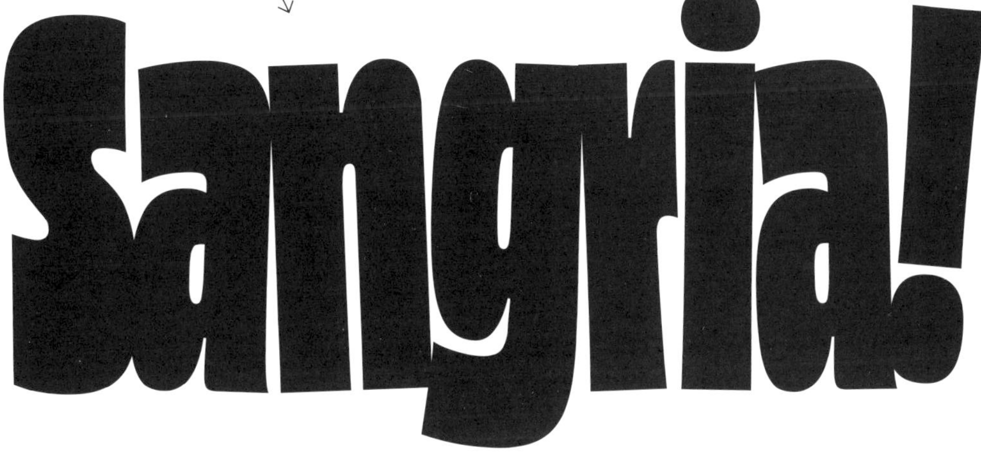

:(

Ugh, faux italics are a heinous crime against humanity. I truly regret publishing them in this book.

OSVKX OSVKX

Edust Onanas Itunas
Edust Onanas Itunas

↑ (top)
The letters on the left are digitally slanted. Those on the right are corrected. It's almost unnoticeable to the untrained eye, but each digitally slanted letter is far from acceptable. The shortcomings of digital slanting are especially visible in round and diagonal strokes.

↑ (bottom)
I showed these two options to my friends Kel Troughton, Tommi Sharp, and Tad Wagner, and the unanimous decision was to opt for the more normal obliques.

Type families can snowball out of control so quickly that I often have entire years of my life scheduled out after five minutes of daydreaming. This is fine if you're the sort of freak that has mastered self-discipline and laser focus. For other human beings who are easily distracted, the project files can end up lying dormant on your hard drive for eternity. I am firmly in the "other human beings" camp, and that's exactly what happened. The workload I created for myself was the very thing that put the brakes on my progress.

Future Fonts and Marty

Around this time (2016–2018), I released some other fonts and I got involved with Travis Kochel and Lizy Gershenzon, two friends who were starting up a project called Future Fonts. I came on board with art direction and recruitment responsibilities, and I put my own projects up on the site as well.

At this time, Ohno was not doing so hot. I was three years in and disappointed that the foundry wasn't even close to supporting itself. Our little girl was going through 150-pack boxes of Huggies at a frightening rate, and I needed to figure something out quick.

I met up with my buddy and mentor Marty Grasser and lamented about some of the stressors floating in my head. Lucky for me, Marty has one of the healthiest approaches to combining art and business of any designer I know. His advice was simple: "You gotta come back to Earth!" Marty's perspective on the Ohno catalog circa 2018 showed me the forest for the trees. There was almost nothing in there that you could use on more than one project. It was all self-indulgent esoteric bullshit. I was completely inspired to make something one step closer to a workhorse. I emailed him a preview of Obviously that night.

The risk of bringing Obviously to Future Fonts was pretty low. I planned a "cooking-show rollout" where I would prepare styles in advance, and update the project faster than I actually made it. Version 1 went up on September 25, 2018, for sixteen dollars. It was just one style.

Future Fonts has been great at keeping me enthusiastic about my own projects. There is some added accountability, and I often receive great feedback from the community. It's relatively easy to get the first version together, and with this project, the first couple of versions were already done by the time I started sharing it with the world.

The Unfortunate Realization of the Inevitable Slog Before Me

Around October, the work I made visible through Future Fonts had caught up with the work I'd done. I had no more additions to the typeface hiding in my back pocket. I was confronted with the brutal reality of how slowly this typeface was going to develop. The diagram on page 99 illustrates the reason why.

Still, it seemed I wanted to make things harder on myself. I shifted the sources around and tried to get the designspace to a place where I could get the most (instance) bang for my (source) buck. This was a decision I'd pay for later, as many of the interpolations didn't go as smoothly as I'd hoped.

At this point, the design work was essentially done, and it became a matter of production work. In general, I like how type design is a mix of about 5 percent creativity and problem-solving and 95 percent zoning out with flow-state production work. Obviously was pushing this ratio closer to 1:99, and my patience was wearing thin. Luckily, Future Fonts income reports were showing that Obviously was my most financially viable project to date, so I kept my nose to the grindstone and pushed out a few more versions.

Ugh, Do I Really Need Italics?

I knew at some point someone was going to ask for italics, but I didn't know if I had the heart to actually make them. After all, this would essentially take the designspace into two dimensions, doubling the number of sources.

Obviously had been drawn with variable fonts in mind from the beginning. I knew that if I drew the romans with a continuous áĕöūñ

ííĭĭïïīīįįĩĩ

↑
The narrower *I* accents. Have you ever felt like you bit off more than you could chew?

ductus, I could interpolate between the romans and italics to give users a fun "slant" slider so they could select the angle of the italics.

This was a particularly boring and isolating operation to perform. The number of sources quickly doubled to eighteen, and I had to go through nine of them and correct the obliques.

Final Polish

I had to fix several stupid things in the final versions of the fonts. For instance, accents over characters like *I* in the wide styles had to be made narrower to avoid collisions, and I added more (perhaps unnecessary) stylistic sets for a *t* with no tail (a "Jesus t") and a single-story *a*.

I Never Thought This Would Be Done

Here's what I want to remember for later: We are running a marathon, not a sprint. As much as I like to work quickly and get stuff out there, there is something to be said for the long and winding road that creates work of considerable heft. Also, a community of people gently requesting additional styles and features can do a lot to sustain development. To do anything, I have to feel like it's *worthwhile* and hopefully *important*. Obviously was already worthwhile—it was a learning experience in font production and self-discipline—but it's up to users whether it becomes important.

↑
I briefly considered making a rounded version of Obviously called Vaguely, but the idea never matured.

OUSLY!

OH no

our doctor about

rhensa

CLOHEPTAPIPERIDINECARBOXYLATEDIMETHYLETHYLAMINE

es the pain
le go away.
ch pain?
f it."

4038

Y TECH
OTIVE
ANIC 1984-2019

CHEROKEE
FREIGHT
LINES

STOCKTON
S DOT 154922

2596

OPEN

HOURS
MONDAY-FRIDAY
10AM–8PM
SATURDAY & SUNDAY
10AM–5PM

FR
PIC
& DEL

WELCOME TO
OBVIOUSLYTO
"THE VIN
CAPITAL

PAID FOR BY THE
OBVIOUSLYTOWN
CHAMBER OF COMMERCE

SANDWICHES SNACKS DRINKS COFFEE BAGELS CANDY

SWEET
CHINITO

SANDWICHES SNACKS DRINKS COFFEE BAGELS CANDY

FRENCH CUISINE

SEPOLITESSE

HAYES VALLEY

1029

AUDROMAT

WASH DRY FOLD

SAME DAY SERVICE

HELLA MACHINES

TRIPLE SIZE DRYERS

OPEN 24 HOURS

7 DAYS / WEEK

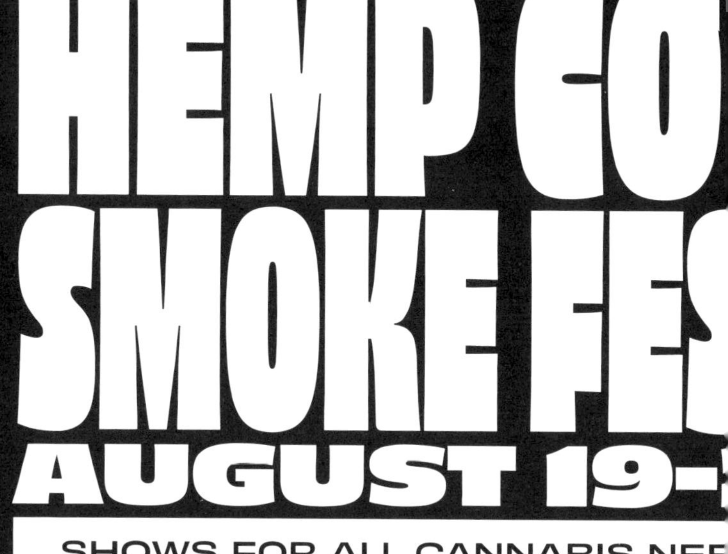

CASH

PLEASE & THANK YOU!

ONLY

THIS "EZC" SUPER

MERCHANDISING DOOR IS

SELF

CLOSING

ZERO COLD INC.

ANAHEIM, CALIFORNIA

PULL

-OR-

PUSH

BOS

MON

THE PROCESS OF

DEGULAR

YEAR	OPTICAL SIZE	STROKE ENDINGS	WEIGHTS	CONTRAST	GENRE
2020	Text to Display	Flat	Thin to Black	Low	Grotesque

In the spring of 2019, I tweeted out a questionnaire that was as simple as possible: (1) Ever purchased anything from Ohno? (2) What's the best thing about Ohno? (3) What's the worst thing? I was most interested in the responses to question 3, and one answer in particular echoed in my mind for months.

This bit of reality hit me like a ton of bricks. At once I had a hunch of how to save our business, and my daughter's college fund.

"It would be great to be able to use an Ohno font more than once."

Ouch.

How Do You Name Your Typefaces?

My studio mate and long-time buddy Kel Troughton and I were walking out of Sparky's Giant Burgers in Oakland, California. We had just polished off an extremely affordable lunch and were singing the praises of this legendary East Bay eatery. Kel summed it up by saying, "The burgers are pretty good here, nothing incredible, just a good, regular degular burger."

Kel's affinity for and impeccable use of slang had stopped me in my tracks before, but nothing hit quite like this. Immediately, I knew I had to return to that unfinished sans project, name it Degular, and bring it to the finish line.

Becoming a Hypocrite

It wasn't so long ago that I made every effort to curb the use of grotesques in graphic design. From my perspective, their abundance is similar to turning on the radio and hearing techno on every station. Sure, techno is OK, but why should a single genre dominate so heavily? I tried to translate this idea into a Twitter-friendly format, and it became my only viral tweet.

The popularity of that tweet was inspiring to me. Maybe people were becoming more aware that mega-corporations assume similar voices to leverage the power of their peers, and maybe that could lead to a backlash of rogue designers embracing the chutzpah of the typographically adventurous. But one night, my mind was changed.

I had spent the day putting off lunch while feverishly trying to finish Ohno Blazeface Italic from a coffee shop. Driving home, my hunger was too much to bear, but in the nick of time, the familiar glow of red Arial letters shining like a beacon in the night entered my peripheral vision. I quickly U-turned and parked beneath the "TAQUERIA" sign deep within a strip mall. While inhaling my dinner, I confronted the harsh reality that Arial (and all similar grotesques) works. They work on tired and hungry drivers. They work from a hundred yards away with a terrible vantage point. Thinking about my distaste for conventional sans, I ate my burrito—and my words along with it.

↑ (top)
I have been on Twitter for ten years and have had exactly one tweet that caught on.

↑ (bottom)
The dimensional, backlit, Arial caps sign that spoke to my soul—and speaks to me still. Recreated from memory.

Save As

I came back to Covik Sans, which was already a distillation of many of the lessons I took away from TypeMedia. I did a Save As and began ironing out all traces of the pen in a new file called Foundation Sans. It was a boring name for what I hoped to be a boring typeface.

I was trying to figure out how to approach the joints. The humanist method of overlapping joints felt more interesting and maintained a nice rectilinear texture in paragraphs, but at every crossroads, I tried my best to steer away from what I would normally do.

The most interesting part of the project was that it was still fun. I was totally enjoying stretching my comfort zone and drawing in a way that shunned attention, rather than commanded it. As it turned out, that agrees with the science. Cal Newport, author of *So Good They Can't Ignore You*, puts it this way:

The United States of America (USA or U.S.A.), commonly called the United States (US or U.S.) and America, is a federal constitutional republic consisting of fifty states and a federal district. The country is situated mostly in

The United States of America (USA or U.S.A.), commonly called the United States (US or U.S.) and America, is a federal constitutional republic consisting of fifty states and a federal district. The country is situated mostly in

↑
I wasn't sure whether to go with joints that grew out of the stems or joints that overlapped. In moments of self-doubt, I remember the mantra "Don't look aloof; make yourself a proof."

We don't have much evidence that matching your job to a pre-existing interest makes you more likely to find that work satisfying. The properties we know lead people to enjoy their work—such as autonomy, mastery, and relationships—have little to do with whether or not the work matches an established inclination.

My established inclination here would be unusual display fonts, but the autonomy and mastery required to produce them is exactly the same whether I'm working on that or something decidedly more neutral. With that in mind, I checked my ego at the door and simply tried to do a good job on the first leg of work: creating the roman family. I renamed the project Disclaimer in an effort to focus the project more on small optical sizes.

Save As . . . Again!

When I paired Disclaimer with Vulf Sans as the companion display font, the inconsistency in the terminals became really distracting, and I began thinking about how to reconcile that. My first inclination was to throw tons of alternates at it!

This simple change of adding alternate terminal options was so fundamental to the feeling of the typeface that it began to derail my initial plan of letting Foundation Sans be the most succinct expression of itself. And besides, I had already done this terminal switching move with Obviously.

Disclaimer sat on my hard drive for quite a while in its unfinished state, and although I wasn't actively working on it, I did find myself using it occasionally. This is around the time when Kel took me to Sparky's and gave me the name Degular, and my enthusiasm was renewed.

When coming back to the project with fresh eyes, I wondered if I could add an optical size axis, since the name was no longer married to the idea of small sizes only.

hea hea hea hea
hea hea hea hea

George, Sylvia, and Clara were careless yet strategic in their social developments.

George, Sylvia, and Clara were careless yet strategic in their social developments.

George, Sylvia, and Clara were careless yet strategic in their social developments.

GSCaces → GSCaces

↑ (top)
Here there are only two sources (complete drawings at either end of the spectrum), and you see some inconsistencies in the middle weights, like the crossbars on *e* and *a*. Also, Kel (my former student) told me this is not enough difference between weights, and he was right! I later switched from eight weights to seven.

↑ (middle)
Three kinds of terminals that would be available via stylistic sets: (1) completely horizontal; (2) more open, at an angle; (3) very open, completely vertical. This kind of experimenting can be tedious, but it helps if I chant my mantra "Make a proof, you frickin' goof!"

↑ (bottom)
Hold on to your butts, a monumental change here! I committed to the more-open-but-not-completely-open angled terminals that seemed to fit within the Ohno catalog a bit better than the other options.

SCHELTER & GIESECKE AG., LEIPZIG C1

BREITE FETTE GROTESK-GROSSBUCHSTABEN

ABCDEFGHIJKLMNOPQRSTUVWXYZ 1234567890

SOLE DISTRIBUTORS: ADAIR, DUTT & CO., 27, POLLOCK STREET THE WORLD-RENOWNED PRINTING MACHINE MAKERS

GROSSBUCHBINDEREI KONRAD SCHIRRMEISTER IN MÜNCHEN LEOPOLDSPLATZ 20. FILIALEN IN WÜRZBURG UND ERLANGEN

ESPOSIZIONE DEL LIBRO E D'ARTE GRAFICA 1930 MATERIALE SCOLASTICO PER GL'ISTITUTI MEDII

ANNUITÉ DE CONVERSION DE L'EMPRUNT FAURE CRÉDIT LYONNAIS, 19, BOULEVARD DES ITALIENS

SOCIEDAD IMPORTADORA Y EXPORTADORA BUENOS AIRES - 68, CALLE DE SAN MIGUEL

MODENHAUS RAIMUND STOLZENBERG, ROSTOCK

BREITE FETTE GROTESK

ABCDEFGHIJKLMNOPQRSTUVWXYZ abcdefghijklmnopqrstuvwxyz 1234567890

Letterpress Printing Machine Manufactory, Leipzig SOLE AGENTS: INDO-EUROPA TRADING CO.

Mode d'Election du Conseil municipal LE MONDE COURSE DE TOULOUSE

Testo-atlante di geografia sacra L'EUROPA NEL XVI SECOLO

Material Eléctrico para Luz PRODUCTOS QUIMICOS

Das Schwäbische Meer

Breslauer Stadtpark

Chansons anciennes et leurs Poètes

North Eastern Railway, Ireland

Drukarnia Anczyca i Spółki

Neue Wiener Moden

Kloster Rodach

160

SCHELTER & GIESECKE AG., LEIPZIG C1

HALBFETTE KURSIV-GROTESK

ABCDEFGHIJKLMNOPQRSTUVWXYZ abcdefghijklmnopqrstuvwxyz 1234567890

Vielen gibt das Glück allzuviel, aber keinem gibt es genug

Everything to be seen and done this month in Liverpool

Fabbricanti di Automobili Costruttori Meccanici 59

Transport en grande vitesse entre Paris-Toulon

The Land and Ocean Scenery of South Africa

Literatur und Kunst in der Türkei

Atlas de Géographie physique et politique Bar-sur-Seine

Collection of British and American Authors

Graphische Kunst der Gegenwart

MEDIÄVAL-STEINSCHRIFT

ABCDEFGHIJKLMNOPQRSTUVWXYZ abcdefghijklmnopqrstuvwxyz 1234567890

Spezialität: Kataloge, Postkarten, Mehrfarbendrucke

Nieuwe Goudasche Algemeen Handelsblad 68

Handlexikon des praktischen Wissens

Notes sur les photographies artistiques

Mémoires des Officiers turcs 45

Modello della germinazione

Handbücher für Drucker

Rhine Boat Company

Une Délibération à Fontainebleau

Los placeres causan pena

Botanisches Lehrbuch

161

↑
Why do the pages of old specimens look so good? Not just the samples but the descriptions, titles, and folios too? One answer is the smell of the book. Another is the feel of the paper. A third answer: optical sizes. Breite Fette Grotesk by Schelter & Giesecke, circa 1925. Did this typeface influence the design of Degular? Only unintentionally.

My Beloved Optical Size Axis

I love designing type with optical sizes and doing graphic design work that uses said fonts. Respect for the intended size of a font truly separates digital design, performed with infinitely scalable vectors, from analog design, performed with physical type at fixed sizes. I used to puzzle over why type specimens from the days of letterpress type look so incredibly good, while any piece of run-of-the-mill modern design pales in comparison.

Despite being a big-time hater of all things Helvetica, I have to admit my fondness for its display usage, specifically when super tightly spaced, with minimal leading.

The big difference between the display and text styles in Degular came in the apertures (the open white spaces found on letters like *a*, *c*, *e*, and *s*). I tried to close them up to an absurd degree, and they created little shards of white space that seemed to dazzle up the texture of words. These tiny windows in the black weight made it feel even bolder, like the shapes were just about to close in on themselves.

Ink traps are the dug-out areas of negative space around joints designed to trap ink at small sizes, avoiding a traffic jam of positive space that inhibits legibility. In Degular Text they are an exaggerated and hard-working feature that is quite noticeable when zooming in but hardly visible when reading paragraphs at actual size. For that reason, the ink traps in the display needed to also be barely visible when viewing them at their actual size.

While the ink trap changed quite a bit, the joints stayed thin. This is a recent trend in type design that I'm quite fond of. I first saw this idea taken to the extreme with the fantastic typeface Media Sans from Production Type. I enjoyed learning that joints are different than the "thins" of a typeface and can be treated as such. You can have something with low contrast and super thin joints that shimmer like a lake under the midnight moon.

A Clarion Book

The True Adventures of Huckleberry Finn As told by John Seelye

3.45

Finishing Touches

The only thing left to do was add a handful of alternates. It's a slippery slope in Alternate Land, and as I previously stated, it was not my intention to solve problems via alternates. The single-story *a* and *g* were no-brainers, as I had to have them in the italic styles. After that, simplified versions of *G* and *t* were all that I deemed necessary. I wish I saw alternates in use more often, so please be aware that these are here awaiting your use!

snug → tight

aces → aces

A huge bonus of working on a grotesque is the relatively minute change between roman and italic. That means you can fit them all within the same variable font. With some substitutions, the italic forms of *a* and *g* show up automatically when you push the slant past 2°.

↑ (top)
Helvetica isn't all bad. In fact, a ton of stuff from early on warms my heart as much as anything else. This particular use (contributed to Fonts in Use by Chris Purcell) is a perfect summary of good Helvetica: tight spacing, tight leading, printed around 1970, with a little reflection to add some chaos.

↑ (middle)
When I did my first tests using Degular for display, I found myself consistently tracking. So why not bake that super tight spacing into the font?

↑ (bottom)
The apertures in Degular, a main difference between text and display.

Failure

When I began finishing up the work on these fonts and showing them to my friends, their reaction was not at all what I had anticipated. They were saying things like "Wild" and "I can totally see your hand in this." In an effort to make something super bland and devoid of emotion, I had completely failed. I wasn't able to remove myself from the work as much as type designers Kai Bernau or Kris Sowersby, but in *trying* to do that, I hopefully created something barely unique.

n n → n n

Managerial
Customs Union

age → *age* → *age*

Gadget → Gadget

↑ (top)
The size of the ink trap in the text styles is about 40 units, which shrinks to about 2 units in the display styles.

↑ (middle top)
I love Media Sans from Production Type. I just wish the descenders were shorter!

↑ (middle bottom)
The italic forms of *a* and *g* show up automatically in Degular Variable when the slant is pushed beyond 2°.

↑ (bottom)
Alternates for *G*, *a*, *g*, and *t*.

→ (opposite)
There are just a few places where Degular has a little bit of fun. The *S*, for instance, is a bit more wide on the bottom, and the *g*'s ear goes flat. Even a simple stylistic decision like that on the *S* is never executed in just one place. Opportunities to echo an idea are usually taken!

I wanted to do a good job, and I would be lying if I said this project wasn't in some way financially motivated. Corporations big and small overwhelmingly favor low-contrast geo-grotesques, and as a small business, I have to throw my hat in the ring. Degular is a conventional typeface that subsidizes work on unconventional typefaces. The other bonus is that it's the first Ohno typeface you can use more than once!

Sg

§2

3

GNE

ar
ar
ar
ar
ar.

Original Release: 2020
Mono Update: 2023

"IT WOULD BE NICE TO USE AN OHNO FONT MORE THAN ONCE."

©1986 STRAIGHT
DEGGIN ENT.

TOR of shipping,
kaging materials

"Most of y
typeface

Ordinary Merchandising LLC

[6] 12×18
[7] 16×20
[8] 24×36

At **Degular Rubber**, we believe that *working hand-in-hand with our clients* is the key to producing high-quality, precision-made products. From the moment we learn about the solution our clients are seeking, we work with them as our partner throughout the process. **This commitment to our partners** is part of what makes Degular Rubber Products so special.

at Services & lanufacturing Inc.

Basic Industries Marketing Group Corp.

THE PROCESS OF VULF MONO

YEAR	CONTRAST	STROKE ENDINGS	WEIGHTS	PROPORTIONS	STRAIGHT LINES
2016	Low	Slab	Light–Bold	Monospace	Nah

It was Sunday, October 8, 2015. My roommate and I were making the drive from a dingy hotel in Rohnert Park to our apartment in the fog-drenched hillside of San Francisco's Outer Sunset District. Bleary-eyed and dizzy from the night before, I lazily opened up my Discover Weekly playlist and randomly selected "Wait for the Moment," a soulfully nuanced groove from some band with a weird name.

We both knew there was something special there, so into the artist page we dove. This is a path I've followed many times before, but often, the remainder of a band's discography fails to deliver the goods. We put on their album *Thrill of the Arts* and were completely blown away. About two minutes into the auditory odyssey that is "Welcome to Vulf Records," I had found my new favorite band. "Funky Duck" made us laugh out loud, "Back Pocket" had the best clarinet solo in existence, and "Rango II" made me grab the "oh shit" handles of the car.

We immediately checked tour dates, hoping a San Francisco appearance might be in the cards. To our amazement, they had a show booked five miles from home that night. It was *hands down*

↑
The IBM Selectric typewriter was a technological milestone not only for the multiple font choices available to it (see the balls of type), but also due to the machine's "memory," which allowed you to type faster than the machine could print.

the best show of our lives. The music gods blessed us that night, and to this day I don't understand why.

You can connect the dots from this story to Rob Stenson's foreword at the beginning of this book. I can't describe my excitement when Jack Stratton, the leader of my new favorite band, reached out looking for the only thing I could provide them: an incredibly specific custom typeface.

Jack was looking for a bold monospace that referenced the Light Italic available as a golf ball for IBM Selectric typewriters. A number of things are interesting here:

- A musician aware of the power of custom type and its relationship to branding
- A relatively young person aware of IBM Selectric typewriters and the fonts available for them
- Someone outside of the type world using the word *monospace*
- A monospace typeface for a funk band? Most definitely not an obvious choice when you consider the rich history of expressive type and lettering on funk and soul record covers.

In addition to his musical contributions to Vulfpeck, Jack is in charge of marketing and design for the unsigned band. For someone

ABCDEFGHIJKLMNOPQRSTUVWXYZ
abcdefghijklmnopqrstuvwxyz

@#$%¢&*()_+ :",.?
234567890-= ;',./

1167014 ± °
1 !

1167032 ± ¼
1 ½

↑ (left)
The inspiration: 12-point Light Italic. Image courtesy of Luc Devroye.

↑ (right)
The simple difference between a geometric square (left) and one with slight bends on all sides (right). A subtle move to be sure, but one that can breathe life into a design when echoed through thousands of outlines.

who can play any rhythm section instrument with impressive competence, he knows his way around the Creative Suite astonishingly well. I was simply happy to be working with the person who would be using the type. It was time to start sketching.

Warmth in Vectors

Putting the same nuance and soul into a monospace that Vulfpeck puts into their tunes became the name of the game. The Light Italic from IBM was fun and lively, but part of its charm was the fact that it gets printed on a sheet of paper in front of you, with all the subtle inconsistencies that are inherent in typewriters. The job was making type come alive in digital outlines, without applying some hacky filter to roughen edges or distress the shapes. I believe those things should be left to the typographer or graphic designer.

One of the biggest challenges of designing monospace type is dealing with the widest and narrowest glyphs. Simply put, *i*, *l*, *j*, *m*, and *w* are a real nightmare. Luckily, with a slab serif design, one can elongate entrance and exit strokes to occupy as much horizontal space as possible.

Another difficulty is consistency in the width of capital and lowercase letters. In most monospace typefaces, caps become a bit condensed, while the lowercase maintains more traditional proportions. Because this was not an actual typewriter face, and because it was not intended for code, horizontal economy was not an issue. We had the luxury of going wide with the minuscules, allowing the majuscules to be more normal.

Broadening the Designspace

Although the bold italic that Jack initially requested would be a sufficient stand-alone, I knew that making the typeface truly useful meant building out the family—not a trivial task, but perfectly within the realm of possibility.

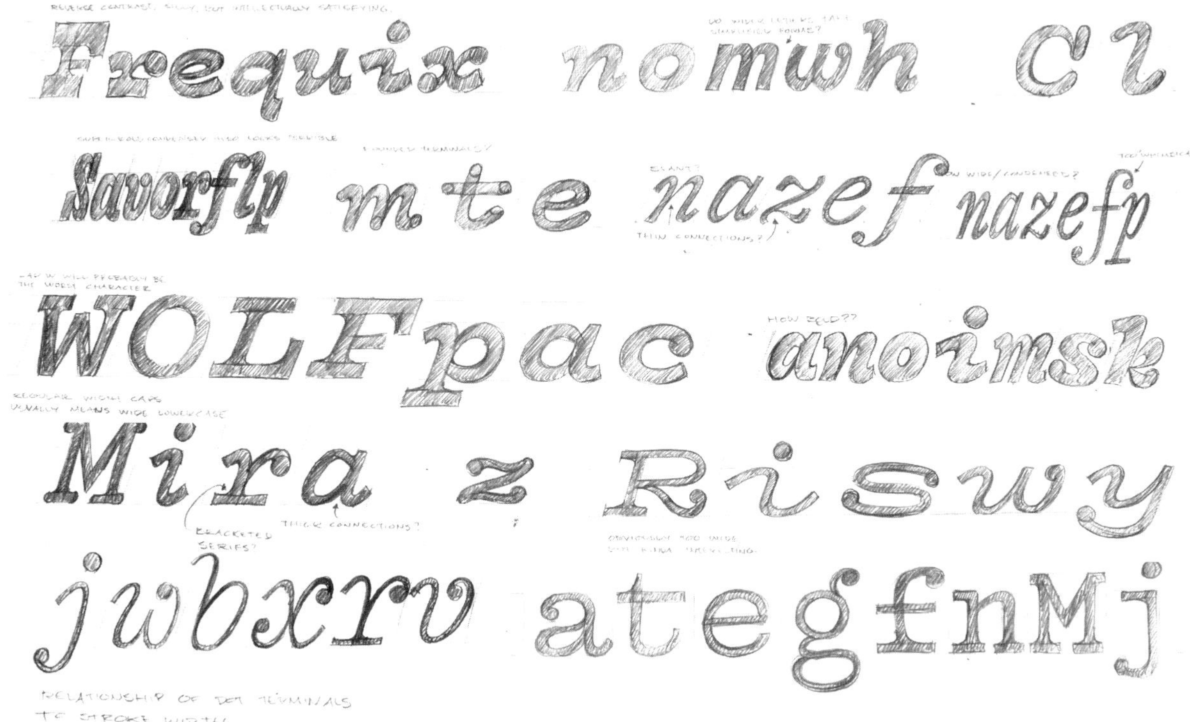

↑ (top)
My initial sketches for Vulf ranged wildly in weight and width. Leaving no stone unturned is always a good strategy for dialing in the variables to find their sweet spot.

↑ (bottom)
Though the vast sketching exploratory revealed a few interesting directions, Jack resisted their novelty and found my first sketch of the Vulf logotype to be more fitting for the band.

fußball ilfmw nnnnn

ABCDEFGHIJKLMNOPQRSTUVWXYZ
abcdefghijklmnopqrstuvwxyz

↑ (top left)
Another opportunity for warmth came from the slant of the individual letters. By making certain letters like *f* and *ß* lean back, they more appropriately filled out their rectangles, minimizing pockets of white space.

↑ (top right)
An early version of the typeface, showing how adjusting the varying slope helps to fill horizontal space more evenly.

↑ (bottom)
The relation in width between upper and lowercase is a challenging give-and-take for monospace designs. This early version of Vulf Mono also shows ball terminals on *K* and *R*, a detail that was later ironed out.

The rest of the process was mostly manual labor, with little room for invention. Luckily, Jack was a pleasure to work with and usually kept his responses to my emails under two words, which is a great sign of respect.

Bringing It Home

Arrows are a feature in typefaces that I find to be quite useful, and because this was for a band that is particularly musically literate, I felt obliged to offer some additional music-related dingbats in all four weights.

In Closing

When you love a band, you are compelled to express that, but you know the limitations in getting your point across. Making Vulf Mono has become my vehicle for appreciating the music and honoring the skill and artistry with which it is made. Whether I'm reading or listening to music, I've always been attracted to the human element. Joe Dart, Vulfpeck's legendary bass player, said,

> My practice regimen for a long time was playing along with a drum machine. I think that having great time is maybe the most important element as a bass player. Now I like playing along with records, getting more of the human element involved in the time.

For me, the parallels to type are obvious: Great rhythm is great spacing—harmonious white spaces from which positive shapes are formed. The human element is something else entirely, but it's exactly what I tried to breathe into Vulf Mono.

incorporated incorporated
incorporated incorporated

Black *Black*
Bold *Bold*
Regular *Regular*
Light *Light*

→↓↔↕ ♩ ♪ ♫ ♬ 𝄞 𝄢 ♯ ♭ ♮

↑ (top)
Starting with the bolder italic in the top left, I considered what additional styles might look like. By drawing just a few characters, one can quickly test ideas to get a feel for the family. Later, the x-height was increased in the bold to help the styles maintain proportions through the weights.

↑ (middle)
As is often the case, I realized that the roman could go even bolder, but then the italic had to be beefed up as well. At this point, we have a nice little happy family starting to take shape.

↑ (bottom)
This part was pure fun. I had predicted that treble clefs would be the new ampersands. (Update: Treble clefs have definitely not become the new ampersands.)

UTS
VOLUME
“No would-be comp
has ever been wil
to lay out the do
—Trader Joe
2
FLINT, MICHIGAN
6 7
5 8
4 9
3 10
2 11
1 12
NORMAL BRIGHT
MORE DRIVE
#♭♮
#♭♮
#♭♮
#♭♮
Ghz
WOODY GOSS
Solo
Rhodes
OG&
ACH
JACK “THE TWO AND THE FOUR” STRATTON
S
L
E
E
P
I
F
Y
U+266C
utiful
ne
...
THE FIRST TED TALK
...
hybrid
mono
prprtnl
spcng
eck • 2016 • 10 songs
SAVED
...

tor
g
..."
ponzi.io
1 1/2 tsp. flour
for dusting
1 cup flour
1/3 cup water
1/2 teaspoon salt
(kosher)
1 tsp. olive oil
→EX
feat. Joey
#THEOKATZMAN
#ALMOST
Outsid
Friday,
2:55-
Panhand
1
4
1
161
TREMELO
on
off
JOE
COMP
WOW
95%
9%
VULFMON
INTERST

THE PROCESS OF CASSEROLE

YEAR	OPTICAL SIZE	STROKE ENDINGS	WEIGHTS	CONTRAST	JOINTS
2023	Massive	Sans, Flared, and Ball	Only Bold	Low	Hairline

In the process of digital type design, there is no physical limitation to stop you from taking an idea too far. The absence of these boundaries can often make concepts snowball out of control before you even place your first point. I can't tell you how many times I've dreamt up a 200-style experimental variable font, only to lead up to the next thought: *Nobody will want this.*

Casserole wasn't a big idea from the beginning. In fact, it started even smaller than type—simply as a piece of lettering for a Vulfpeck concert in Los Angeles.

Cheee and Eckmannpsych had the same origin. While both of those projects explored additional styles through interpolation (placing the same points in different locations, allowing for a blend between styles), Casserole grew in another, even more labor-intensive way.

Louis Minott and His Son David

I began with Davida Bold, an extremely popular font from 1965. Louis Minott, most likely inspired by Victorian-era display fonts like Ringlet and Hogarth, lettered a prototype and submitted it to a contest by Visual Graphics Corporation (VGC). It won, earning Minott a thousand dollars. Davida Bold was a runaway success, but unfortunately, zero royalties were part of the deal. Louis's triumph of winning the contest and having his work published gradually turned

→ (opposite)
The Los Angeles date for the 2018 Vulfpeck North American Tour poster series, designed by James Edmondson.

VULF
PECK
THE REGENT THEATER ////////////////// JUNE 2 & 3 ////////////////// 2017
LOS
ANGELES

That part halfway up the R where the ball meets looks a little heavy.

↑
Louis Minott (*left*), designer of Davida, with his son David.

into bitterness, and every use of his Davida reminded him of a lousy deal with VGC.

Experimentation

The Vulfpeck poster series was an excuse to experiment with my own versions of a bunch of ornate display typefaces that I loved, including Davida. I began by tweaking many of Davida's characteristics. First was the width. Going super condensed, as I did with *Angeles* for the Vulfpeck poster, wasn't working, so I went slightly wider than the original. Because the poster used the type at such an absurdly large size, I got to add a bit of drama by emphasizing the contrast throughout. The serifs became razor sharp, and I made the

PASSIVE
AGGRESSIVE
INCOME

ABCDEFGHI
JKLMNOPQR
STUVWXYZ
abcdefghijklmn
opqrstuvwxyz
1234567890

OOOO
BB
QQQ
ggggg
aaaaaa
XX

The lowercase g is a subtle nod to Hobo, one of my favorites.

↑ (top)
In this early iteration of Casserole, I began for a moment to think that my ideas were better than the original. They weren't!

↑ (bottom)
At some point, I ventured into the lowercase. That's where the real fun was! Davida never had one, so each glyph became a puzzle to solve, with no easy answer. Not every glyph needed a ball terminal, but some were too easy to pass up.

ABCDEFGHI
JKLMNOPQR
STUVWXYZ
abcdefghijklmn
opqrstuvwxyz

NITCH
QUASI
NAZIR
TOKAJ
RIGHT

ABCDEFGHI
JKLMNOPQR
STUVWXYZ
abcdefghijklmn
opqrstuvwxyz
012345678

From cheesy fiesta chicken and cajun shrimp to classic baked zi and a kid-friendly tater tot cass role, there's no way you won't fi something to try on this list of 5 casserole recipes.† We've got a to get through, so let's jump righ in. §2 Cracker Barrel® Hash Bro Casserole I don't know if there is better combination than potato cheese, and sour cream. This tri works well in every form, but thi hash brown recipe is extra speci To be honest, I'd be happy with just those three ingredients. But like I said, this recipe is special!

↑ (top)
The Flare style was simply a lack of ball terminals, with a few crossbars redrawn to swap in a conventional horizontal stroke.

↑ (bottom)
The Sans style required a bit more work and was spaced more generously to encourage use at a broader range of sizes than the Classic and Flare styles.

connections between branches and ball terminals as thin as possible. I added a bit of gravity—emphasizing the trapezoidal nature of *D*, *G*, *O*, and *Q*.

I quickly began asking myself if the ball terminals were something that could be messed with. I attempted alternate versions that ditched the balls in favor of little flourishes shaped like shards of aluminum or other bizarre and illogical shapes.

After I returned to the idea of classic ball terminals, the working files just sat on my hard drive for years. Every once in a while, needing to use the typeface in a presentation, I'd quickly add a handful of glyphs. Then on our holiday cards, and eventually over time, the classic style blossomed into an actual typeface, but only as a single style.

↑
Lombardic capitals are a truly underrated genre and don't have a ton of representation in digital type. They are found in churches, pubs, and Tolkien fan fiction but have generally been out of vogue for a few hundred years. Initially, they were intended to serve as drop caps. But I mean, c'mon. These are a sample drawn by Frederick Goudy designed to complement his blackletter, Goudy Text. I looked at them quickly, then forgot they existed.

Normally, with any typeface that has thin thins, I'd add another small optical size (a redrawing of the same outlines intended to excel at around 14 points). Beastly and Ohno Fatface follow this idea, but it didn't feel right for Casserole. Variable fonts aren't always the answer, after all! That's when I got a really simple idea: What would happen if we just took off the balls? Would all be lost? Would the typeface make any sort of impact?

The Classic and Flare styles made for a nice mini family, but Ohno would not be Ohno if we didn't scrape the sides of the can for every drop of cream of mushroom soup contained therein. The next step was to strip the Flare down to a Sans. This simple move was actually a more substantial undertaking because with no contrast to play with, accents and certain bits of punctuation had to be entirely redrawn.

It Gets Funkier

A family of three styles can be pretty useful, but there was still plenty of soup in the can. While we were adding lowercase letters to each style, it dawned on me that no genre is more hospitable to the ball terminal than script, in both capitals and lowercase. It seemed completely obvious that this was the new expedition on which to embark.

But there's also a subgenre of blackletter that (contrary to how broad-nib pens work) actually embraces the ball terminal as a visual motif. We set out to accomplish both.

↑
While I used to sketch mostly by hand, I'm totally comfortable doing loose drawings on the computer these days. I don't recommend this, though, especially to students. And sometimes I just can't figure out how to put an idea on the computer without doing a little doodle first.

ABCDEFGHI ABCDEFGHI
JKLMNOPQR JKLMNOPQR
STUVWXYZ STUVWXYZ
abcdefghijklmn abcdefghijklmn
opqrstuvwxyz opqrstuvwxyz
012345678 012345678

↑ (top)
The Script and Blackletter styles fully fleshed out the Davida-centric universe in which we were operating.

↑ (middle)
The Script and Blackletter styles required many attempts at some of the glyphs before we got to a place that felt natural.

↑ (bottom)
On occasion, something would click on the first try, but more often than not, a few attempts were required before things started to make sense.

The family had a nice symmetry to it, with the Classic as the fulcrum, and the sober combination of Sans and Flare balancing out the completely bonkers combination of Script and Blackletter. So, with absolutely no reason to add anything else, I delved into the most lawless genre I could think of: Lombardic capitals.

Tightening the Screws

Everything was in its place, and we had a concept: a thorough exploration of the Davida style through the lens of Ohno, splitting off into six styles. It's essentially a mixed bag of different flavors of varying intensity, all getting cooked in the same dish. Obviously, only a name like Casserole could bring everything together.

But despite solving the naming issue, we still had the arduous task of ensuring that all the forms were correct. Classic, Flare, and Sans all had fairly easy answers, but Script, Blackletter, and Lombardic were chock-full of question marks. Everything needed to be cooked from scratch, and we couldn't just look up the answer in the back of the book.

The Lombardic style was frankly too insane, but extreme problems called for drastic solutions, and we were forced to play with the size of the ball terminal. Whereas in other styles, the ball hovered around a similar size, the Lombardic just needed another element that wouldn't distract too much but still add a good amount of sparkle in an otherwise empty pocket of negative space. These became particularly handy on *X*, *V*, and *Y*.

Not a Revival

Davida is a classic, and no one can argue with that. Its vast usage is a testament to how compelling and adaptable a mood it can create. But to honor this contribution to type history, a simple revival would not do! To revive is to relive or to look at the past. We wanted to resuscitate, bring new life, and put all of our love into every style, every glyph, and every curve of Casserole.

Louis Minott is gone. His son David is too. But Davida will continue to live on for decades to come. I haven't given much thought to the fact that my typefaces could outlive even my children or me. My hunch is that they will be long out of fashion way before I meet my maker. But fashion is cyclical, and there's nothing new under the sun. Casserole is a project about a combination of flavors, built around familial love. And those are both things that will never go out of style.

↑
My greatest triumph in my entire career:
The *S* in Casserole Lombardic.

obo
ley

E-AMERICAN
SINE

NE NIGHT ONLY

CEINO
INGADERA

ERIA

OVER
FORT

THE PROCESS OF

YEAR	OPTICAL SIZE	STROKE ENDINGS	WEIGHTS	CONTRAST	STRAIGHT LINES
2018	12–72 Point	Slab Serif	Only Black	Reverse	Yes

Beastly began as a simple suggestion from Alexander Tochilovsky while we were working on a logotype for the Herb Lubalin Center's Lubalin 100 project. While it imbues many of the qualities of the signature styles of Lubalin's team of lettering artists, it's a completely new design. Alexander and I agreed it was simply too expected to ape an existing typeface, so we tried to create something new.

The year prior, I had done some lettering for the Typographics conference that slowly snowballed into several other ideas for typefaces. The most basic of those was something generically titled Ohno Fatface.

After completing the logotype, I started drawing out the rest of the capitals. My thinking at the time was that it might be useful to have a full alphabet for various collateral for the project. Also, numbers were needed in a smaller optical size, so I took a crack at those as well.

Around this time, David Jonathan Ross's Rhody came out, so I had a good reference for how a slab treatment could be applied to numerals. This was not the first time I've ripped off DJR—and it won't be the last.

I had nothing driving this project except my own curiosity. I wondered what a lowercase for this super slab design might look like, so I played around with making the slabs absurdly enormous.

LUBALIN 100 YEARS

OFHERB

Typo-
graph-
ics'17

Sometimes it's impossible to resist making typefaces out of lettering.

TYPOGRAPHICS 2017
New York, United States

↑ (top left)
The kernel of the idea, hastily drawn in less than a minute.

↑ (top right)
After Alexander suggested an Italian (which is an old-school term for a reverse-contrast slabby design), I simply squashed the middle, then pulled out the serif into enormous slabs. It struck the right balance of impactful and familiar, so we used it for the project's logotype.

↑ (middle)
This design was printed on T-shirts and sold for around twenty dollars a pop. It did not sell out.

↑ (bottom)
The resulting display face from the Typographics lettering.

→ (overleaf)
The gauntlet of obvious solutions we explored for the Lubalin 100 project.

100

1918 LUBALIN

LUBALIN
100

Lubalin 100

100

'18

1918-2018

LUBALIN CENTENNIAL

100

LUBALIN 100

Lubalin 100

100 LUBALIN CENTENNIAL

Lubalin 100

Lubalin
/100

LUBALIN
100 YEARS

100BALIN

Lubalin
OneHundred

100

OF
ONE HUN-
DRED
YEARS
B

Lu100alin

ONE
HUN
DRED

Lu100alin

LUBALIN
100

1 HUN-
DRED
YEARS OF
B

100

100

1918
OneHundredYear

100 LUBALIN

100 DAYS
ST. PATRICK'S DAY BIRTHDAY

VIDEO
LECTURE
IMAGES

LUBALIN100.COM

LUBALIN

LUBALIN
CENTENNIAL

NUMBERING
1/100
WATERMARK
CROSS PLATFORM

Lubalin

A CENTURY OF LUBALIN

100 LUBALIN

HERB LUBALIN CENTENNIAL

NUMBERS SET OF

LUBALIN
CENTENNIAL
100 YEARS
1918-2018

ANIMATION
CARUASE
ALAN P

10×10

1 Lubalin

LUBALIN 100

100 2018

Lubalin

100 100

Hundred

1/100

Lubalin

LUBALIN 100

Lubalin's
100th
Centennial

100 Lubalin

Lubalin

100

Lubalin

26 good reasons to celebrate Herb's 100TH

Lubalintennial

52/100

1918 2018

Lubalin One Hundred

1918 -2018

018

1918 20

1918 2018

00

LUBALIN

Lubalin One Hundred

LUBALIN ONE HUNDRED

MARCH 17
FEB 17 (24)

LUBALIN ONE HUNDRED

HERB!

LUBALIN/100

LUBALIN ONE HUNDRED

NO

1234567890

1234567890

I love how DJR threw a slab on the bottom of 7–a figure that doesn't typically indulge in a slab.

↑ (top)
The wonderfully slabby figures from Rhododendron by David Jonathan Ross.

↑ (bottom)
The slabby figures from Beastly diverge from DJR's model slightly.

In all of the classes I teach, I like to talk about the Counterspace Equals Letterspace technique for achieving consistent spacing in type or lettering. Basically, this approach involves a blackletter-esque concept, where there is no difference between the space inside an *n* and the space between two *n*'s.

Picking Up Speed

This project moved a lot faster than most of my typical original designs do. Usually, due to a lack of deadline, those projects can sprawl on for months and years with no end in sight. This design, however, was just so much fun to work on that I couldn't deny myself the indulgence!

For a brief moment, I explored a width change. I can't quite pinpoint what exactly felt wrong about this, but after a few unenthusiastic hours of pulling points around, I simply lost interest. My gut was telling me this was a waste of time. I decided that I might approach this idea again in the future, but I also knew that just because something is starting out slightly wide, that doesn't mean it should get narrow. Maybe Beastly would be a wide typeface that only gets wider! (Update: It didn't.)

The pinching was a tricky thing to navigate, and there aren't really obvious conventions to follow for many glyphs. The 2 and the *N* proved to be especially problematic, and I persistently banged my head against the wall until the correct forms were discovered. This part of the process requires a lot of patience and some brutal honesty. I'm still not sure about the final form of the *J*, but at some point, you have to move on!

highlighting

HIBADE

At a glance, this drawing feels like it was digitally squished, even though it wasn't. Whenever I get that feeling, I know I'm heading down the wrong path.

↑ (top)
An early version of the slabs on the lowercase, which were so big that they were pushing other letters too far away. It's really annoying to hear your own voice in your head as a teacher talking to students! I knew that to move forward with spacing that actually worked, my beloved monster serifs would have to be trimmed. This actually helped achieve an even bolder weight, so the work still looked monstrous.

The switch in priorities here is pretty much the name of the game in type design. The word always trumps the letter, the paragraph trumps the word, and the page trumps the paragraph.

↑ (middle)
An instructional image I show to students displaying the relationship between letterspaces and counterspaces.

↑ (bottom)
An early exploration into the condensed side of things just wasn't as interesting as I thought it would be.

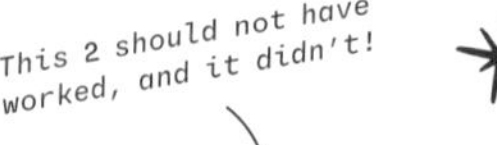

It was a good effort.

woof.

yeah nah.

↑ (top)
I was trying waaaaay too hard with early versions of the *2*.

↑ (middle top)
N was one of those letters that I thought would be simple, but it took forever.

↑ (middle bottom)
A more in-depth view of some failures for other glyphs. Particularly humiliating are these laughable attempts at the *S*, *$*, and *§*.

↑ (bottom)
For the hairline call, I had to go Goldilocks (see page 80). Also, a traditional italic style for the *@* was swapped in at the last minute.

I wasn't quite sure how to handle the punctuation, but taking some notes from Tânia Raposo's beautiful work on Coryn Didot, I utilized the hairline punctuation technique. Sometimes I wonder if I should include two sets of punctuation in an example like this, but eventually I settled on simply making it part of the design. At their worst, alternates are a way of saying "I'm sorry" or "This might be a mistake, so here you go." Beastly has no alternates and makes no apologies!

It was fun to see the type in use as I was designing it. While type legend Jim Parkinson was working in-house at the *San Francisco Chronicle*, he used to test his typefaces daily in print when each new paper was printed. That sort of stress testing is amazing, but I had to settle for new versions of web fonts being loaded and used (in this case) on Lubalin100.com.

The Name

Why Beastly? Well, what else was I supposed to call it? Just like many of my contemporaries in font marketing, I lament the process of naming typefaces perhaps even more than kerning.

In 2011, the best band in the world released its first EP. *Mit Peck* by Vulfpeck was the delicately named culmination of six tracks, four insanely talented musicians, and just enough 2-inch tape. I can't say why, but all the songs were named after movies released that year. The first track, "Beastly" (named after a film with a 20 percent Rotten Tomatoes score), features one of Vulfpeck's most recognizable grooves and a mind-blowing bass solo that single-handedly garnered the band their first wave of major attention.

Seven years later, "Beastly" holds up as one of the funkiest things Vulfpeck has ever done, and it is my belief that the song will cauterize a permanent place of honor in the history of funk. It was with the utmost respect for the band that I humbly named this riff on Lubalin-era typography in homage to their tune.

Let's Wrap This Up

Like all of the retail typefaces I release at Ohno, I am not sure how many people are going to pony up the greenbacks to license these fonts. But for those who do, I hope they do not think of the continuous sequence of failures that brought this design into existence. I hope the optical sizes make it useful, and I hope that interesting brands and organizations will want to align themselves with Beastly's warm and aggressive tone. I hope it's not simply nostalgic, but that it brings something new to the conversation. Lastly, I hope you like Vulfpeck as much as I do.

→ (overleaf)
For this photo, I delicately positioned all of these kerning proofs like a real jackass. Kerning comes late in the process, after the final shapes have been drawn and spaced. For a really heavy weight with such a large intended size, there can be a little less room for error, so you have to nail it.

«t» «u» «v»

‹w› ‹x› ‹y› ‹z›

»r« »s« »t« »u« »v« »w

u‹ ›v‹ ›w‹ ›x‹ ›y‹ ›z‹

u&v&w&x&y&z&

u@v@w@x@y@z@

uR vR wR xR yR

xC yC zC

ADD MORE
SPACE

2,159[87]

URCHASE
BEASTLY.

ADMISSION: £5

idly] amid the "noise" and the
nd @remember what #peace
ay be in 1957–2013. As far as
e, without ½surrender, be on
rms with (all) persons. † Speak
th› quietly and clearly; and
others—even to the dull and
orant; they too have their story.
loud and aggressive persons
ey {vexatious} to the ©spirit. ¶
mpare/contrast yourself with
ers®, you may become vain |

AN ITALIAN?

LITTLE MUCH

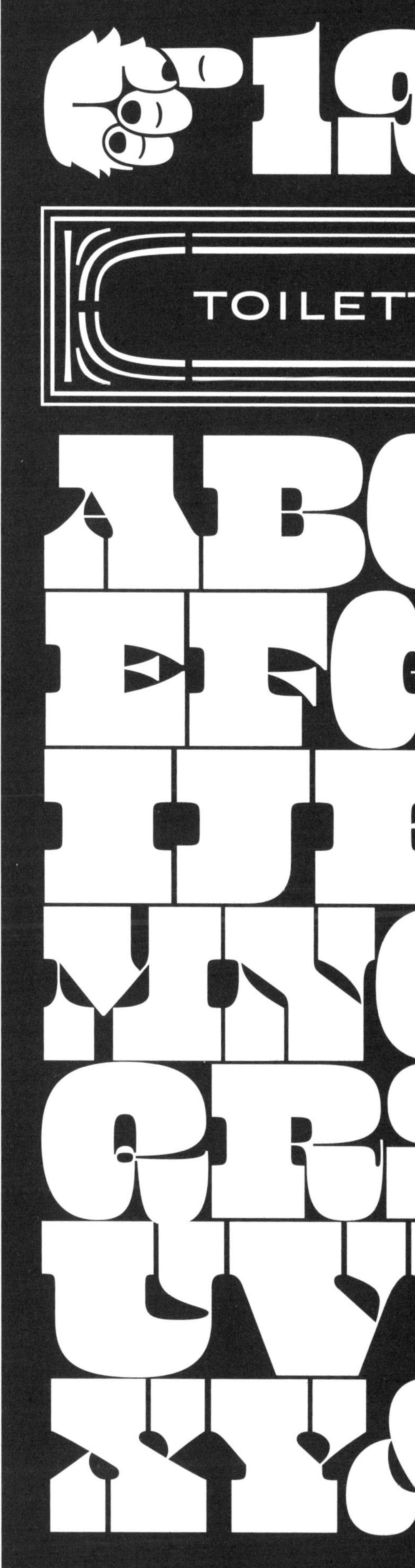

THE PROCESS OF REGRETS

YEAR	OPTICAL SIZE	INSPIRATION	STYLES	PROPORTIONS	STRAIGHT LINES
2023	Huge	Art Nouveau	Major and Minor	Dramatic	Some

Half the time, the origin of a typeface is really obvious. For instance, with my first Ohno typeface, Hobeaux, I knew exactly what it was trying to do, right from the beginning. But as I work on more typefaces, like Regards, our twenty-second, I'm finding it fun to create from a more abstract or nebulous origin idea.

Lighter Is the New Bolder

Around 2019, I started sketching in a monolinear fashion on my iPad. I was trying to see how quickly I could make a word that looked somewhat typographic—a sort of middle ground in between lettering (drawn) and calligraphy (written). I found the most effective trait to be confidence. A confident line knows where it begins and where it ends. Both things are clear decisions, and that doesn't leave any room for debate. An insecure line wanders, wiggles with trepidation, and trails off indecisively. The shortcut to a confident line, I found, was to use the Procreate app—and specifically the primitive shapes function, which allows you to quickly draw straight lines, perfect circles, and ellipses. Frankensteining these shapes together gets a word out with less effort than any other method I've had success with.

My favorite Motter fonts are Motter Femina, Tektura, and Ombra, but check those out on your own time!

This sketching exploration coincided with a trip down memory lane recalling some of the display typefaces we had created at Ohno. Everything was so bold! Why? Is it my fondness for the designer Othmar Motter (aka Meister der Extrabold)? Is it the fact that advertising and branding seem to prioritize positive space?

I think we can look at an image like this and see which lines look insecure and which feel more confident.

↑ (top)
A more expansive iteration of the previous sketches and an introduction of contrast and the pen angle.

↑ (bottom)
This baby announcement was made for my sister-in-law's sister—which basically means she's my sister—which basically means she gets free graphic design. Wesley also always buys our merch.

↑ (overleaf)
The method of digital sketching on the iPad in Procreate was the genesis of our typeface Irregardless.

RuPaul's
Eleganza Extravaganza
24 Hour Laundry
Blue
Mariposa
Eggs Any Style
$500
Gaston
Tummytime
Free Shipping Always
Baby
Alonzo
Johnny
Bad ideas
well executed
Lunchbucket
Brother

Abstract
nope
MACHINE WASH
STOP
PROBLEMATIC
Pest Control
Dang!
Ark
Blueberry
Lavender
YOU FIND WHAT YOU CAN
LOVE WITHOUT IT
ABOUT IT
go on not thinkin

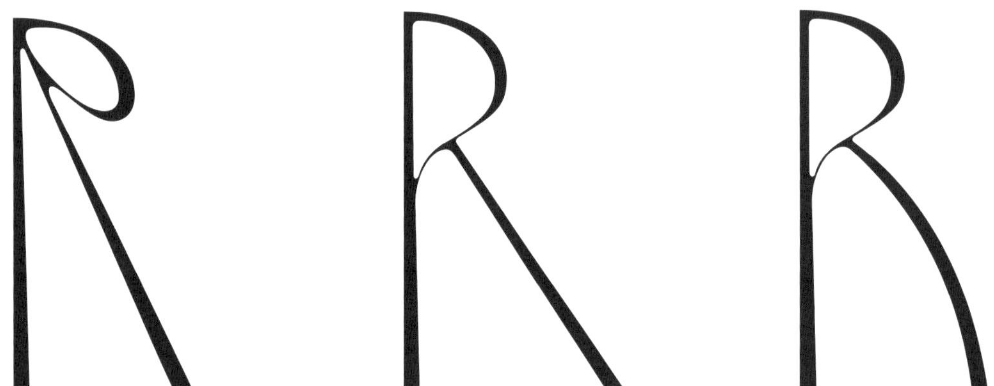

↑
The capitals came fairly quickly, and each answer was obvious. The *R* was the only glyph that gave me significant trouble, as the first version created too chaotic a texture, and the straight leg then pushed everything else too far away. The classic art nouveau or Hobo *R* seemed to space nicely and fit stylistically.

Or do I simply enjoy the challenge of drawing things as boldly as possible? I had no idea, but whenever a tendency is discovered, it's healthy to consider the opposite. My new challenge: to make an impact while keeping things light.

I immediately came back to my monolinear sketches and examined a few details that didn't make their way into Irregardless: a broad nib contrast model, ornate detailing, and an art nouveau influence. That seemed to be enough to go on, and it was at that moment that my sister-in-law asked for a baby announcement.

It's always funny when I go diving into my old sketchbooks to see at what point I thought it was best to jump on the computer and figure out the problems in digital form. It seems that more and more, drawing on the computer is so natural that it's easy for me to "sketch" in RoboFont, even though at that point it looks more like drawing. It's a shame, really, that I have a job where I could be using analog tools but I'm choosing to work digitally. The indulgence of analog work should be embraced! But eventually I get the feeling that things could go quicker on the computer, so I jump.

A Regrettable Choice

This was one of the most difficult fonts to name in our (at the time) seven-year history. Our list of potential names included Ennui, Foible, Malaprop, Menthol, Misgive, Misanthrope, Xylem, Qualm, Impolite, Manners, Dissociate, Gravure, Calamity, Spite, Deceit, Contempt, Disdain, Diaphane, Casement, Gravicide, Lament, Feign, Dispirit, Pariah, Venge, Sympathy, Malinger, Slander, Rumours, Shade, Maladroit, Malevophane, Filament, Vanity, Atrocious, Fiend, Heinous, Unspeak, Philophane, Enclave, Ingrid, Rhain, Graves, Ageless, Apleat, Contraire, Ashade, Please, Desperate, Relax, and Fleetwood Mac.

ABCDEFGHI	ABCDEFGHI
JKLMNOPQR	JKLMNOPQR
STUVWXYZ	STUVWXYZ
abcdefghijklm	abcdefghijklm
nopqrstuvwxyz	nopqrstuvwxyz
0123456789	0123456789

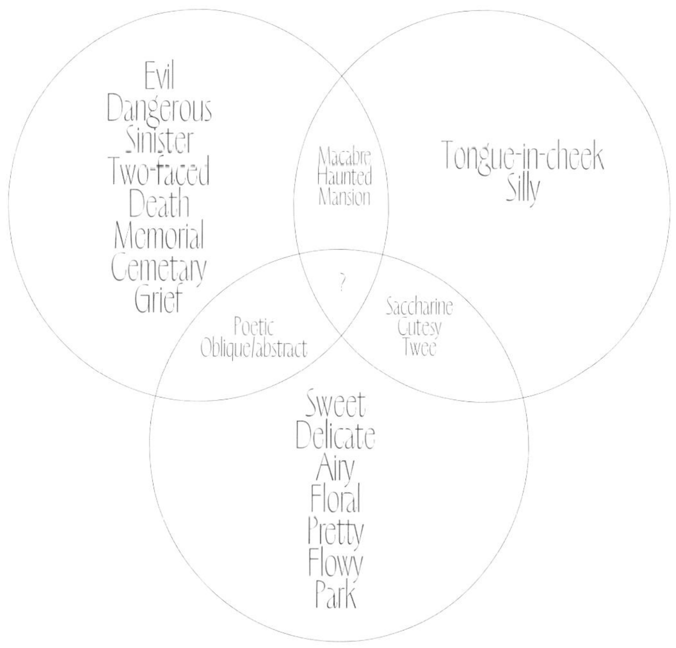

↑ (top)
After an expressive single style was created (left), I stripped it of all the frills and made a companion style (right). It was still just as high-contrast and light, but simplified.

↑ (bottom)
At one point, the naming process became so bleak that I tried a Venn diagram that combined a few of the ideas we were circling around. Ultimately, this led... nowhere.

It was too obvious to hint at an art nouveau or French influence, and I didn't want something that sounded too much like a font name. Does that make sense? Eventually, the name Regrets felt right, was a good combination of letters, and most importantly, was available. Our style names became Major and Minor, but a piece of the puzzle was still missing.

I just like the idea of classifying regrets as big and small, Major and Minor. Plus it had a connection to music that I liked. I appreciate that this typeface leaves people with more questions than answers.

If Ornament Is a Crime, Lock My Ass Up

A perusal of any type specimen from around 1900 will show you some of the sickest borders and ornaments you've ever seen, and we wouldn't be the first to give some of them new life as digital artwork, but there was a nice cohesion when we brought them alongside Regrets. A sad-sounding typeface needed some flowers to cheer it up! The motif of rounding every interior corner in Regrets was a perfect detail to put into the drawings of plants, leaves, flower petals, and a few animals.

The digital expression of these sketches surfaced as a series of repeatable tiles, a series of plants and flowers on a common baseline, and about twenty different border treatments.

The End?

It wasn't until three weeks before the release of this typeface that everything seemed to fall into place with the overall concept and the artwork. This is a bit unusual for us, but ultimately it was a testament to the fact that we were working in a slightly uncomfortable genre. Yes, there are other things in our catalog that share a 1900s organic-looking influence, like Hobeaux and Eckmannpsych, but this is a lot less derivative. I am hugely grateful to Jamie Otelsberg, who handled the accents and punctuation, and Colin Ford, who helped Jamie, completed countless improvements, including the final version of *R*, and suffered through the naming process with me. When I think about hiring those two, I have no regrets! Only Regrets!

→ (opposite)
Working on the ornaments was a true joy and a good excuse to take pictures of flowers on walks. It made my daughter ask, "Why are you doing that?" I told her I needed pictures to add to my collection. Now every time we pass a flower, she says, "Papa, do you wanna add this one to your collection?"

→ (overleaf)
Making these images in Photoshop and not hiring a real airbrush artist to do them is my only regret.

rmas

Regrets

REGRETS
REGRETS

TYPE
ANY
SPACE
2023
XOTIC
TYPE
NO ONE WANTS
SWAN DOTH CALL
PHIC
ODY
DAWN
VELY

Ornamented
VACACIÓN
(805)489-2371
REVISITATIONS OF THE
PAST WITH DISDAIN
FOR OUR OWN CHARACTER

THE PROCESS OF EckmannPsych

YEAR	OPTICAL SIZE	STROKE ENDINGS	CORNERS	PEN ANGLE	STRAIGHT LINES
2018	Small–Large	Round	Nah	Yes	Nah

Eckmannschrift was of course originally drawn by Otto Eckmann, but the seeds were planted in 1899 as the masthead for the illustrated weekly magazine *Die Woche*. Eckmann then translated that lettering into a full typeface, but it seems that type was just a single facet of his many skills. Trained as a painter, Eckmann ditched his purely artistic pursuits later in life to focus on applied design. It's wonderful to see the influence of a true artist on his type. His eponymous work remains one of the most original and enduring art nouveau contributions in type design history.

The psychedelic poster artists of the late sixties had a way of swiping art nouveau and Vienna secessionist work and tailoring it to fit their needs. I had been particularly inspired by their adaptations while working on the Vulfpeck North American tour posters a few years prior. I got to explore some of my favorite historical display faces, reproducing the letters to excel at huge sizes and fit justified across the entire 24" by 36" sheet.

The process for actually translating Eckmann's work was embarrassingly simple: I drew his version, pinched the middle, and rounded every corner. With surprisingly few moves, the dust was blown off a turn-of-the-century German relic, and a surprisingly funky child was born.

For a while, my psychedelia-infused version of Eckmann sat dormant on my hard drive until Rob Stenson asked for a customization with a few more letters. I was happy to oblige and even made a little animation for a project that never got off the ground.

At that point, the working title of Eckmannpsych was assigned to this bizarre design, and it went back into hibernation again until Future Fonts got closer to launch. I wasn't sure exactly what typefaces I wanted to put up there, but I tried to include a mix of things that covered a diverse range of styles. My goal was to make Future Fonts the home for Ohno's more daring designs, and Eckmannpsych fit the bill perfectly. All I had to do was finish the capitals.

The immediate response was way more positive than I ever could have expected. In the first few weeks, Eckmannpsych (the working title became the actual title because I couldn't think of anything else) was my top earner, despite its meager price tag. The enthusiasm was very surprising considering just how crazy it looked—and how impractical it was to use. The first update came a few weeks later, when I added some numbers to the mix.

Through the magic of @mentions on Instagram, I started seeing people actually using the font for real work, often on the psychedelic side. I was thrilled to see someone actually hand-carving the letters out of linoleum for letterpress posters. Seeing things like that while the fonts are still in progress does wonders to maintain my enthusiasm.

↑ (top left)
The front cover of *Die Woche* (German for "This Week"). The masthead and other type used on the cover appear to be a prototype of Eckmannschrift.

↑ (top right)
An advertisement for Eckmann-schrift graciously provided by Florian Hardwig, who says, "In a way, the original Eckmann was a Future Font itself, too. In the first official specimen, Rudhard'sche Gießerei proudly mentions that the typeface was already acquired by a large number of companies, although it had been advertised in an advance showing only, and lists twenty of the early adopters, with several leading printers among them: 'By the time this specimen is released, the typeface has become a household name already, and has been introduced by more than a hundred print offices in Germany and abroad!' On the next page they add: 'While this specimen is being printed, the typeface has been acquired by the following companies, among others,' and lists another eighteen addresses from Brussels to Riga."

→ (overleaf)
I chose Eckmannschrift for the Portland show, which seemed to be a nice fit for a city that celebrates idiosyncrasies and individuality.

VULF
PECK
FIRST AVENUE ////////////////// MAY 1 & 2 ////////////////// 2017
MINNE

VULF
PECK
THE OBSERVATORY ////////////////// JUNE 4 //////////////////

VULF
PECK
THE REGENT THEATER ////////////////// JUNE 2 & 3 ////////////////// 2017
LOS
ANGELES

VULF
PECK
MCMENAMINS CRYSTAL BALLROOM ////////////////// MAY 26 ////////////////// 2017
PORT

VULF
PECK
THE OGDEN THEATRE ////////////////////// MAY 30 ////////////////////// 2017
DEN
VER

VULF
PECK
THE PHOENIX CONCERT THEATRE ////////// MAY 8, 9 & 10 ////////// 2017
TOR
ONTO

This S eventually changed to something that referenced a broad-nibbed pen more. Sometimes I see people are still using this version because of the telltale S.

TARQUIN ZBEVIT FRUGTEN DEBAJO GRIT OBJEKTU SPALTEN COMPUTE

4 FOR $32.59—7:00 6/3/18

↑ (top)
The first version of Eckmannpsych on Future Fonts was extremely bare bones. There weren't even numbers, but it was only six bucks.

↑ (bottom)
If the letters are going to be crazy, the figures oughta be completely bonkers. I started playing with contrast a bit more here by illogically adding thins and swells where there were absolutely none.

Think Small

One annoying thing about single-style typefaces is that they lock you into a very limited spectrum of use. Something with really high contrast is pretty useless for every size except huge, so I thought more control over the thins would increase the utility of this one-note song. While decreasing contrast, I also increased the width to allow for larger counters that wouldn't be in danger of filling in when set at a tiny size. This gave way to an optical size axis that made Eckmannpsych quite a bit more useful. The character set was still tiny at this stage, so each update wasn't an intimidating overhaul. This let me feel at ease expanding the family at a comfortable pace that wasn't getting in the way of other work.

Gradually, accented characters came into the mix, and my friend Dan Reynolds had some thoughts. Dan is a bona fide historian and happened to be working on a dissertation concerning, among other things, Eckmann's work. His email read:

> I love Eckmannpsych, but as I tweeted, I wish it had a Ü ;-)
> Attached is a drawing in the Klingspor Museum from Eckmann for the Ü; it is probably close, but not exact, to what ended up in the original metal type. The idea of a little /e inside the /U was not as extreme as it seems today. Like other German founders, Klingspor cast its capital letters so that their tops went all the way up to the top boundary of the sort. The German Umlauts…every typeface got some sort of individual solution. For foreign languages, other diacritics were made on little sorts that you had to put on top of the letters (and then you had to put spacing material on top of all other letters in that line), which the compositors must have totally hated.

I was very grateful for Dan's incredibly well-informed critique, and I happily added the suggested *Ü* as a nod to Eckmann's original work and the typesetting technology of that era. Also, in a design this far out, I feel like one has a bit of freedom. As a native English speaker, I'm always afraid to play with accents because I don't want to look like an idiot. Dan might not be a native German speaker, but his German is certainly better than mine, and he's no slouch when it comes to type. (Just some Matthew Carter collabs. No big deal.)

At some point, a lowercase seemed to be a fun exploration. There is a huge problem with fun explorations: They can quickly grow into a lot of work. I try really hard to keep most typefaces as minimal as possible, but the lowercase opened new possibilities of setting Eckmannpsych in (challenging) paragraphs, and I was all about that.

Finally, I added a few alternates to make things a little less insane if desired. Just like the descending alternates in Hobeaux (a design famous for the lack of descenders), I don't really recommend using these. I think if you want to use Eckmannpsych, you have to commit. On the contrary, I'm making just a small effort to be mindful of other people, who are trying to please clients whom I will luckily never talk to.
If one issue can get resolved by swapping in one of the boring alternates, then it was worth it.

↑ (top left)
Around this time, the amazing design team Online Ceramics took a John Mayer album cover design to unprecedented levels of absurdity, and the *N* from Eckmannpsych made a cameo.

↑ (top right)
Although most in-use cases fail to alter my heart rate, I (without irony) love John Mayer and was mucho stoked to see this.

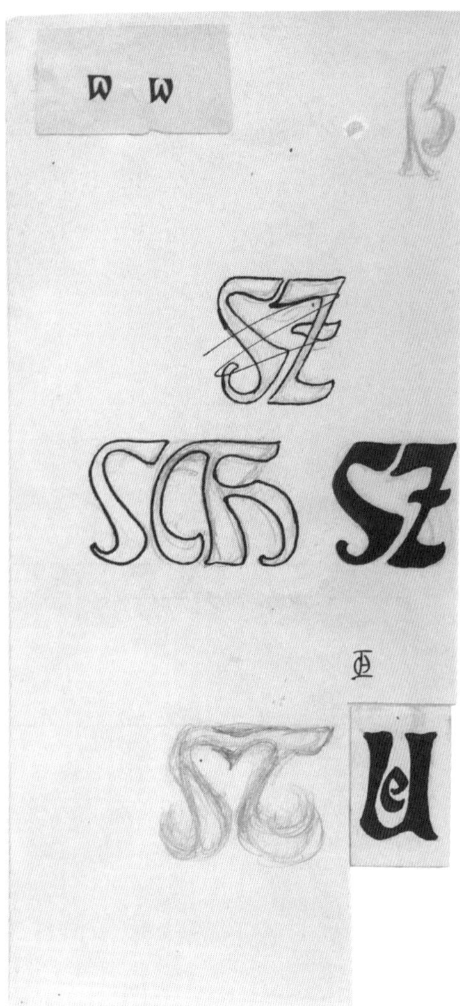

↑
Dan Reynolds's photograph of an original Eckmann sketch at the Klingspor Museum in Offenbach, Germany.

Thanks to Future Fonts, Dan, and Florian
Eckmannpsych would never have happened without the Future Fonts ecosystem. Dan would never have weighed in with his thoughtful suggestions. Worst of all, John Mayer would look like a complete moron with a different font for the *N* on his record cover. I hope that this family of fonts continues Eckmann's original vision of art influenced by humanity and nature and that it turns on the current generation to his amazing work.

Money really can buy happiness, as it turns out—but you might not need as much as you think.

Well, I have a surprise for you. It turns out that when it boils right down to it, your time to reach retirement depends on only one factor: Your savings rate, as a percentage of your take-home pay. If you want to break it down just a bit further, your savings rate is determined entirely by these two things: How much you take home each year and How much you can live on. While the numbers themselves are quite intuitive the relationship between these two numbers is a bit surprising.

"LIFE'S A THRILL FONTS ARE CHILL."

"LIFE'S A THRILL FONTS ARE CHILL."

↑ (top)
The lowercase was born from a more faithful adaptation of the Eckmann model.

↑ (bottom)
Alternates are available, but I hesitate to recommend them.

WAIT—STO
“SHOWN & T
TERRIBLE*
HTTP://OHN
PHIL@SERE
B-W $2.57-
ABOUT×COM
om // May 26 // 2017

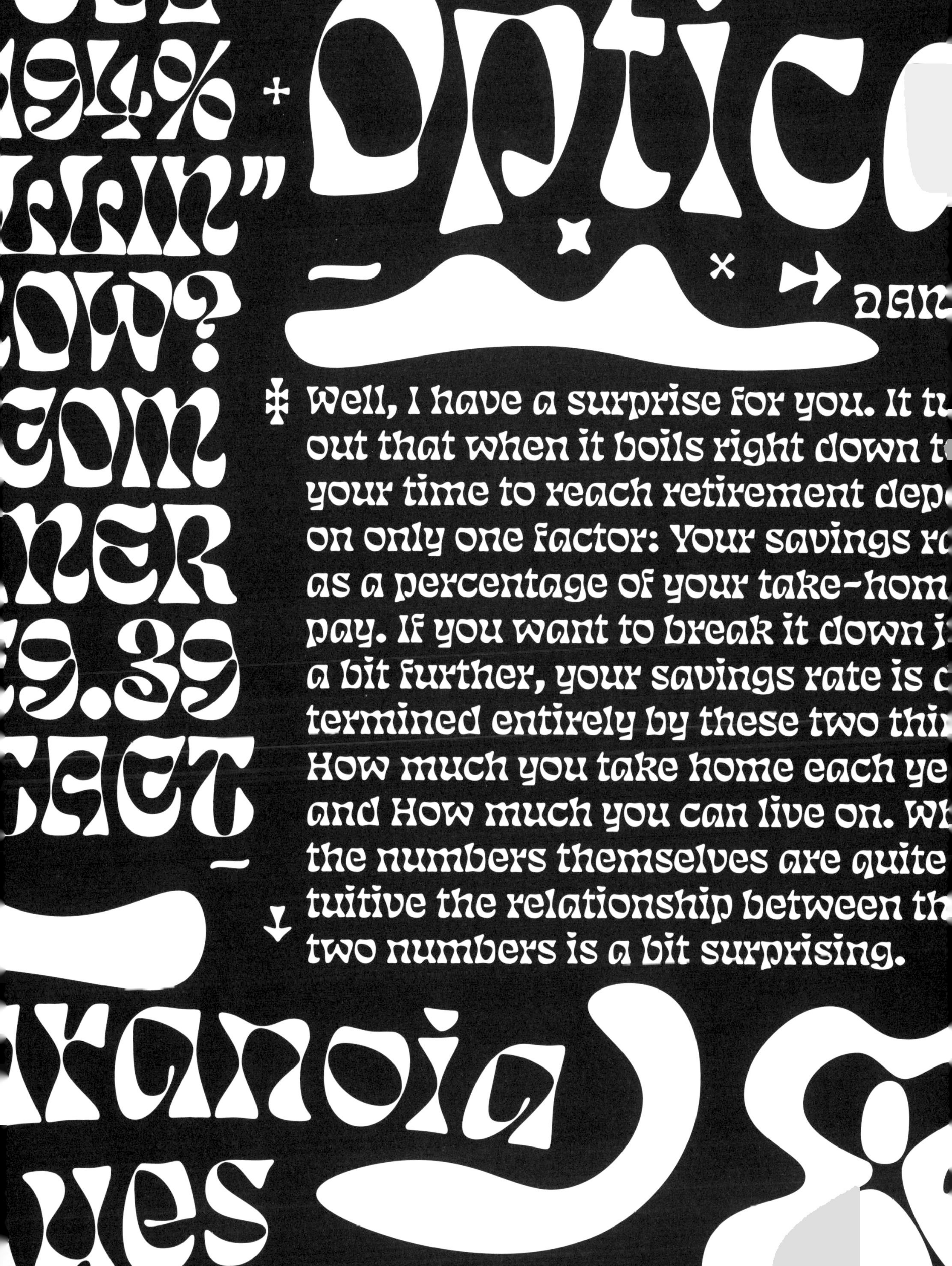
Well, I have a surprise for you. It tu
out that when it boils right down t
your time to reach retirement dep
on only one factor: Your savings ra
as a percentage of your take-hom
pay. If you want to break it down j
a bit further, your savings rate is d
termined entirely by these two thi
How much you take home each ye
and How much you can live on. Wh
the numbers themselves are quite
tuitive the relationship between th
two numbers is a bit surprising.

THE PROCESS OF

YEAR	OPTICAL SIZE	STROKE ENDINGS	WEIGHTS	BONUS	TOOL
2020	Text–Banner	Bracketed Serif	Thin–Black	Inverted Contrast Italic	Flat Brush

The impetus for a serif text face could come at any minute, and a type designer must always be ready.

Gen Ramírez had invited me to teach a workshop and give a talk at Letrástica, a three-day type, calligraphy, and lettering conference in Guadalajara, Mexico. Because I am a lover of all things Mexican (and have a wife who enjoys traveling more than I enjoy type design), we packed up our kid and headed south.

The first night of the conference, I was reunited with many old friends, met some new ones, and got the overwhelming feeling that Letrástica is the greatest conference ever.

The students were hungry and enthusiastic, and a few of them had backgrounds in calligraphy that far exceeded my own. At various points in the conference, a fresh sheet of butcher paper was laid down on the tables, and Gen and others got an opportunity to flex their brush skills. It was at one of these sessions where I learned how a certain twist of the brush could render an italic with an unfamiliar contrast.

I was encouraged to take a crack at it, and of course I fell on my face in front of everyone. But it didn't matter! I was too many Coronas deep to care. Suddenly, I multiplied my already massive respect for Vincent de Boer, the avant-garde calligrapher who takes the brush rotation to a whole other level.

I shared a classroom with Vincent's buddy (and another personal hero of mine) Julien Priez for the duration of the conference. I had met Julien a month prior in France, which quickly solidified my

↑ (top)
Works by Vincent de Boer from the *Stolen Goods* exhibition in Denmark. In both calligraphy and abstract expressionist art, Vincent has a way of rotating the brush like no other.

↑ (bottom)
A humble page from one of Julien Priez's magnificent sketchbooks. He indeed makes the paper boogie.

↑
The good news: The flat brush is capable of creating magical forms. The bad news: In the hands of an impostor, there is no such magic.

hunch that he might be the chillest dude around. A look through his sketchbook left me speechless. This guy was also doing things with brush rotation (among other magic tricks) that were mind-blowing.

God was telling me something during that trip: The flat brush was the tool that is capable of producing expressive forms like nothing else. Spending time with it became my top priority.

Sketching

It wasn't long after I started practicing with the flat brush that I realized I was never going to gain mastery over this tool. Fun as it may be to practice, at the end of the day, I'm a type designer, not a calligrapher.

In an attempt to crystallize some of my experiments, I began sketching in a more traditional way—building letters up as drawings and attempting forms with a standard broad nib. Unfortunately, this mundane approach was producing mundane results.

↑
Early sketches of Swear that had a long journey ahead of them.

Display First, Text Later

Drawing a text face is always impossible for me. I came to type design through logotypes and advertising, not through the higher brow path of text fonts and literature. Perhaps this is the reason my attempts to start a small optical size design failed in grad school. It was there I learned that, for me, display comes first, and designs for smaller sizes can be born out of them.

The brush twist became the bedrock of the design, and this crazy italic was the first digital incarnation of Swear.

Tariffs on Serifs

A distinct feature of Swear came out of sheer necessity. I always appreciate the menacing effects of exaggerated, razor-thin serifs, but they also cause a lot of problems. Particularly on letters like *A* and *V*, the exterior serifs can push out neighboring letters to an absurd degree, creating large pockets of white space that distract the reader. I usually try to keep the interior serifs large and the exterior serifs small, but here I pushed it to the extreme.

Pairing with Italics

Drawing a serif italic is as simple as nailing the *n*. Many of the lowercase letters follow the decisions made in that one glyph, and the rest of the character set is just slanted from the roman. But just because it can be simple doesn't mean it's easy!

Backpedaling Toward the Finish Line

At this point, I had the first glimpse of what the family could actually be, and how it could work. I went to the bold italic of Future Fonts thinking, "Yeah, the italic is weird, but guess what? Some italics should be weird, OK?!" The wisdom of the crowd trickled in as more and more users (who actually paid me money) began to request an italic that was more traditional. I was reluctant at first, thinking that would dampen the impact, backpedal on the concept,

angst
evac
ycnn

← (top)
Letting go of the need to create a text face first allowed me to ease up, have a little fun, and remember that way of twisting the brush.

← (middle top)
Way too much. This is the definition of "try hard." Swear had to feel less labored.

← (middle bottom)
Maybe the entry strokes were a bit too much? By going with a flatter option, would the texture be tamed?

← (bottom)
Finally, rounding out the downstrokes to be a more elegant shape gave me everything I was hoping for: a classic enough structure for legibility, with fun contrast modulations to make words sparkle. I was curious if it was even possible to maintain such an intense flavor in the roman, and after a bit of noodling, it came out much more reserved.

This looked fun as a sketch.

aunoe

ginrs

The perils of making an r too narrow. It's quite rare to see, as most of the time it shows up too wide.

aegost

This terminal of g was just a little too much.

It's subtle, but all the exterior serifs on the bottom are just a little longer, which pushes out the neighbors a little more than necessary.

AVENGERS
AVENGERS

↑ (top)
Swear tries to solve the spacing problem by making the exterior serifs tiny fractions of the interior ones.

↑ (bottom)
Superexaggerated serifs unencumbered by the rules of spacing.

and water down the whole project. But after really listening and seeing how folks were intending to use this typeface, I got to see things from their point of view and thought a more normal italic might be cool. The new, more reserved italic filled the role of "italic," and I renamed the previous italic Cilati (italic spelled backward), hinting at the reverse contrast and unorthodox forms. I was informed that it sounds very awkward in Italian. To be honest, it sounds awkward in English too. It feels justified, because it looks even more awkward than it sounds.

At this point the family was beginning to make sense, but it was time to return to my sketches of the small optical size and see if it would actually work in paragraphs. Usually, I think about four things that generally need to happen when moving from display to text:

1. **The x-height increases.** To prevent small shapes from enclosing on themselves, increasing the x-height can provide a bit more real estate for countershapes to grow.
2. **Letterspace increases.** Similarly, the tracking (the distance between characters) increases, also allowing for more white space. This seems to be especially the case for punctuation like the period, comma, and quotes.
3. **Details get chunkier.** For something to show up at a small size, it has to get clunky. Fine bits of elaborate ornamentation are simply not going to render, so we have to edit down the shape to the core of its architecture.
4. **Contrast goes down.** Similarly, any stroke that was once quite thin has to become thick enough that it is guaranteed to show up at 8 point.

Retain Coin Isentropic

Oes Rang Cougars

Knurs 56, Disponed Lackey.

↑ (top)
The roman seemed to want to be a bit more normal. Maybe it was OK to have a standard roman and a much more extreme italic.

↑ (middle)
When I first took a crack at adding weight, the roman was essentially standard, with a few moments of irreverence to balance out the weight.

↑ (bottom)
How many times must I learn that even when forms are not crazy, I still enjoy designing type?

Everything seemed to work in the interpolation department, with just a few exceptions. When the dollar and the Euro symbol get really small, they're just unnecessarily dark. To fix this, we had to create an alternate version of those symbols and have a way of automatically substituting out the correct version in the variable font. This was also the case with *W*, as the overlapping apex was just getting too complicated at smaller sizes. An alternate was drawn to clean up that mess.

As the text versions began to take shape, I committed to the decisions by adding small caps, old style and tabular figures, fractions, and various other typographic accoutrement to get it functioning as a real-deal, workhorse typeface—even if it's a bit outspoken. It was nice to realize that the Cilati styles were working just fine and were surprisingly acceptable in text. Hopefully, this can provide something useful for designers. I always enjoy playing with multiple italics or experimenting with different ways of creating emphasis.

anz
anz
anz

↑
The differences between the styles aren't always this dramatic.

IDORA

NOPE

ne "noise" and the
ber what **#peace**
7–2013. As far as
rrender, be on
ll) persons. †
quietly and clear-
ers—even to the
nt; they too have
loud and aggres-
hey {vexatious} to
compare/contrast
thers®, you may
, for always there
esser persons than
your achievements
s? Keep **interested**
$13.00, however
possession in the

CONCEPTUALLY M

OHNO

AESTHETICALLY O

OAKLAND, CALIFOR

EPISTOLAS RUDIS MATERIA SUN

®

ever

E. NEROZUMĚLA

Gyre

INIMAL

MINAL

WHITE DENIM/IN PERSON

1	BS	3:08
2	SHORT SHAKE	0:08
3	MOVES	3:09
4	DORGS	3:04
5	MIRRORED 2	2:12
6	MIRRORED 3	2:06
7	MIRRORED TOO	1:21
8	SKY B	2:51
9	STRIKE GOLD	2:46
10	DARK	3:50
11	FARM	3:35
12	SAY	3:47
13	DD	3:18
14	ZIN	3:38
15	YU WANTED 2	1:46
16	THX U!	4:26
17	RIVER 2	7:10
18	ALL CONSO	1:44

THE PROCESS OF HOBEAUX ROCOCEAUX

YEAR	OPTICAL SIZE	STROKE ENDINGS	WEIGHTS	FANCINESS	STRAIGHT LINES
2016	Massive	Fancy	One	Extreme	Nope

During my year in the TypeMedia program, my classmate Mark De Winne was exploring display styles for his soon-to-be-released Morris family. I was enamored with the callipygous stencil and thought some ornamented forms would be a valuable drawing exercise.

↓
An ornamented capital I drew in grad school. At the time I thought this was so sick. Now I think it's "mid."

Our instructor, Erik van Blokland, was unimpressed, and he pointed out the distinction between decorative display faces that were simply old designs filled with pattern, and designs where the shape and construction of the letter were informed by the ornamentation. Indeed, the latter are almost always more challenging, compelling, and beautiful.

Later, when the opportunity came to take a second crack at an ornamented version of De Winne's Morris, I omitted the outline, allowing the edges of the illustrations to define the letter.

Recently, a few display faces have employed programming to generate dazzling effects that respond beautifully to the letter shape. Andy Clymer's work on Obsidian and Ben Kiel's sublimely executed Dala Prisma are stunning and well-crafted examples

↑ (top left)
Morris out of the box.

↑ (top right)
A combination of flora and fauna filling the positive space.

using code to automate tasks, thus turning the impossibly tedious into surmountable challenges.

Unfortunately, my programming abilities are not on par with these heavyweights, so to focus on my strengths, I searched for an ornamental style that could not or should not be programmed.

Rococo, Roccoco, and Rococeaux

While working for Photo-Lettering, Paul Carlyle designed many famously ornate typefaces. Among them was the absurdly intricate Carlyle Roccoco. As soon as I laid my peepers on this remarkable beauty, I knew a hybrid of Carlyle Roccoco and Hobeaux was in the cards.

Creative Freedom: A Blessing and a Curse

A while back, I was tasked with creating a poster to be given away at a lecture. Occasionally, a designer is faced with a horrifying prompt: "Do whatever you want." Because most designers thrive on

I wanted Hobeaux Rococeaux to reduce a little better than Carlyle Roccoco, but in the end, my efforts in that department didn't move the needle.

ELABORATELY EMBELLISHED ROCOCCOS AND VICTORIANS – The ultimate in flowery styles of the period. The more intricate designs do not lend themselves to extensive reproportioning. Excellent for color break-ups where ornamentation is required. Some styles fill up when reduced.

HAPPY ANNIVERSAR

4252n
Jester Ornamental 0* Vol.3 p.348 Do not use in Small Sizes

6032n
Carlyle Roccoco 0* Vol.3 p.350

↑
Images of Jester Ornamental and Carlyle Rococco (and Roccoco) from Photo-Lettering's *One Line Manual of Styles*. I enjoy how Jester Ornamental comes with a warning against use in small sizes and Carlyle Roccoco does not.

constraints that narrow the realm of possibility, complete freedom only induces anxiety and paralysis. Luckily, when you have nothing to say, you can just take something someone else said.

For this poster, I went back to basics. My first reading assignment in art school at California College of the Arts was Beatrice Warde's *The Crystal Goblet*. Her essay argues for the invisibility of type, and as someone with a deep adoration of emotionally expressive letters, this quote stood out.

As a personal challenge, I attempted to choose a different display style for each word in the quote and fit it over a skeleton of Hobeaux Black. Needless to say, by the end of the citation, I was running dangerously low on ideas. That was when I remembered the fantastic work of Paul Carlyle.

After the poster was complete, the response to the rococo style was unexpectedly positive. Because I am a slave to praise, finishing the alphabet seemed like a good idea.

Pencil, Ink, Vector, Repeat

Sometimes these tasks seem overwhelming. If one character takes upward of three hours, you know you have your work cut out for you. Fortunately, as you gain momentum, you can develop processes and techniques that minimize the headache as the flow takes over.

Many typefaces can be somewhat componentized—there are serifs, stems, bowls, or other features that can be copied and pasted or otherwise shared between glyphs. Unfortunately for the batteries in my mouse, this was not the case with Hobeaux Rococeaux. Most characters needed to be drawn from scratch, scanned, vectorized, and tweaked one by one to produce adequate results.

The sheer amount of Bezier drawing encouraged a reevaluation of the character set. Thus, the lowercase was ditched.

→ (opposite top)
A bizarre tapestry of styles: regular, shadow, script, balloon, horror, icy, inline script, chrome, paint, drip, script (again), mosaic, overlap, highlight and outline, drop line, dots, top heavy horror, tiger wood, and finally, rococo.

→ (opposite bottom)
The initial attempt at this style reveals many inconsistencies in stroke width and style. The outline one is too thin compared to *W*, and the *r* is too elegant compared to the haphazard twists and turns of *a* and *e*.

"There is nothing simple or dull in achieving the transparent page. Vulgar ostentation is twice as easy as discipline."
-Beatrice Warde

The only drawings for a lowercase Hobeaux Rococeaux were for the letters a, r, d, and e.

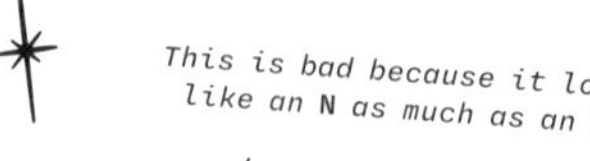

The dimension was a good effort, but I thought that designers could easily do that themselves.

↑ (top)
Sketches don't have to be pretty.

↑ (bottom left)
After struggling with the letters, the figures revealed themselves with considerably less torture.

↑ (bottom right)
With a typical project, we'd get to the back of the character set and begin copy/pasting to arrive at most forms, but with Hobeaux Rococeaux, every glyph had to be drawn from scratch.

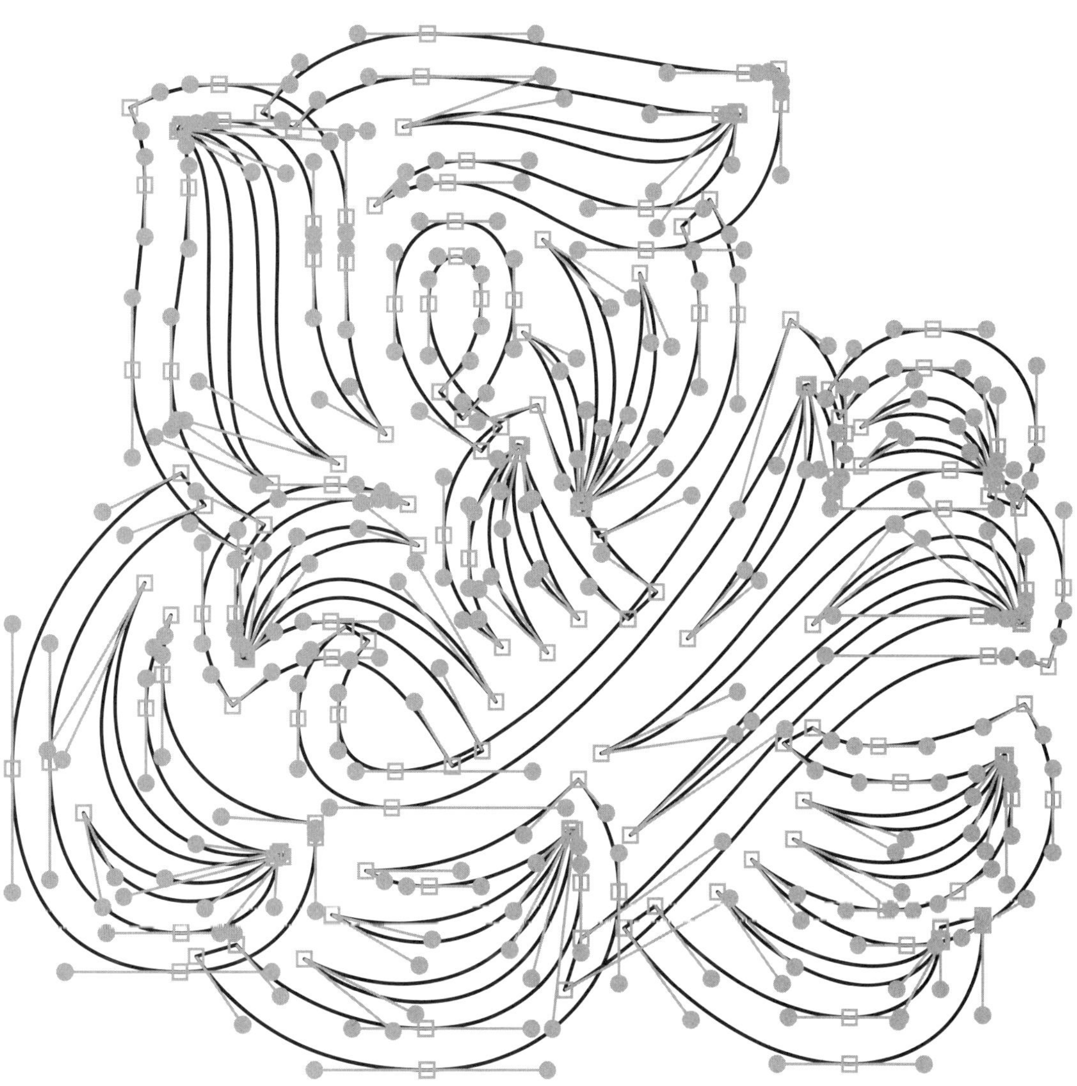

↑
Drawing Hobeaux Rococeaux took a while.

Designing the System

In addition to the basic style, Hobeaux Rococeaux Background was drawn to be used as a background color in multicolor settings. Ideally, this layer would operate well on its own, but alas, it makes absolutely no sense without the linework on top.

Repeated testing revealed that something was lacking. The essential idea behind the rococo movement was that more indeed is more—the frame becomes as important as the art itself. I began imagining what the ideal border for this style could be. A quick round of experiments led to a system of repeatable horizontals or verticals, corner pieces, and center pieces.

↑ (top)
Hobeaux Rococeaux Background and Hobeaux Rococeaux Regular layered on top of one another.

↑ (middle)
A flexible system of interchangeable corners and borders could allow designers to achieve absurdly ornate or toned-down results.

↑ (bottom)
Hobeaux Rococeaux doesn't go overboard with OpenType features, but superiors were added to spice up the figures. Other ligatures or alternates were not necessary because the letters do not touch, and repeated letters do not cause the same hesitation and disappointment that they do in handwriting fonts and the like.

The only caveat was what a pain in the ass it was to typeset the border in graphic design software. Enter DrawBot, a simple yet powerful application that takes Python code for input, and outputs graphics. Using the small amount of Python I was comfortable with, I wrote a simple script that allowed the twenty-five border styles to be painlessly typeset for any word or phrase. The borders automatically adjust to fit the size of the word or words, and once you're satisfied, DrawBot can generate PDFs that can be further manipulated in the graphics application of your choice.

When to Say When

It's funny to think about how a simple idea can quickly get completely out of control. That seems to be a recurring theme in this book. There is no doubt that other styles and additions to Hobeaux Rococeaux would be fun to design, but after a certain point we

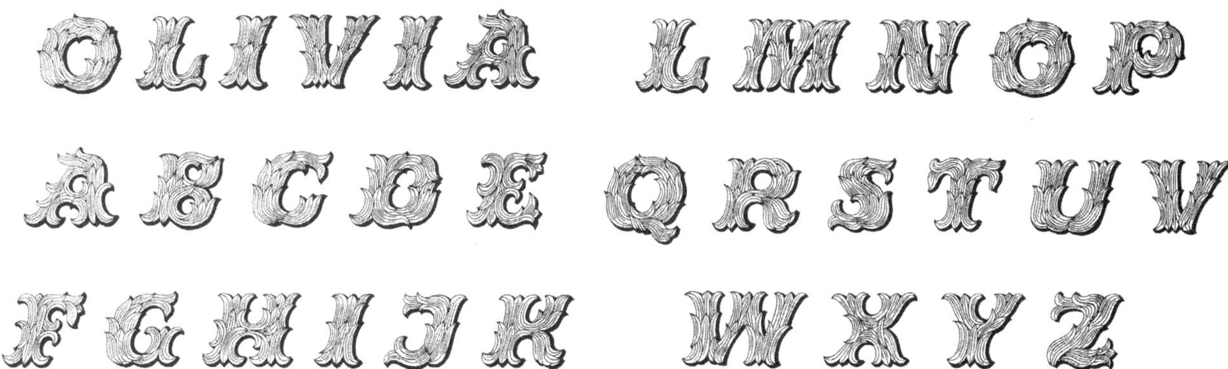

↑
Olivia came out in 1954 and was designed by Alex Stocker. From *Lettera*, no. 1-4, copyright Armin Haab and Co.

must call it a day and see if our work was actually useful to anyone. (Update: It wasn't.) This minuscule drop in a sea of type will almost certainly not be a bestseller, but it can perhaps show that the horizons in type are vaster than we might think. We are only at the tip of the iceberg in terms of what is possible, especially with typefaces for display.

If you choose to purchase the fonts, have fun! Play and experiment! I have put a lot of love into these typefaces as a system, but rules were made to be broken, and nothing would thrill me more than to see this family used in unexpected ways.

Finally, a note for those who say, "James! You have wasted a lot of time here. Your typeface is hard to read!" Remember, it's not a matter of whether or not people can read it; it's a matter of whether or not they want to.

Update

My former instructor from TypeMedia, Peter Verheul, was doing some research on the effect of art nouveau ornamentation in mid-century type designs. In the Swiss series *Lettera*, he came across an image of a typeface called Olivia, which was quite similar to Hobeaux Rococeaux.

Before Peter sent the image to me, I had only seen a single word of Olivia set in a Solotype catalog (with typical Solotype resolution), and that was *after* Hobeaux Rococeaux came out. It seems as though there is nothing new under the sun. I don't recall seeing Olivia prior to the design of my typeface, but did I somehow save it in the hard drive of my subconscious? Who knows? It's funny, though! Even the most outrageous typefaces have a precedent. The good news is that this does very little to take the wind out of my sails. The bad news is that I can't go have a beer with Alex Stocker.

THIS LEGAL AGREEMENT BETWEEN A LICENSEE ("YOU") AND JAMES T. EDMONDSON D/B/
SOFTWARE, YOU AGREE THE TERMS OF THIS AGREEMENT. IF YOU DO NOT AGREE TO THESE T

SECTION 1

GRANT OF LICENSE

Upon payment in full, OH no Type Company grants You a non-exclusive and terminable License to use the Font Software and the designs created by the Font Software but your use must be in accordance with the terms and conditions of this Agreement. You are not allowed to use the Font Software

SECTION 2

TWO BACK UPS

You are permitted to make two (2) back-up copies of the Font Software. Unauthorized copying, creating derivative works, sharing, lending, renting, sale, or other unauthorized use is not permitted. Unless the law of your country states otherwise, You are not permitted to decompile, reverse

SECTION 3

EXCLUSIVE OWNERSHIP

OH no Type Company together with any successors and assigns retain al right and title to the Font Software, trademarks, copyrights and the designs embodied in the Font Software. You hereby agree that this term is contractual in nature and tha the unauthorized use of the design o

TYPE COMPANY. BY DOWNLOADING AND/OR INSTALLING, COPYING, OR USING THE FONT
O NOT PURCHASE THIS LICENSE, OR DOWNLOAD, OR INSTALL, OR USE THE FONT SOFTWARE.

SECTION

LIMITED DISTRIBUTION

You are permitted to make a temporary copy of the Font Software for use by a commercial printer or service bureau solely for use in the production of your own materials. You are also permitted to include a temporary copy the Font Software with a document solely for the

SECTION

OTHER USES

If you are a design consultancy, advertising agency, or purchasing this License for use by or on behalf of such an entity, the actual end user must purchase an appropriate License. Specifically, if your client will use copies of the Font Software, your client must also purchase a License.

SECTION

LIMITATIONS TO USE

Use of the Font Software, as noted below, is NOT permitted without first obtaining a special license:
a) ALPHABET OR LETTERFORM-RELATED PRODUCTS FOR RESALE OR LETTERFORM CREATION PRODUCTS OR DEVICES;
b) EMBEDDING IN ELECTRONIC

↑
Perhaps the most absurd end user license agreement in existence, featuring all the styles of Hobeaux Rococeaux singing in harmony.

HOB
©2

CHAPTER EIGHT

FAQS & FINAL WORDS

The FAQs

Here are a few questions my students have asked me over the years. I found myself in the classroom saying the same things on repeat all the time. It was difficult to say the same stuff constantly without starting to sound less enthusiastic. That's when I realized all of my favorite teachers had similarly regurgitated their same set of points over and over, year after year, decade after decade. What a talent to say the same thing you've said a million times in a way that feels fresh and believable! In an effort to repay the debt I owe them, unto you, I present the FAQs.

What Makes a Good Concept for a Typeface?

A strong concept begins and ends with one idea. An "idea" to me could be something as simple as "high-contrast Caslon," as in the case of Big Caslon by Matthew Carter. It could be "impossible geometry," as in the case of Macula by Jacques Le Bailly. It could be "responsive, with minimal negative space," as in the case of Fit by David Jonathan Ross. A common affliction among students is that their enthusiasm gets the best of them, and they try to pack their typeface full of so many ideas that the concept gets muddied. As jazz guitarist John Scofield says, "If you don't got a concept, you got a misconception."

Concepts are at their best when they make decisions for you. Single- or double-story *a*? Does this need a light weight? Would an overlapping form of *W* be good here? Should I add in alternate swash capitals? Throw all your questions to the concept, and if a clear answer doesn't arrive, then perhaps the concept hasn't been clearly defined yet.

How Faithful Should a Revival Be?

Revivals are reinterpretations of older typefaces. They are among the most educationally beneficial projects that a student can undertake, and for that reason they are often incorporated into type design curricula.

At many points in the process, it's normal to question just how much creative freedom the designer has and how much they should simply trace the original to the best of their ability.

There are no wrong answers to this question, as both extremes and everything in between can be educationally viable. For the newcomer, it can be too much to learn the software and how to draw and space *while* imbuing the revival with a personal touch. These three things compete for our attention, and we must free ourselves from at least one of them. Software and drawing and spacing are the prerequisites for everything else, so that only leaves the designer's creativity as eligible for omission.

But as students become comfortable with the tools and best practices, I'd encourage them to approach everything with a point of view. It's a thrill to work on something where you *can't* just look up the answer in the back of the book. Many of the glyphs in our fonts—particularly Casserole Lombardic—had to be attempted many times before the solution presented itself. I look at all those failed attempts more like going to the gym than getting a last-place trophy. If we can get comfortable looking for solutions, then there's no genre of type that can mystify us for long.

So the short version of this answer is, "Up to you."

For our typeface Hobeaux, I opted to alter the *T* and *L* to be a lot narrower. In general, I've let spacing be my north star in many decisions. *T* and *L* can be surprisingly narrow before they present

legibility issues. Minimizing unnecessary white space around those painfully white space–laden glyphs goes a long way in creating even texture across a word or paragraph.

For our typeface Casserole, which is a reinterpretation of Davida, I pushed this idea to the extreme. We changed how everything was drawn (how thin the connections to the ball terminals were, how trapezoidal the round glyphs were), we added a lowercase, and then we created five more versions covering everything from a sans to a script to a blackletter.

Should I Add Alternates or Other Features to My Project?
I have released enough typefaces to know that, by and large, the alternates that get built into our painstakingly manufactured font packages are rarely used. My opinion is that most of the time, when designers are choosing typefaces for a project, they are simply going down the list of the fonts installed on their computer and are not considering the wealth of alternates and other bells and whistles the type designer has hidden under the hood of the font in question.

But simply because these are often overlooked does not mean that they aren't worth the time of building into our projects. I've found that for many of our typefaces, like Forevs and Polymath, the suite of alternates becomes an important part of the project's goals. They're useful for marketing and generally make me really excited to show off our hard work to the font-loving public.

I think the worst alternates arise when the type designer simply cannot decide between two viable options. The best alternates, in contrast, do an efficient job of completely changing the vibe while only swapping out a few key glyphs.

Polymath FOREVS
Polymath FOREVS
Polymath FOREVS
Polymath FOREVS
Polymath FOREVS

↑ (top)
Forevs and Polymath include so many alternate forms that our designers asked me, "Is this really necessary?" The short answer was "No, not really."

When Do You Give Up on a Project?

My childhood friend Daniel Montellano had won a couple of BMX races, and several impressive trophies adorned the walls of his bedroom. One trophy featured a sick statue of a bicyclist doing a wheelie, with the phrase "Don't dump it, pump it!" engraved onto the aluminum plaque underneath. That phrase always stuck in my mind, and I utter it to myself whenever I feel I'm on the verge of giving up on an idea.

There is always a way of saving something. There is nothing truly destructive about editing digital outlines, and so the only things that are in our way are the thoughts and ideas we have about the project. A simple repositioning and a Save As can go a very long way in reinvigorating our projects and our enthusiasm for working on them.

What Should Be Going On in My Head as I Work?

I have seen students cry. I have taught workshops where students go off to lunch and do not come back. I have seen students look around the room and feel terrible that their classmates seem to be doing a better job. I know because I've been that student too!

As much as possible, speaking to yourself in the same way you'd encourage your best friend or even a child can give you the best shot at enjoying the work in the early stages. Celebrate all wins, and never deprive anyone of a pat on the back.

There are so many things to keep in mind while you're working on a typeface. With each character you add, more relationships are built, and the intricacy of your system snowballs. It gets overwhelming, especially for beginners. For this reason I think someone's first font should be a doable project that builds confidence. Maybe it's only five letters! Maybe it's not even a font at all—just a piece of lettering. Don't bite off more than you can chew, and remember that (as *This American Life* host Ira Glass has so elegantly articulated) in the beginning, your taste far exceeds your skill level. Just try to make every subsequent project a little bit better in some capacity. We are here to have fun, after all.

What's Your Number One Best Tip for a Good Result?
Space as you draw, and draw as you space. The tricky part about type is that as soon as you get the letters how you want them, someone comes in and jumbles them all up! This simple fact—that type can be rearranged in any sequence—means that we have to evaluate all our micro decisions on a macro level. As type designers, it's too easy to keep your eyes on a single glyph at 5,000 percent scale.

Evaluating your decisions in a more realistic context gives you the awareness and perspective to be confident about your design decisions. Finally, the negative space inside and around letters is just as important as the positive spaces—if not more so. The more we think about this, the more we realize that drawing and spacing are the same activity and should happen at the same time.

When Is a Project Done?
This question seems to come up more frequently than most frequently asked questions, and I think that's because many students struggle with perfectionism and are perplexed by people who willingly stop working without a client deadline looming overhead.

First, I believe that I am someone who finishes things. That's just my belief, but I also have to remind myself of it. It's a lot like every time I'm in the self-checkout line at Home Depot. I have to remind myself, "I am someone who does not steal." But I still think about shoplifting every single time.

There is one liberating thought on finishing things I heard from Erik's brother, designer Petr van Blokland: "Everything is done. It's just done at a different version." I like this software-driven approach because there is a time when fonts go from the designer's computer to the designer's friends and then to everyone else. Even at that

point, things can be updated again, styles can be added, and more languages can be supported. Everything is always done because nothing is ever really done!

There is also the idea that our enthusiasm for a project eventually runs out. With every typeface, there is a point where I feel like I have given it all I've got, and the reality is that it's not much fun to work on anymore. That's how I know it's done. If I can't justify or get excited about more work, the project dies. And if when it dies it's ready for public use, then we release it. But there are plenty of projects that die long before that!

Before I Go

I've read a lot of self-help books, and they're all fairly similar. Take 100 percent responsibility for everything in your life; align your thoughts, words, and actions; and break overwhelming things into manageable pieces. I still love self-help advice, but there seems to be a glaring omission from the "How do you get good at something?" sections.

I've found that the best way to improve at something is to place an irrational amount of importance on it. In confined groups, it's easier to obsess about the same things, inspire one another, and generally get the feeling that what you're working on is super important. In reality, type design and lettering rank extremely low in terms of real-life importance. That reality is detrimental to your improvement, as you'll begin to think of all the time spent devoted to learning this craft as time wasted.

But with the right group, friend, or accountability partner, you can think in a less rational and much more fun way about this stuff. You can see it as an extremely important thing for you personally—and even for the world.

And honestly, that's not far from the truth. While the fate of the world doesn't lie in the hands of the type designer, having a hobby to get you out of bed in the morning is worth its weight in gold.

The Business of Type

I was twenty-three when I first designed a complete (to me, at the time) character set. It was a font called Wisdom Script that I designed in Bob Aufuldish's Graphic Design IV class, and I spent about a week working on it. I put it on my website and asked people to email me for a copy. About three people asked.

Then I put it on Riley Cran's website Lost Type, a pay-what-you-want font distributor that had about eight projects on it at the time. Immediately after releasing it, my phone began buzzing every five minutes with small donations coming in through PayPal. I made $726 that day, and my life changed forever.

This book is not about running a business, but I can share some basic points.

The vast majority of what we work on at Ohno can either be classified as contributions to our library or projects for visibility. The library is our catalog of fonts, and visibility is everything related to how people find us. If no one knew who we were, we'd be dead, and if everyone knew us but we had nothing to sell, we'd be dead as well. So our library and visibility projects work hand in hand to keep us afloat.

In our library, we've found it helpful to have a combination of fun things that explore a genre, bring something new to the conversation, or revitalize old typefaces to exist in a contemporary context. We basically made it through the first handful of years of Ohno with only those projects. But as they say, what got you here, won't get you there. We then began experimenting with adding typefaces to our library that could be used over and over and could exist in more corporate environments. That has been hugely effective at giving us more stable income that isn't so closely tied to trends.

On the marketing side, we've experimented with the most effective way to get a large number of eyeballs on our work for very little money and not too much time. So far, the best way seems to be using video and getting people to subscribe to our newsletter. These methods will change over time, so I'm hesitant to put them in a book. But there is a principle that's a bit more timeless: There is always a way for artists and designers to market themselves that isn't painful; you just have to find what works for you. Just saying words like *marketing* or the even more detestable *content creation* is enough to get many artists and designers to roll their eyes in disgust, but for me, it's been fun to experiment and work in other design-adjacent disciplines like video editing, writing, and storytelling.

—BOB AUFULDISH

The Type Community

I was still an undergrad when I first started going to type meetups in San Francisco, attending conferences all over, and reaching out to designers I admired and hanging out with them in real life. I can't say enough positive things about making that leap from bedroom enthusiast to member of the worldwide type community.

Perhaps because there isn't too much money at stake, the type community is blessed with countless folks all over the world who are completely genuine in their adoration for this niche subgenre of design. It's amazing to see that a love of fonts is something that doesn't discriminate based on age, culture, ethnicity, or gender.

The most important thing I've learned, especially from those older than I am, is that there is always a new area within type design to explore and get better at. I always appreciated my type design heroes who seemed to keep releasing type well past the point that they needed to for financial reasons.

No matter your interest, there is something tremendously valuable in getting out into the world and speaking with people who share your interests. It's definitely scary putting yourself out there in that way, but the benefits are more than I ever could have realized at the outset.

This Is Supposed to Be Fun

Bob Aufuldish began his Graphic Design IV class with a simple phrase: "This is supposed to be fun." It's something that always stuck with me. If I had to guess, Bob has too often witnessed stressed-out students, suffering from lack of sleep and desperate to end the semester with a decent project, fall victim to the art school blues. But he's right, this *is* supposed to be fun, and if we're not having fun, then it's up to us to find some way to change that.

The best way I've found is to point my canoe downstream. Bringing other obsessions or interests into my type design work has been a recurring theme that has kept me having fun. Every band, hobby, or piece of art I love has worked its way into an Ohno specimen in some capacity.

Ran Ran
Ran Ran
Ran Ran
Ran Ran
Ran Ran

↑
A curly tail on an *a* can be a very cute decision in the light and regular weights, but it can be nothing more than an eyesore in the heavier part of the weight spectrum. Sometimes designs can account for this and switch between more outspoken and subdued decisions where appropriate.

Even just designing and redesigning my workshop to be a sacred space surrounded by the tools and supplies that I love goes a long way. This takes up more time than you might think, but it always puts me in a good mood.

Tidying a drawer, putting on a favorite record, starting a new font, lighting a candle, checking something off a to-do list—there are many instant wins that can bump my mood up a few points. I've learned to employ one or more when the art school blues come back for a visit.

Fun is the coal the makes this train roll! It's only through having fun that we can successfully pick ourselves up off the ground and recover from the failures that a student of type design is bound to experience. Fun can carry us through the mistakes, corrections, and myriad versions of that first typeface. Conversely, a lack of fun can expose type design for what it is: monotonous labor. More fun increases patience, and more patience increases quality.

Doing a Bold

At some point along a type designer's path, they will be tasked with taking something they've drawn already and adding a new style to it. The most common form of this type of iteration would be drawing a bold. And so the question invariably arises from the blossoming young designer, "Where does the weight go?"

The answer is another question: "Where does the weight *not* go?" In short, weight goes everywhere. Mass gets added to the left, the right, and even on top of some glyphs. The x-height tends to grow a little bit in heavier weights, because adding weight only to the left and right tends to leave the lowercase feeling *wider* than it was before. Our challenge in all of these iterations is to change what we intend to change and leave everything else the same. Bolder styles usually have tighter spacing, because their smaller counters have a relationship to the distance between characters.

Doing a bold is more than just a technical challenge and a stop along a type designer's education. For anyone, the bold can inform many decisions about what the regular and light weights of a design need to do. This is why type design instructors often encourage students to experiment with drawing a bold as a way of stress-testing their system. Almost always, doing the bold shows us details that are too delicate or unnecessary or that are simply going to create spacing problems as weight increases.

Save As

I've mentioned it a few times in this book already, but it bears repeating. There are few creative moves as powerful as the Save As. For some reason, our puny human brains feel some emotional pull to not disturb too much as we're working. In an analog environment, it totally makes sense, as a sweeping change across a drawing would be an uncomfortable amount of eraser dust to sweep off the page. But I notice that even in a digital scenario, designers don't want to experiment with a change if it means that the work they've already completed would be undone.

The Save As is there to save the day. There is something incredibly liberating about saving a version of the font you're working on and leaving it in the dust as you branch off, taking a new version into the next phase of your design process. With a clean version, everything is delightfully up for grabs, and you have the comfort of a safety net below to bail you out if things go completely haywire.

While sketching, a Save As might be a new rough trace of an existing drawing. On the computer, it might be an experimental form of a glyph or a new font or an entirely new typeface or designspace. The important thing to remember is that the nagging voice in your head—telling you that the x-height is too low, the capitals are too wide, or whatever the case may be—isn't going away. The only way to get that critic to pipe down is to do a quick Save As and determine if the voice was right or wrong. And it's almost always right.

An Argument for a Creative Practice

When I was a kid, I really wanted to be in a cool band, and I didn't have any aspirations other than to play a single song at the end of *Late Night with Conan O'Brien*. At the time, that was the coolest thing I could think of, and surely something that would impress my older brother Cam.

Years later, I see how truly shortsighted that was! I didn't realize it at the time, but the finish line is not quite the point. I believe that committing to a practice has served me better than playing one song on television, but that idea has never been fully tested.

Even within type design—a field I love and am constantly finding new avenues to learn and grow in—I can't do it all the time. I have had so much fun learning and playing with new interests along the way. When these budding interests first entered the

~~Safety net~~
~~Backup plan~~

picture, I was hell-bent on finding a way to combine them and feed them back into type design. There were a couple of obvious answers, including woodworking with lettering and type design with music. Both things have been satisfying, but at the end of the day, I'm happy to let those interests simply exist alongside type, and not try to combine them forcefully.

Ohno is my only shot at employment. I have no backup plan or safety net. I have no choice but to work in a way that is sustainable. A combination of interests and influences, with no finish line in sight, helps build the framework for me to gradually cruise up to retirement and slowly fade out until I die (probably of prostate cancer).

Working Fast

Watching someone with a mastery over their tools is at once impressive and discouraging. Students in their first few weeks of Font Software Suffering move so slowly that each decision to overhaul even a single glyph requires an overwhelming amount of labor.

Software mastery is a goal that can only be achieved with practice and with a commitment to learn as many keyboard shortcuts as possible. Type them up, print them out, and pin them next to your desk. Write them on Post-it notes and stick them up all over the place. Do whatever it takes to learn a new shortcut every day, and gradually you'll move with speed and grace around your font editor of choice.

At the beginning, it's a little too painful to constantly wonder, *Should I be working on this or that? Is it time for figures yet? Or should I redraw the caps?* But as we get comfortable finishing more projects, the most efficient order in which to work becomes more and more clear. We don't want to fill up empty glyphs just because they're empty. We need to be sure that each shape we add has a sturdy foundation underneath. There is no reason to draw a lowercase *h* when our *n* and *l* haven't been resolved. We can't tackle a *w* until our *v* is set. Other letters need to be drawn *around* the same time, but it doesn't matter exactly if we draw a lowercase *c* or *e*, as long as we have already committed to the weight, x-height, contrast, and width of our *o*. With that in mind, I propose the most controversial point in this book: a new order for the alphabet.

n o i p l a v c e s g r t f z u m b d q h k j w y x

The order for the capitals is different. This will make life a lot harder for preschool teachers, but it will be worth it when their students invariably grow up to be productive type designers.

H O I D N V A E M L T S P B R F U Z C G K J W Y X Q

As you can see, this order emphasizes copy-and-paste-able shapes early on and moves the glyphs that are built with their components to the end. Is it perfect? Of course not! These shapes are all so random that a truly logical sequence does not exist. The most important thing is that you are working in a way that is efficient and comfortable for you.

The two factors in speed are your facility with tools and the ideal sequence of events. With those two things working together, you will meet every question with a liberating sense of ease. Changing the x-height? No big deal. Making the uppercase slightly heavier? Only takes a minute.

When you're not overwhelmed with the workload, when you have mastered your tools and devised a procedure that works for you, you can face challenges with calm confidence.

ABC

GHIJ

OPQ

LET

UVW

DEF
KLMN
STHE
ERS
Y&Z

APPENDIX

THE LETTERS

In the beginning of the pandemic, I started doing a series on social media where I analyzed one letter at a time and talked about the common pitfalls I saw students falling into when attempting to draw each glyph in their typefaces. People seemed to appreciate the content, and I appreciated the ability to tell them without telling them why fonts cost money.

As with most of my projects, the first part of the alphabet was quick and easy, but finishing up all twenty-six posts started to feel like quite an undertaking. Eventually, we were all done, and the information was soon translated into Russian and Spanish.

To be completely honest, I don't see much of a point in going in the order of the alphabet. In fact, just a few pages ago, I proposed a new order for the alphabet strictly for the purpose of being more hospitable to type design.

But there's something about the order of the alphabet that is approachable to nearly everyone. We learn it at such a young age and familiarize ourselves with the shapes so thoroughly that they are absorbed into the deepest recesses of our subconscious. Learning type design forces us to examine these fundamentals that we take for granted and learn them all over again. In a way, the student of type design is a child once more.

Raising kids myself has been an illuminating experience. They need constant help, encouragement, and guidance. In the blink of an eye they can put themself into a completely life-threatening situation, with almost zero effort. Parents have to hover in a way that is exhausting for them and the kid, but they both get used to it. The kid needs help, and the parent needs to know the kid is safe.

But just when you least expect it, you realize you're not needed anymore, at least not in the way you once were. I've found this to be one of the toughest parts of parenting: stepping back and letting your kid fall short.

The rules and suggestions in this book, and especially the ones in the following pages, are a similar sort of guidance. They might help you get on your feet and give you a win. But sooner or later, you won't need them anymore. At that point, the thing that would serve you the most would be to go out there and make your own mistakes.

So is going in the order of the alphabet important? Not at all. It's simply there to make you feel like half the work is done already, which if you've read this far, it definitely is!

Have fun. We're here for a good time, not for a long time.

James Edmondson
San Jose, California
January 2025

Some Tips on Drawing Type *from A to Z*

cap-height

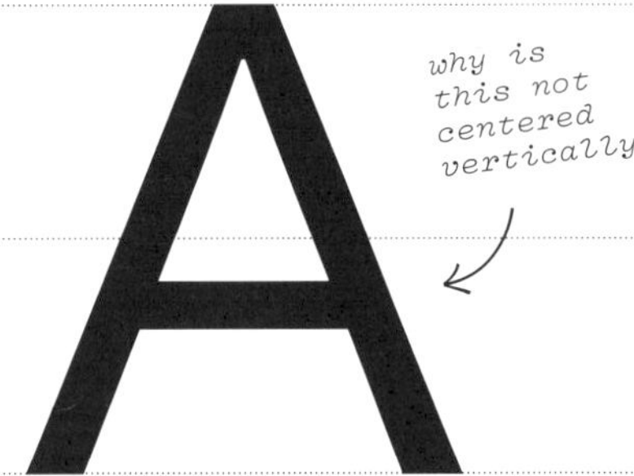

kinda
fugly

center

baseline

You might expect the *crossbar* on A to hit exactly at the center, but nah…

That leaves A feeling really *high-waisted*, and ugly AF. What we want is a balance between the top and bottom negative spaces.

Call it water, air, sand, crushed hopes and dreams, whatever! The important thing is that those two negative spaces are visually close to each other in size.

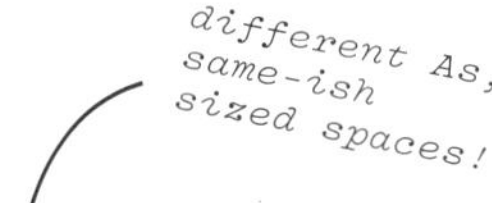

x-height

Another failure of geometry is the stroke weight where *joints* occur.

yowza, that
looks like
dog shit!

Completely even stroke weight would give us a joint that appears way too heavy!

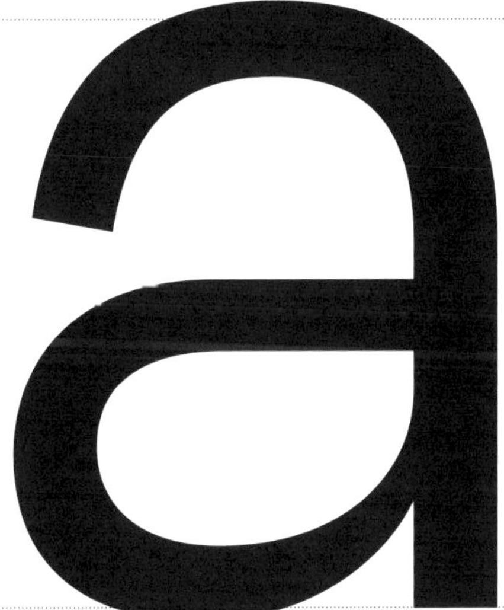

much
better

I can get carried away with this, but you don't have to be so dramatic. Important: Joints should thin out a bit, and they don't define your contrast.

To be honest, I'm usually singing the gospel of "it's not the letters that matter; it's the words." Let's continue on and visit some things about spacing and more macro-level concepts in a bit.

REVIEW

- **Geometry will fail you!**
- **If it looks wrong, it is wrong.**
- **A high waist should be intentional.**
- **Don't get stuck with an expensive car payment!**

Glyphs should always be proud of what letter they are! This becomes even more important when designing type for smaller sizes.

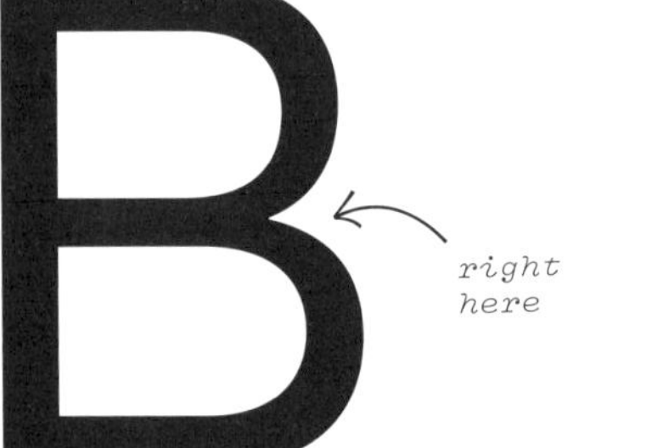

Let's talk about the most important feature of the letter B: the *buttcrack*.

A failure to really *dig in* to the buttcrack creates a dark spot, but even worse, it de-emphasizes the B-ness.

★ denotes buttcrack

ok, smartass, can you explain this?

Also, the top *bowl* is a little smaller, helping the letter stay balanced. We see a similar thing on K, S, X, and Z.

If you don't do that, your B looks weird! Almost like it's going to fall over. Boring! Let's move on to the lowercase.

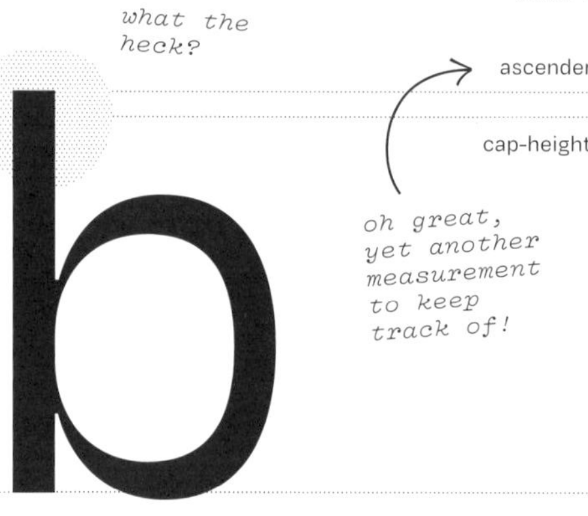

An ascender overshooting the cap-height lets us differentiate I from l and 1 and so on. And could very well get you laid. OK, maybe not!

b has an *ascender*, or a *stem* going above the x-height. But why does it go past the cap-height?

REVIEW

- **Dig into the buttcrack.**
- **Uppercase top bowl is a little smaller.**
- **Ascenders are higher than cap-heights.**
- **Invest your savings in low-expense-ratio mutual funds like VTSAX.**

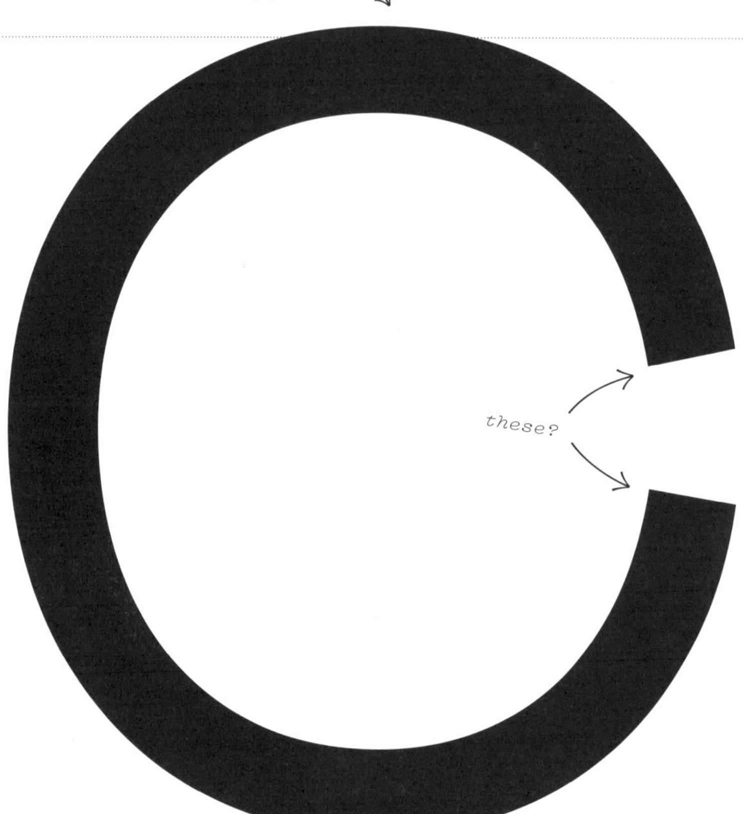

C is a good opportunity to talk about two terms that make you sound fancy: *terminals* and *overshoots*.

no overshoot

ICH

with overshoot

ICH

First, here's how C would look compared to I and H with no overshoots. Because only a tiny speck of C touches the cap-height and baseline, it appears ◈optically smaller◈ than letters that have solid mass at those areas.

Going a bit above or below the guides compensates for the perceived smaller size.

less overshoot

ICH

more overshoot

C

In condensed styles, you need less overshoot, and in wide styles you need more. Why? Because changes in height are more and less obvious, respectively.

Sometimes people ask, "How much overshoot is the default amount?" They think they can trick me into giving them a definite answer. I can't and won't.

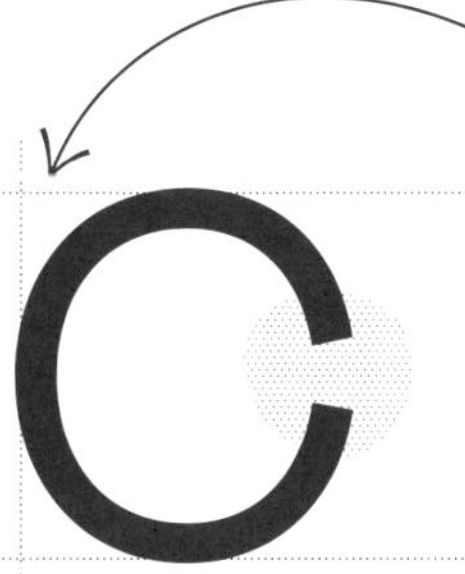

sidenote: did you notice there is also overshoot in the vertical alignment of the C and the paragraph below?

terminals: not just for airports, restaurants, computers, and illnesses

Moving on, *terminals* are the beginnings or endings of strokes. The terminals on C relate significantly to terminals on G and S.

Sometimes the *aperture* of C can be quite open, and the terminals can be cut vertically or at whatever angle your heart desires.

CGS CGS

CGS CGS

CGS CGS

CGS CGS

Across all kinds of styles, terminals on C, G, and S relate in similar ways. How closed or open are they? Is there a serif? Where's my mommy?

Lowercase is pretty much the same in sans stuff. But in serif typefaces, there is usually an omitted bottom serif.

REVIEW

- **Overshoot round shapes.**
- **Get your C, G, and S terminals on the same page.**
- **Drink and eat as much as you want during quarantine.**

are you kidding? D is booooring

wow, that's fascinating. really on the edge of my seat here.

Get ready for a deep dive into d most interesting character there is to d-mystify.

D is a little bit wider than an H, and a little narrower than an O, and you can see how it's basically built out of a *vertical* and a *round*.

In many styles—even script—the left of D is exactly the same as the left of B.

Copying and pasting is not cheating and is an efficient path to a consistent alphabet.

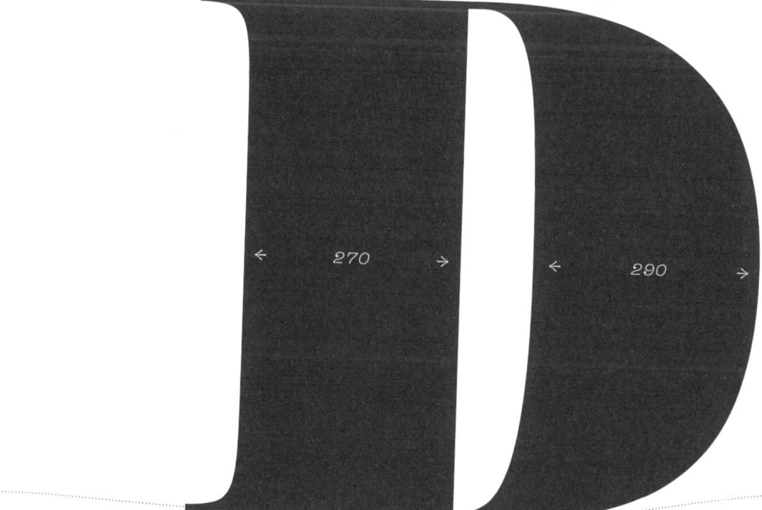

that D is so heavy it dented the baseline!

In letters with *contrast*, the vertical is thinner than the round at its thickest. Since the vertical is thick for the entire cap-height, and the round is thick just for a moment, you must compensate.

db db

In the lowercase, the d and b look like mirror images of each other. But don't believe everything you see.

In other styles, we see that is not the case! You must rotate the b for the foundation of the q, and add a bottom right serif.

bdpq

bdpq

bdpq

bdpq

The bdpq relationship is a holy union, and those four can be drawn pretty quickly, since (again) you're mostly copying and pasting.

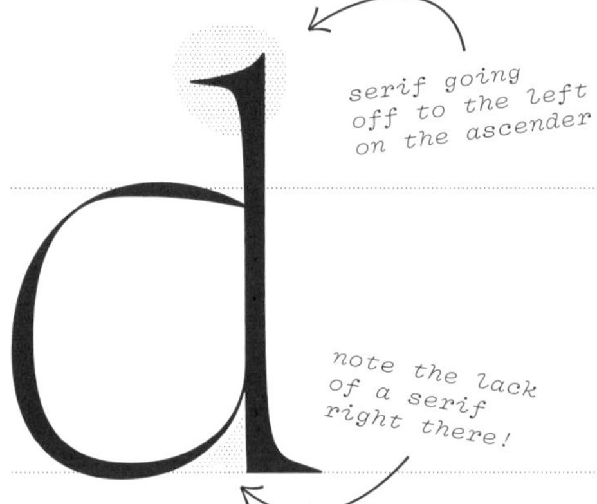

Imagine the path your pen would take when writing a cursive d. That explains the vertical asymmetry in the round. Finally, the negative space at the baseline is very important, so we make it loud and proud.

REVIEW

- **Copy/pasting is OK!**
- **bdpq are related, but not mirror images. Rotate, don't flip.**
- **Don't even think about putting tomatoes in the fridge.**

191

203

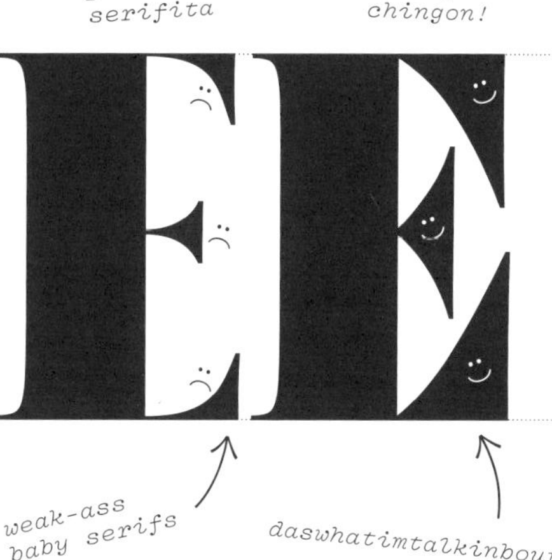

E is full of absolutely wild optical adjustments. The crossbar is slightly higher than geometrically centered, because if it wasn't it would appear to be too low. Isn't that weird?

In serif land, E has *horizontal serifs* on the left and *vertical serifs* on the right. Vertical serifs should follow the weight and width. If the design is bold and condensed, so should be the vertical serifs!

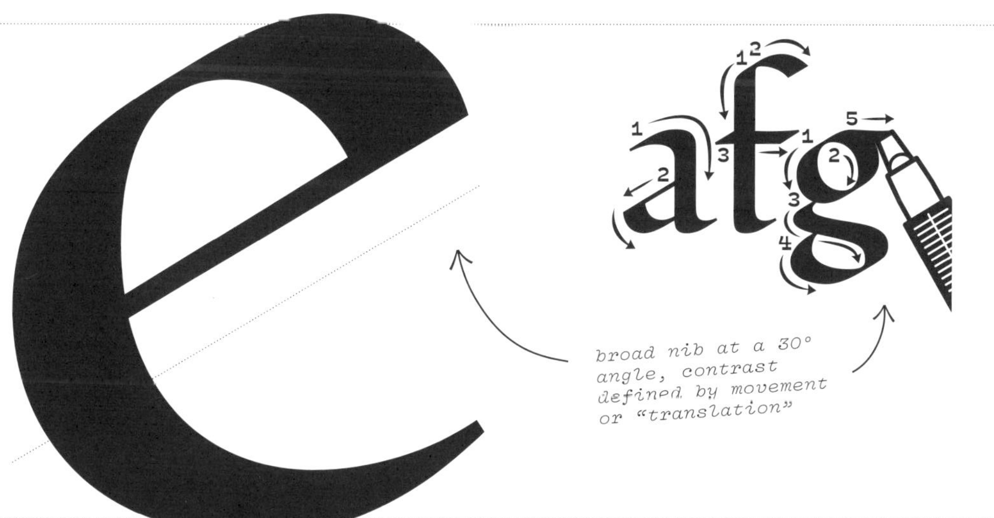

In the lowercase, e is a great opportunity to bring up a massively important topic in type design: *contrast type*. Imagine this e being drawn with a *broad nib*. Most historical typefaces with this contrast model keep the pen held at around 30°.

Garamond, Jenson, and many logotypes for German beer employ the conventions of this contrast model.

pointed pen held straight, contrast defined by pressure or «expansion»

thin

translation:

broad nib, «diagonal stress»

The other main contrast model is called *expansion* because of how the *pointed pen* creates a thicker line when more pressure is applied. With some exceptions, the thinnest point is usually exactly at the top or bottom of any round shape.

Bodoni, Didot, and many logotypes for fashion magazines and cigarettes make heavy use of expansion.

But back to the e! Translation and expansion have so many terms attached to them, it can get really confusing, but the simple trick is to look for the thins!

thin

expansion:

pointed pen, «modern»

Honestly, it took me so long to fully understand the differences between the two, so be patient. Figuring this out unlocks a lot of possibilities and makes you feel like you could work in any style!

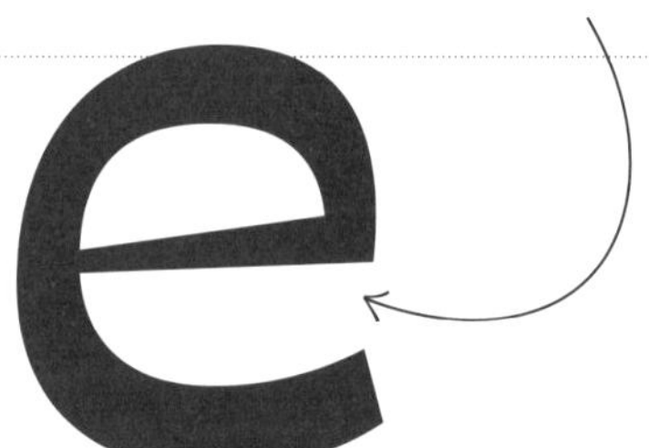

The e contains so much DNA about the typeface—weight, width, contrast, contrast type—it's like a good friend about to give you some juicy gossip! And you can tell, because it's always smiling.

REVIEW

- **Vertical serifs respond to weight and width.**
- **Type is inextricably linked to calligraphy. Thank you, Noordzij!**
- **Expansion and translation are the two main types of contrast.**
- **I went to middle school and high school with Zac Efron.**

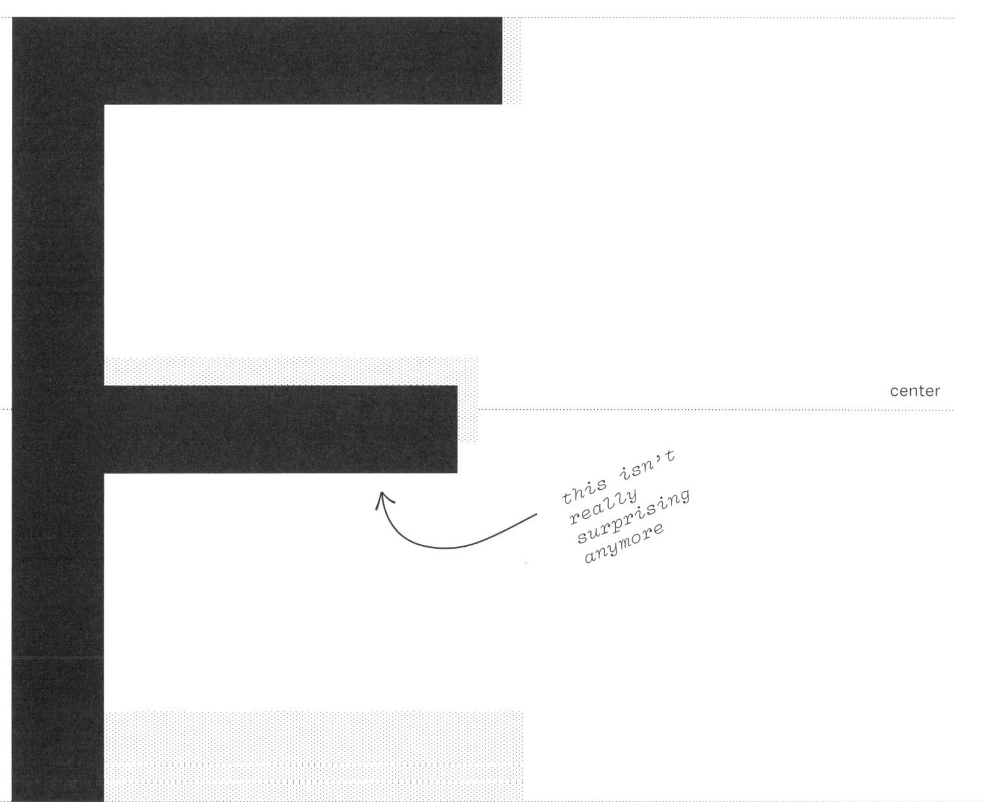

The middle horizontal on F appears to hit right at the middle, and it does... on Opposite Day!

Because F has no horizontal bottom, you can drop the middle horizontal a bit to equalize the two pockets of negative space.

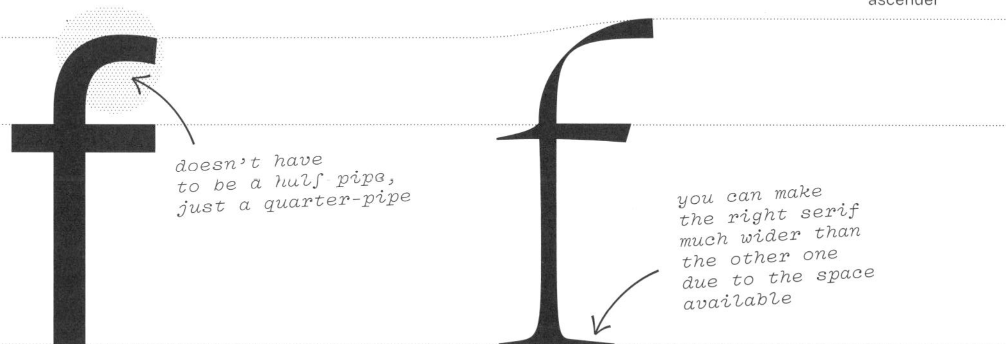

Lowercase f has a crossbar that hangs from the top of the x-height, and an ascender that makes a right turn as it reaches the ascender line.

If you were going to draw a really high-contrast, translation, serif f, you might want to make it look a bit like this.

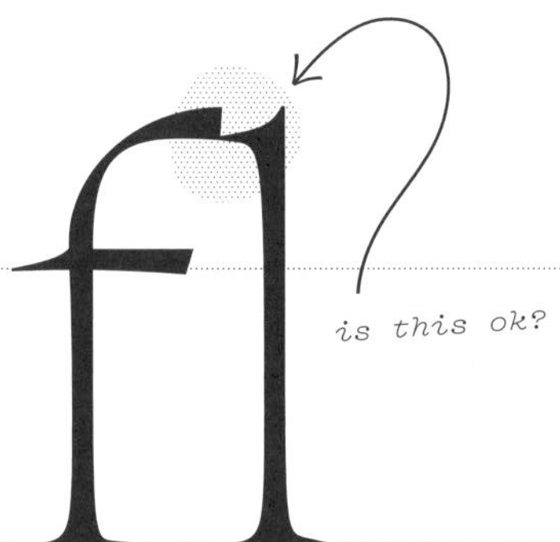

Be careful to make your f narrow enough so that it doesn't collide with anything else. Alternatively, you can draw *ligatures* for all colliding pairs. But type design is about building a system of players that work *in any sequence*. Sometimes ligatures draw too much attention and interrupt the reader. But some people think they're cute?[1] Honestly, I avoid them like the plague.

It occasionally requires some advanced trickery to get bold fs into a compact form, but with patience, it's always possible. And you'll always be glad when you don't have to build a bunch of stupid ligatures!

REVIEW

- **Lower the crossbar on F.**
- **Ligatures aren't always the answer.**
- **A Dyson V7 Animal+ Vacuum changed my life and could change yours too.**

this G has a very closed aperture

G can take many forms in both upper- and lowercase.

---

① If you're a ligature lover, please just go for it. Take my opinions with a grain of salt and ligature it up.

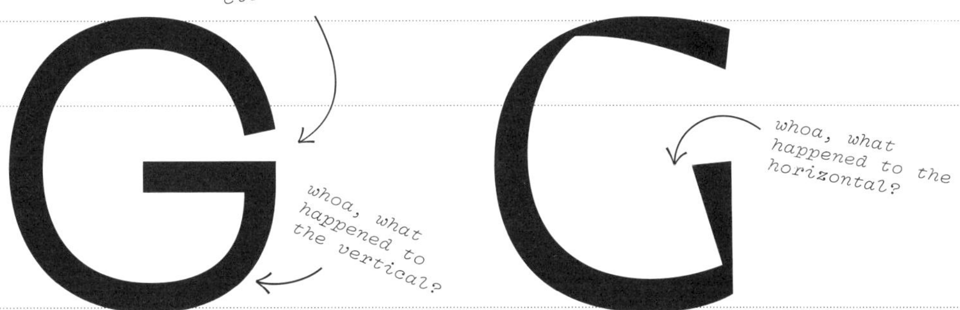

Degular has this as an alternate, which can be read just as easily, but it evokes a different feeling. Futura and many other geometric sans opt for this form.

Oddly, G's salient feature, the horizontal, turns out to not be necessary in some humanist designs.

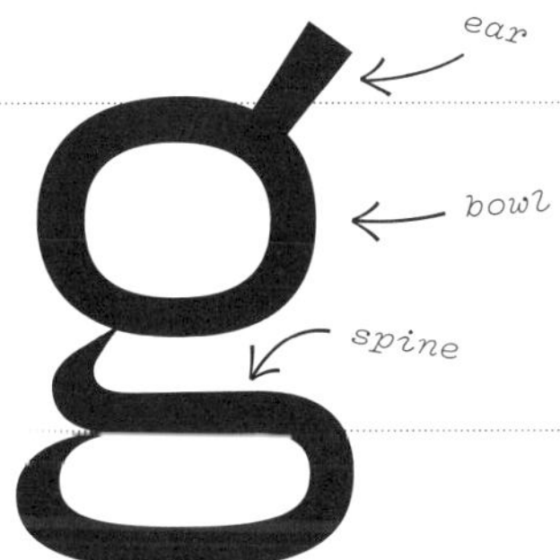

Lowercase g is just a little o that hangs from the x-height, then an s that grows out like a weird tail and turns into an 8. And it has an ear. g is outrageous in every way and makes no apologies.

Perhaps due to g's wild nature, students of type design often take the opportunity to throw out every rule in the book and make the weirdest gs you've ever seen.

That's why I challenge you to make really boring gs. It's much harder than making an expressive g, but not so hard when you can look to your o and s for some cues and inspiration.

the three pockets
of negative space
are of similar size

I often opt for a flat ear, as a sort of nod to calligraphy, but what's *way more important* is the size of the three areas of negative space.

If you crave ✧the ultra boring,✧ the deceptively titled *single story g* is the answer — but maybe not in a high-contrast serif. That wouldn't be boring enough!

REVIEW

- **Prove you can handle a boring g.**
- **The three negative spaces in g should be similar in size.**
- **Our family bought a computer at Costco in 1996 and returned it every year for a decade.**

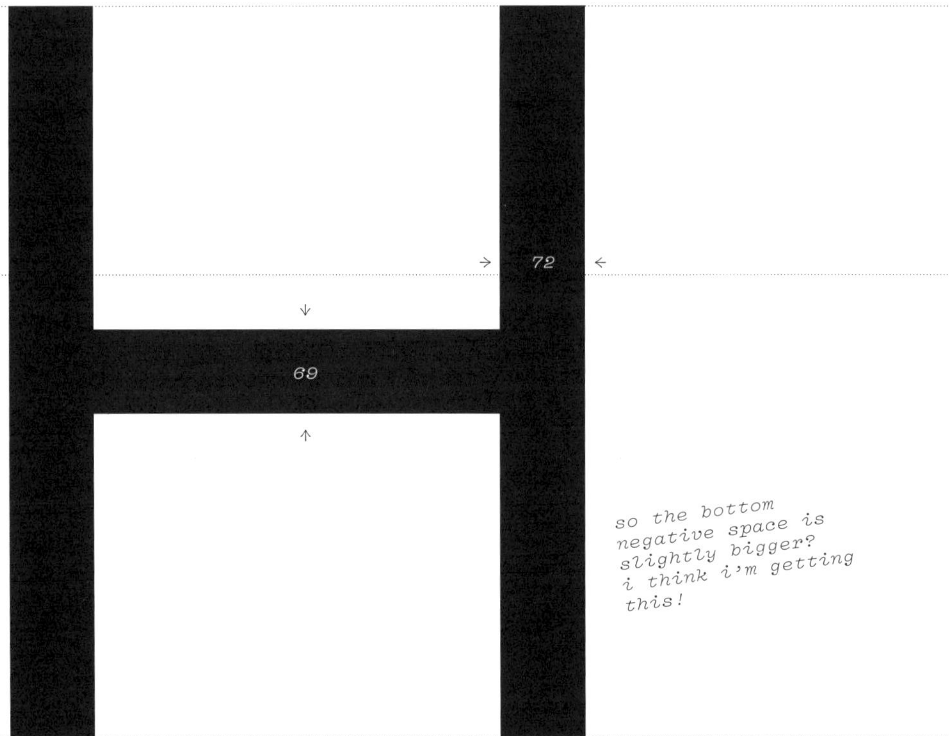

To the untrained eye, H is the definition of *remarkably unremarkable.*

Human eyes tend to perceive horizontals as *thicker than verticals.* Low-contrast designs worth their salt compensate for this by making horizontals slightly thinner.

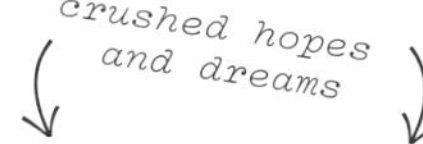

H is a controlling character!

a^2

b^2

a^2 + b^2

But the real beauty of H is how it defines spacing for the entire typeface.

If you want to figure out how much space to add before your next stem, you simply repeat the space inside of H.

see how many channels of negative space are similar in size?

so that's how you named the foundry? for spacing!?

what a nerd!!

HERS

OHno

I call this the Counterspace Equals Letterspace rule, and it's *powerful*. You find it all over the place. Script, blackletter, sans, serif, narrow, wide—this rule doesn't discriminate!

H is a control character, meaning that its characteristics define a lot of the design and spacing. Other control characters are O (for rounds), n (for straights in the lowercase), and o (for lowercase rounds).

h is just an n with an ascender, and we haven't gotten to n, so I won't ruin the dramatic conclusion!

REVIEW

- **Horizontals appear thicker than verticals.**
- **H can define your spacing.**
- **During high school, a bacterial infection spread through the local water park. It was called cryptosporidium and gave everyone uncontrollable diarrhea. Now, in every conversation and news story related to Bitcoin, I think of diarrhea.**

serifs do make it a little bit more interesting...

What is there that could possibly be interesting about this letter?

I is so devoid of character that you have to throw some serifs on it, in particular sans typefaces, just for legibility. It's the only letter that does this.

here's an I that is backslanted, extra bold, bottom-heavy, calligraphic, and reverse contrast with ink traps and exaggerated entry and exit strokes

Remember my rant against wild gs? If you want a wild typeface, make a wild I!

But I is significant as a building block. The reason is because the vertical stroke of I immediately echoes through a type system in a pretty gnarly way.

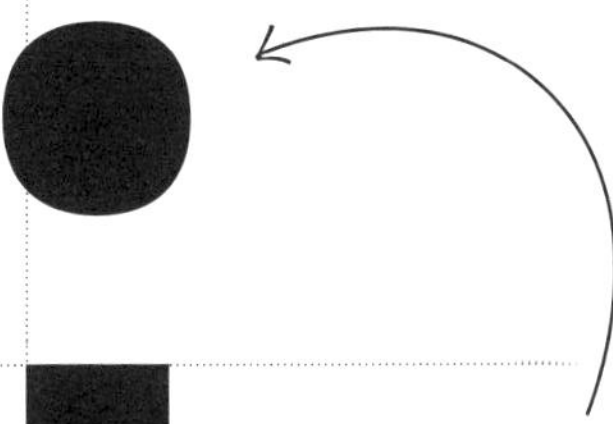

to make the dot appear the same weight as the stem, it actually overshoots

Lowercase `i` appears humble as well, but it functions as a building block just like its capital counterpart.

entry and exit strokes usually relate to the weight and length of serifs

In monospace typefaces (where each glyph occupies the same horizontal space), `i` has to really stretch out to fill the space.

poor m has to sacrifice a few serifs to fit the space, while i is chillin in first class

This is even more dramatic in italics, where there are no serifs, only entry and exit strokes.

REVIEW

- **If you want a weird design, make a bizarre `I` or `i` and let that modular piece ripple through the system.**
- **Listen, I like IPAs as much as the next person, but to be honest, I'm kinda over it. I'm moving on to drinking nothing but German wheat beers this summer. Prost!**

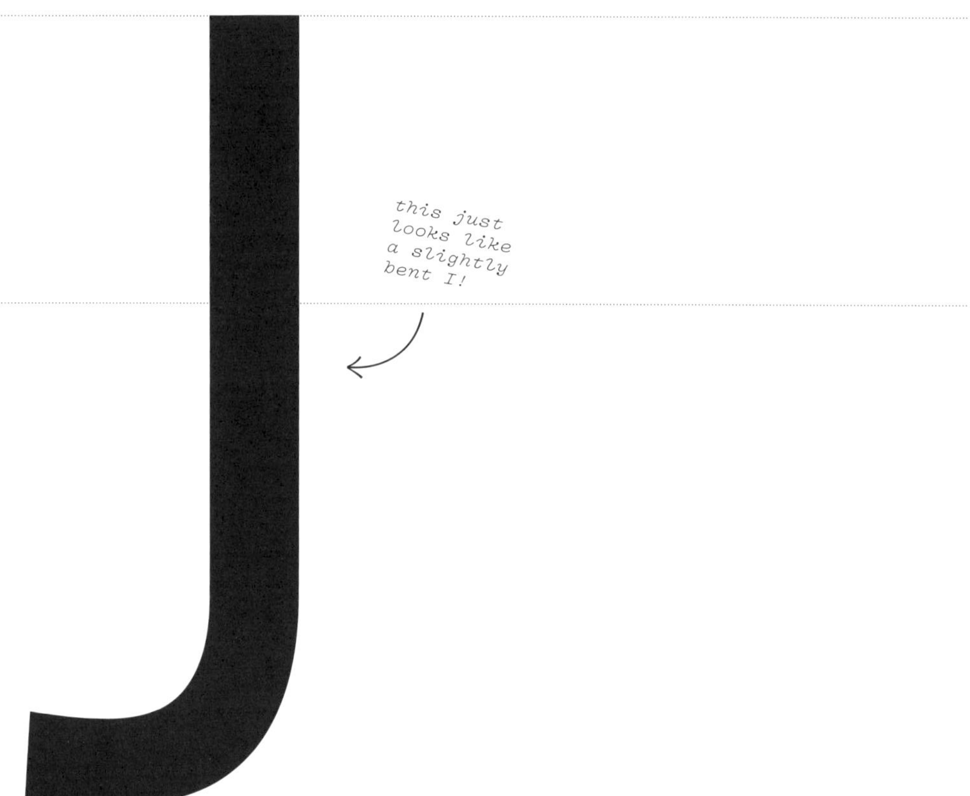

It's ridiculous that J qualifies as a letter.

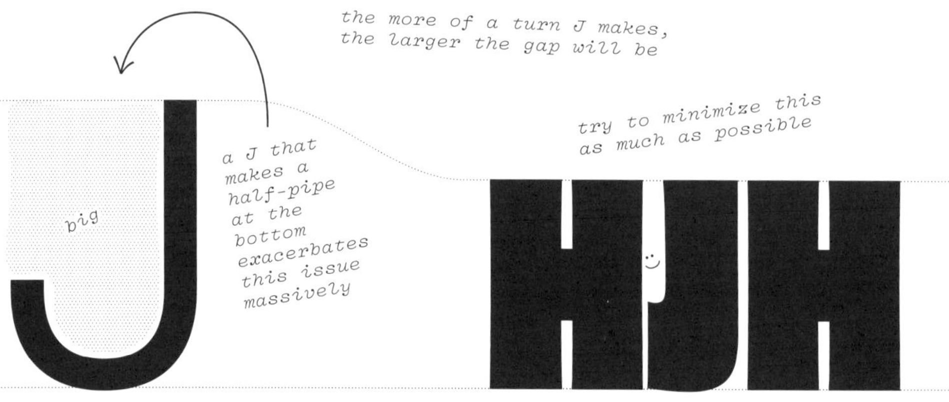

It's also annoying because it creates a large pocket of white space when it falls in the middle of a word.

It might not bother us in light styles, but when things get really bold, spacing needs to tighten up (Counterspace Equals Letterspace) and gaps stick out like a sore thumb.

The lowercase has the same issue. A quarter turn is all you need!

Sometimes, especially in translation designs, j curves even less than that!

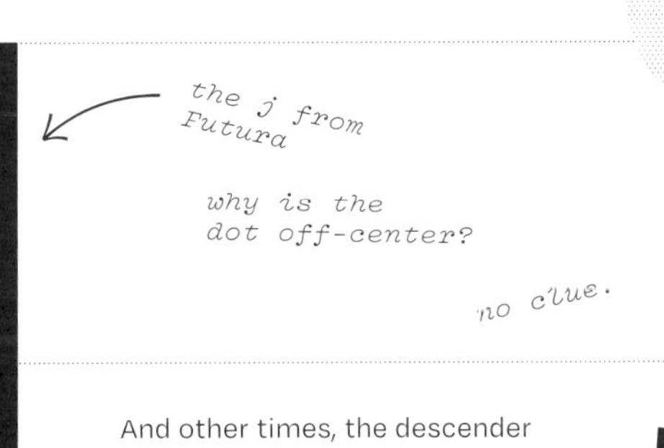

And other times, the descender on j doesn't even curve at all, and it remains perfectly legible in text.

So make your J and j a team player! Monospace J and j have space to fill, so those can go nuts (like in Vulf Mono). But for the most part, I think we should save our half-pipes for the X Games.

REVIEW

- **J and j only need a little turn.**
- **Spacing is the most important thing in type, and life in general.**
- **My daughter has just surpassed her father in intelligence and social awareness. She's two.**

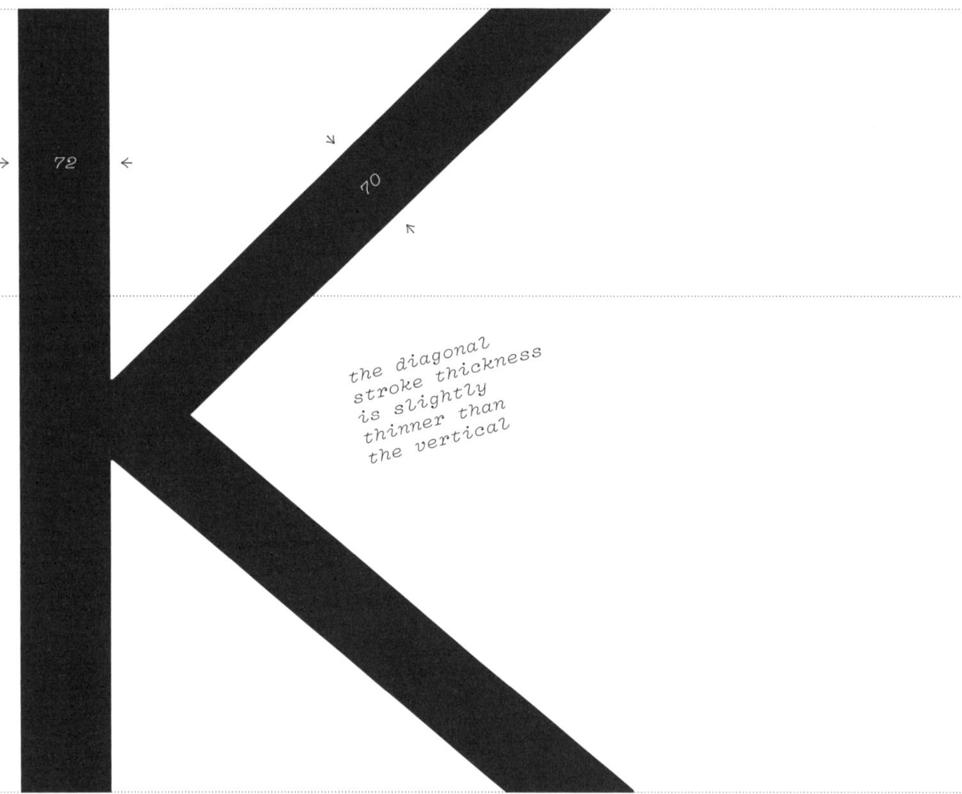

We already know that horizontals appear heavier than verticals. The same is true (albeit less so) for diagonals.

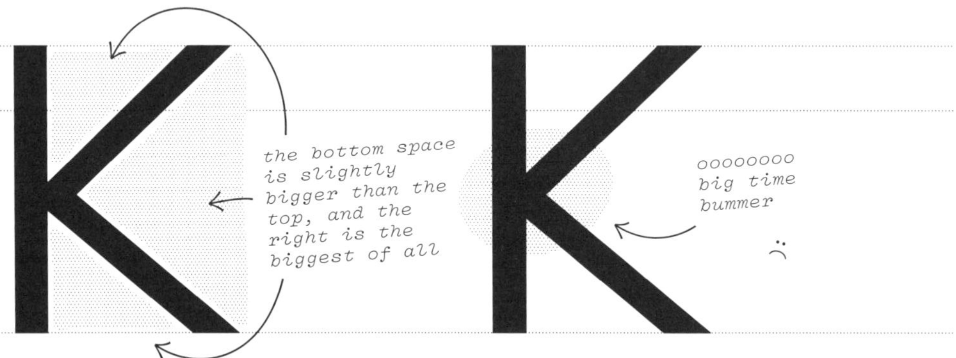

But the real secret to a successful K is the careful consideration of the three pockets of negative space.

If you're not careful about how the diagonals join, you could end up with a K that has a bulky joint and the negative spaces all out of whack.

here the waist was raised to minimize this area

the top diagonal doesn't even have to connect in some styles

In all sorts of styles, we look for a way to equalize the three negative spaces.

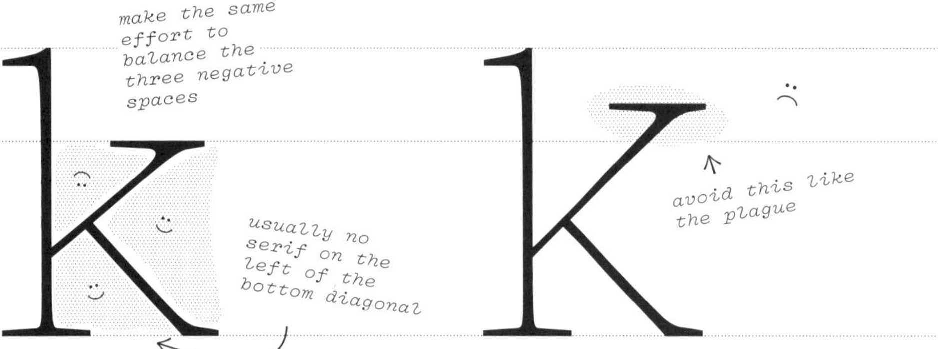

In the lowercase, k is very similar to K, but it has an ascender, and the right doesn't go beyond the x-height.

For some reason, it's extremely common for students to let k's top diagonal extend beyond the x-height. I have no clue why.

K is really tricky and can be extremely frustrating. Just like every glyph, attempting a bold version can help stress-test your solutions and refine your system. Now go work on a bold, k?

REVIEW

- **The secret that unlocks a good K and k is the careful consideration of negative space.**
- **The right of k lives within the x-height and doesn't ascend.**
- **Remember that life is a journey, and know how much I love you.**

but it gets worse!

voids like this are quicksand for eyeballs

L's huge negative space makes it a pain for spacing.

In TypeMedia, I learned that difficult combinations are not the *exception*; they should be treated like the *rule*.

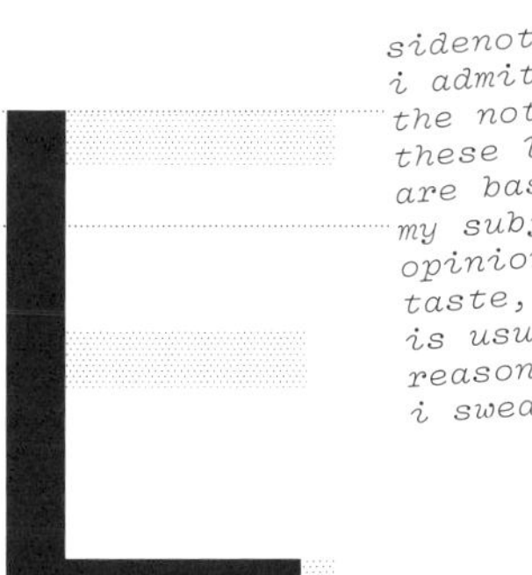

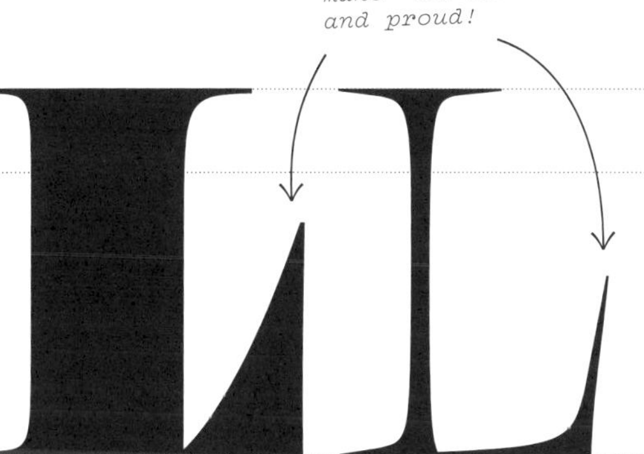

For this reason, an L that is relatively narrow creates the fewest spacing problems. L can get narrower than you might think without impacting legibility.

We can do a pretty gnarly job of filling the space if we have serifs to play with.

casual and fancy!

In script, the capitals have all sorts of options for how fancy they get, but the basic architecture remains the same.

effortlessly fancy!

l hkdb

l is essentially half a letter and ripples through the lowercase

In the lowercase, l's exotic form will blow your mind.

lhb

you can often use l as a component for ascenders, but not in this form, obvi!

Often, adding a curve at the baseline aids in the differentiation of I, l, and 1.

l1

and the slope of the flag can be quite different

In serif styles, l has a serif placement very similar to 1, so having a higher ascender than your figures helps out when writing down Wi-Fi passwords.

REVIEW

- **Try making an L that is a bit narrower than you might think.**
- **Differentiate your I, l, and 1.**
- **The Ernie Ball logotype is tied with the House Industries logotype for the greatest of all time.**

the grotesque:

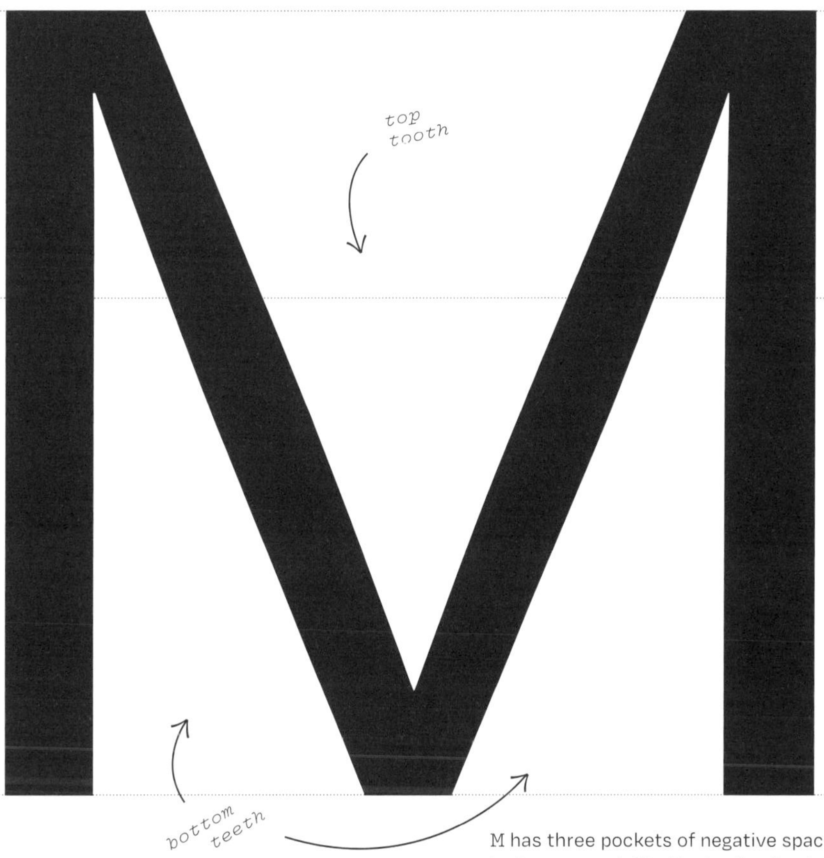

M has three pockets of negative space that look very much like the teeth of a vicious animal biting down.

the humanist:

see how the bottom teeth are the same height?

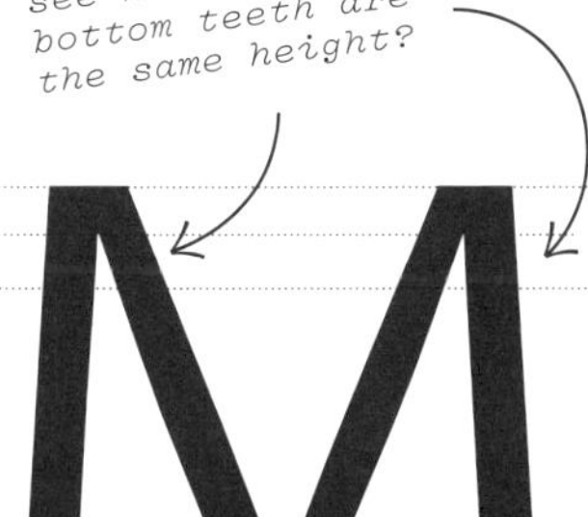

the geometric:

the two bottom teeth now touch, but they are still the same height!

In *humanist* designs, sometimes we see sloped stems. This helps balance out the sizes of the three teeth.

On occasion, in some *geometric* sans, the vertex in M doesn't hit the baseline. This is also the case in *monospace* styles because it allows for a more narrow form.

no serifs here (usually)

thin
thick
thin
thick

Keeping the bottom teeth the same height helps in pretty much every style. Also, the contrast goes thin, thick, thin, thick.

the stuff nightmares are made of

Sometimes, we see students pulling crazy-ass shit like this.

oh god make it stop!!

And other times, even crazier shit like this.

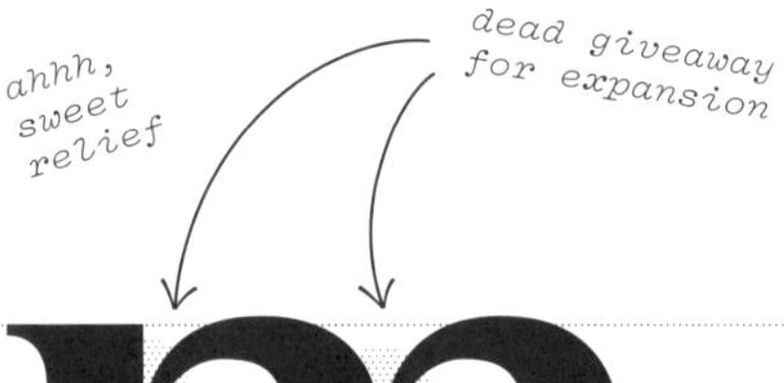

An *expansion* m has branches that grow vertically out of stems.

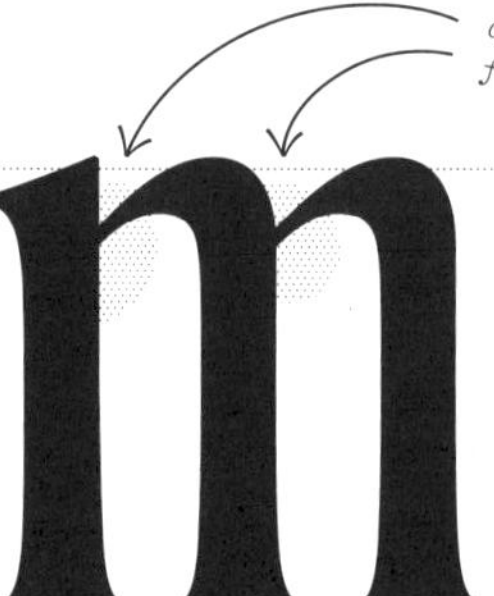

In *translation*, branches join in a more perpendicular fashion. When contrast models change, we see things like joints change, but the same rules apply.

Actually, even when everything changes, the rules still apply.

REVIEW

- **Make the bottom teeth the same height in M.**
- **In m, a middle stem that goes halfway, or any bonus serifs, are heartbreaking.**
- **Pop quiz! Is Beastly expansion or translation?**

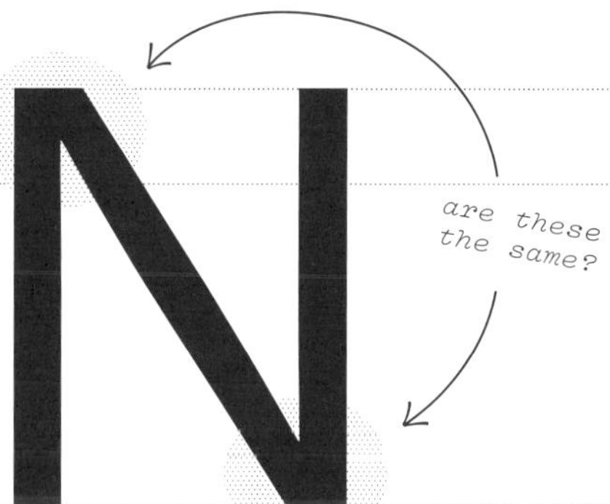

Even the most basic N has some interesting subtleties.

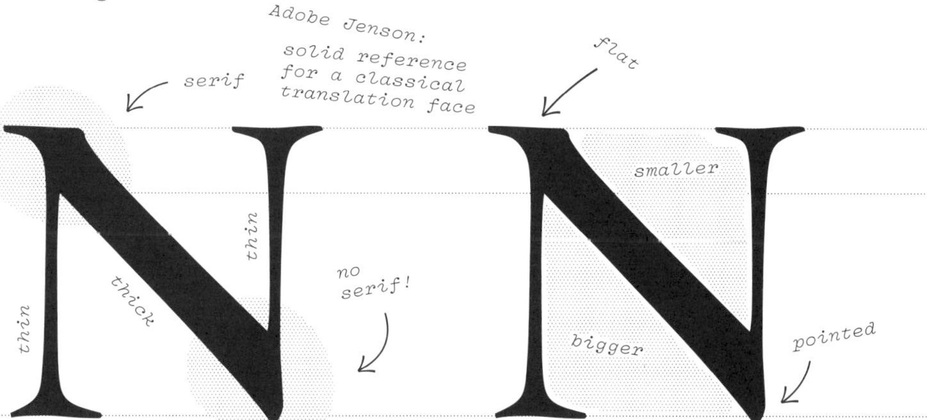

To answer that question, we have to go back in time! Taking a look at Jenson, we see some interesting details.

Also, check out how the construction makes a discrepancy in the size of the negative spaces.

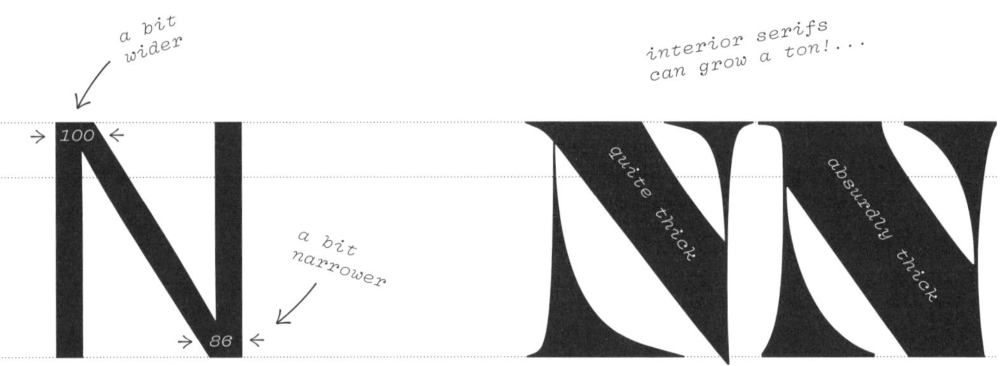

The same inconsistencies between the top and bottom joints occur in sans land, and again, it results in a slightly larger bottom negative space. This always makes a shape feel balanced.

In really heavy designs, I love making the serifs huge, so negative space is minimized.

but exterior serifs can't, as they push the surrounding letters away

and bold stuff has to be tight! because counterspace equals letterspace!

Now, we are on to the bedrock of type design: the lowercase n.

nn

n determines the spacing for the lowercase. In italics, the n is useful for even more letters than in romans.

ihmyujl

counterspace equals letterspace all day in italics

bpadqgrx

Just look at the ridiculous number of letters that share some anatomy with n. For this reason, some folks find italics easier for their first design.

just make sure the middle letter is optically in the middle

animal

But Counterspace Equals Letterspace fails often. When type is really light, without serifs, intended for huge sizes, or all of the above, we have to space tighter. That's when we use the Three at a Time rule.

REVIEW

- **The diagonal in N is heaviest, and the bottom space is bigger.**
- **n determines spacing, and much of the alphabet.**
- **Counterspace Equals Letterspace fails on occasion.**
- **French cleats are a fantastic storage system for garages and workshops. Flexible, adaptable, modular, and DIY.**

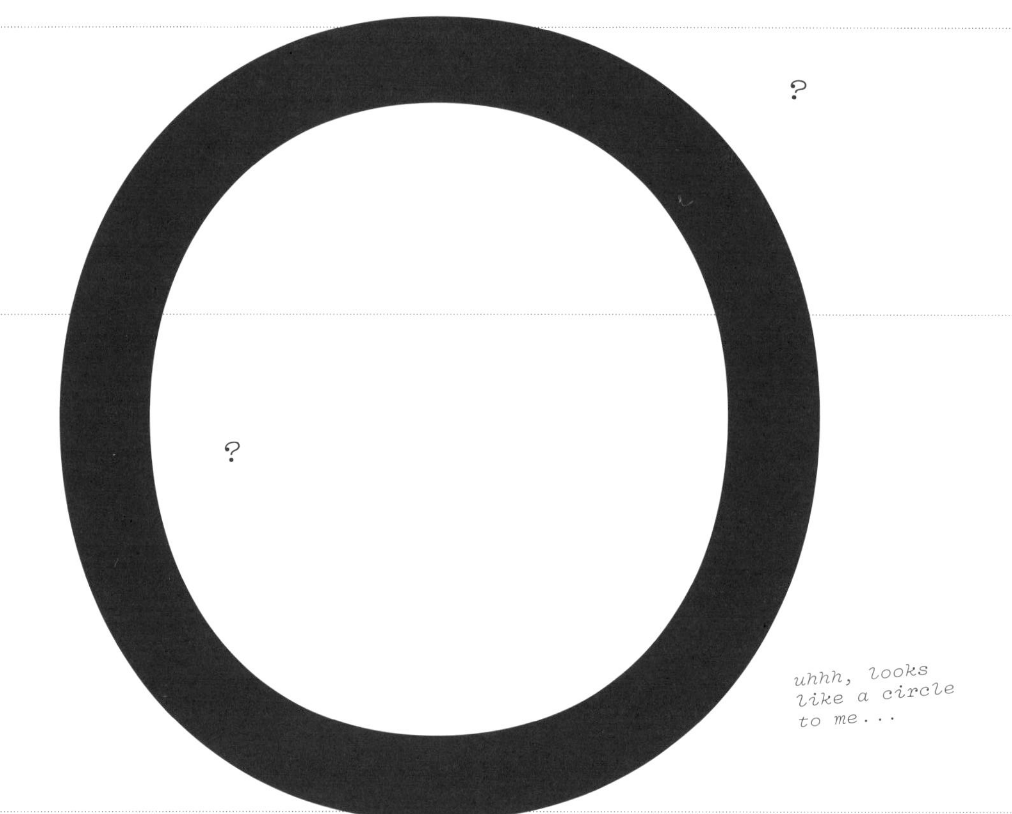

O is another control character, meaning it lays the foundation for the typeface's design and spacing. The first thing to notice about O is that it's not really a circle.

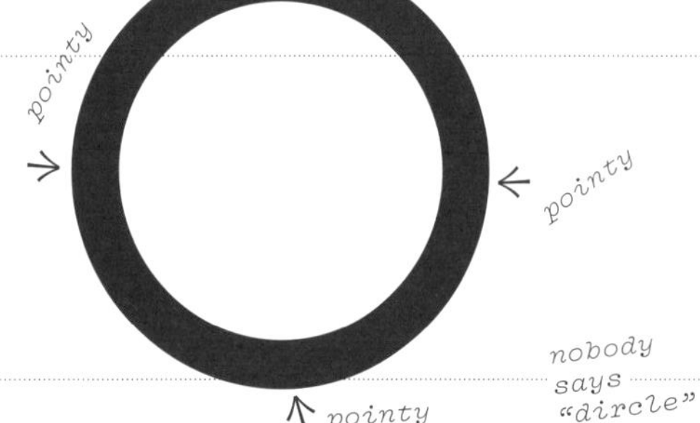

Here's an actual circle. Do you notice how it looks a bit pointy on the extremes? A bit like a *diamond* and a *circle* combined. A dircle.

Even the most "geometric" typefaces do a little optical adjustment to get the O to appear more round.

thin

thin

remember expansion? it's the contrast model based on the pointed pen

ah, just a quick rotation, then it's beer-thirty for me!

remember translation? it's the contrast model based on the broad nib

For *expansion*, the O is thinnest at 12:00 and 6:00.

And for *translation*, you might think you could simply rotate the counter to get your thins in the right spot, right?

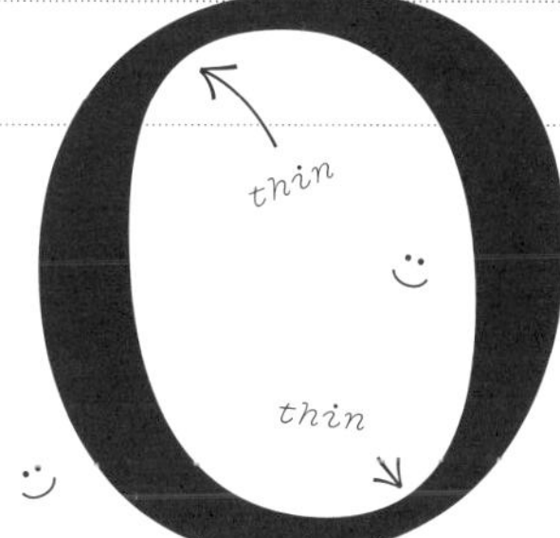

here's how translation actually works

Not so fast! That strategy, while getting the thins in the correct place, ignores the way the broad nib creates contrast.

lowercase isn't gonna blow any minds here

translation

expansion

Source Serif by Frank Grießhammer

But then you could say, "Um, I'm seeing a lot of typefaces that contain elements of both expansion and translation! What are these jabronis doin'?"

Here's a typeface that contains elements of both contrast models. It's called "transitional" or "hybrid," and really, it's nbd.

O is not just a letter; it's a building block that defines what all the round parts of your typeface will be, so take your time, and don't (bl)O it!

REVIEW

- **O is just a tiny bit more square than a circle.**
- **In expansion, the thinnest parts are at 12:00 and 6:00. In translation, the thin placement relates to the pen angle.**
- **I was recently spooked by a rat that presumably lives in my garage and is presumably also a freelance designer.**

The P seems simple enough, and it really is, pretty much.

P usually has a bigger bowl than R, because it has no leg occupying the bottom negative space.

The higher the waist of P, the more awkward it will appear next to letters like T and V that have large areas of negative space on the bottom left.

Using both of these moves to extreme degrees makes for funky-looking Ps, but they space much easier.

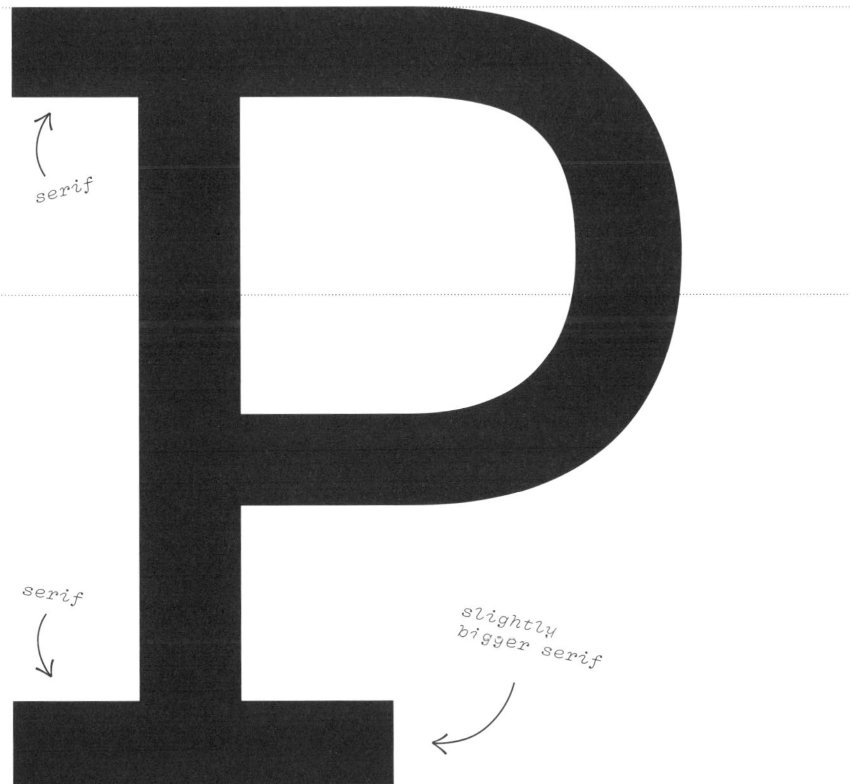

Because we have plenty of room for it, the bottom right serif on P can get pretty big.

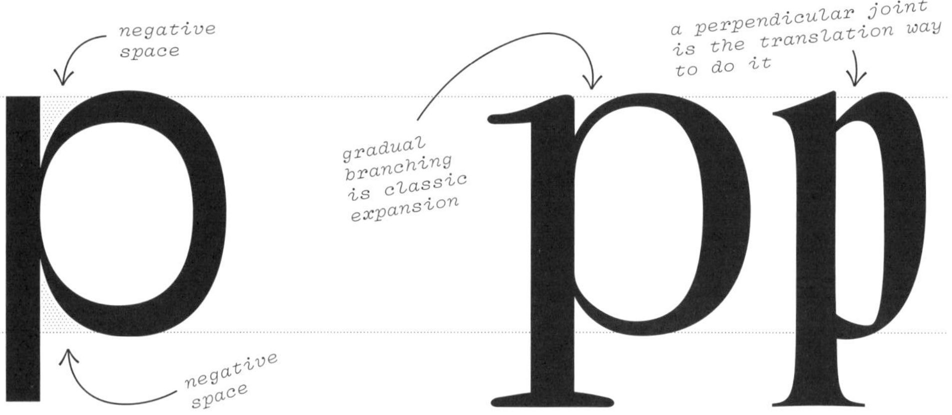

The lowercase p looks so similar to the uppercase, but the key differentiation is the way the bowl connects.

The bowl of p is vertically symmetrical in expansion, but translation shows a big difference top to bottom.

On occasion, in *translation* italic designs, we get to see this cool form of p with the stem overshooting the x-height, and an entry stroke leading into the bowl.

And in *expansion* italic, we sometimes see this lovely form that also features the overshooting stem. P and p are not so stale after all.

REVIEW

- **P relates strongly to R but has a bigger bowl.**
- **The construction of p depends on the contrast model.**
- **I bought 12 pairs of socks and feel like a totally new person.**

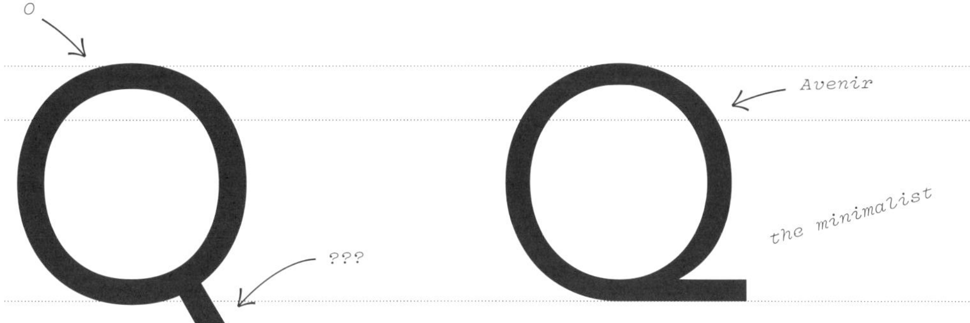

Q boils down to two components: the O and the diagonal/squiggle/swash/magnifying glass handle/tail/chingadero. Component 1 has limited options, but the options for component 2 are infinite.

It's amazing how you can put nearly anything in the bottom right and have no trouble reading the Q.

Trajan
the og

In English, the Q is almost always followed by a u, so you might think, "Well, I can just make that tail as long as I want! After all, it's insanely long in Trajan!"

Vulf Mono Italic
the show-off

Depending on how expressive the rest of the alphabet is, you can try some fun solutions.

Eames Century Modern by Erik van Blokland

But Trajan was designed without a lowercase, so there was no risk of the tail colliding with a descender. For most designs, a modest Q can still be quite attractive and legible.

it's just a d with the stem moved down!

q belongs to the bdpq group, and the *agbdpq* group in italic.

not too much going on up here

pretty basic

In serif land, the q usually has nothing on the top right, and a normal serif at the descender.

whoa, what the hell is this thing?

there are many variations on the umbrella form of q

Somewhere along the line, we must have been taught to make our qs like this. Maybe elementary school?

a boring q is a happy q

While it's a quaint form, it probably does more to distract and mess with spacing than aid legibility. So mind your ps and qs, and keep 'em boring.

REVIEW

- **However freakish or fancy your Q tail is, it should relate to the general concept of the family.**
- **Lowercase q has a normal descender. No need to get cray.**
- **I'm sorry to report I got pranked today.**

R's got
the look!

R has it all: a vertical, a round, a diagonal, and a certain je ne sais quoi that makes all letters want to be R, and all punctuation want to be with R.

R is similar to many letters like A, E, and H, in that we try to balance the size of the top and bottom negative spaces.

Sometimes we see this bummer version of R. I think it looks too close to B and too bold in the connection.

R

a little love goes a long way

(still slightly fugly tho...)

Miniscule edits to thin out the joint, and add a bit more diagonal, help tremendously.

R

usually no serif coming off the left of the diagonal

In most cases, there are four serifs on R.

Rat

In expansion, the bottom right serif can turn into an exit stroke that relates to a and t.

r

to paraphrase Erik van Blokland, all r has to do is not be i

Similar to j, f, and others, r's curve only needs to make a quarter turn! This can help spacing *a lot*.

except in monospace, the leaky faucet r is easily avoided

r

this jumbo pocket of negative space will create uneven texture in words

I had some tough teachers in school who would draw water droplets coming out of r with this form. Their critique was indelibly scorched in my mind.

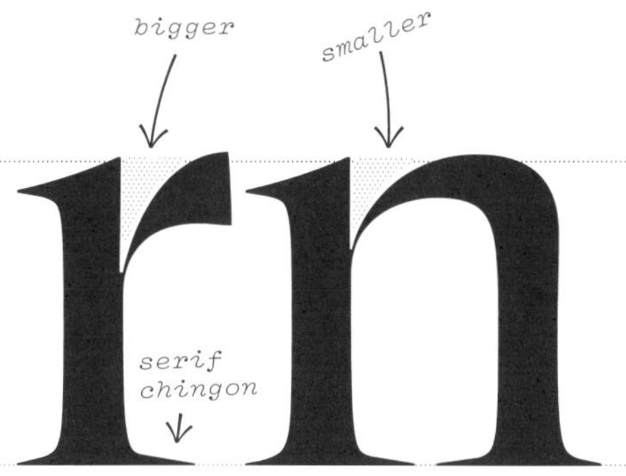

Comparing these two, it's easy to see how the r is derived from n, so I always make my n first.

REVIEW

- **Make your R proud to be an R!**
- **Make your r narrow but still proud to be an r.**
- **Ignore me and form your own opinions whenever you want.**

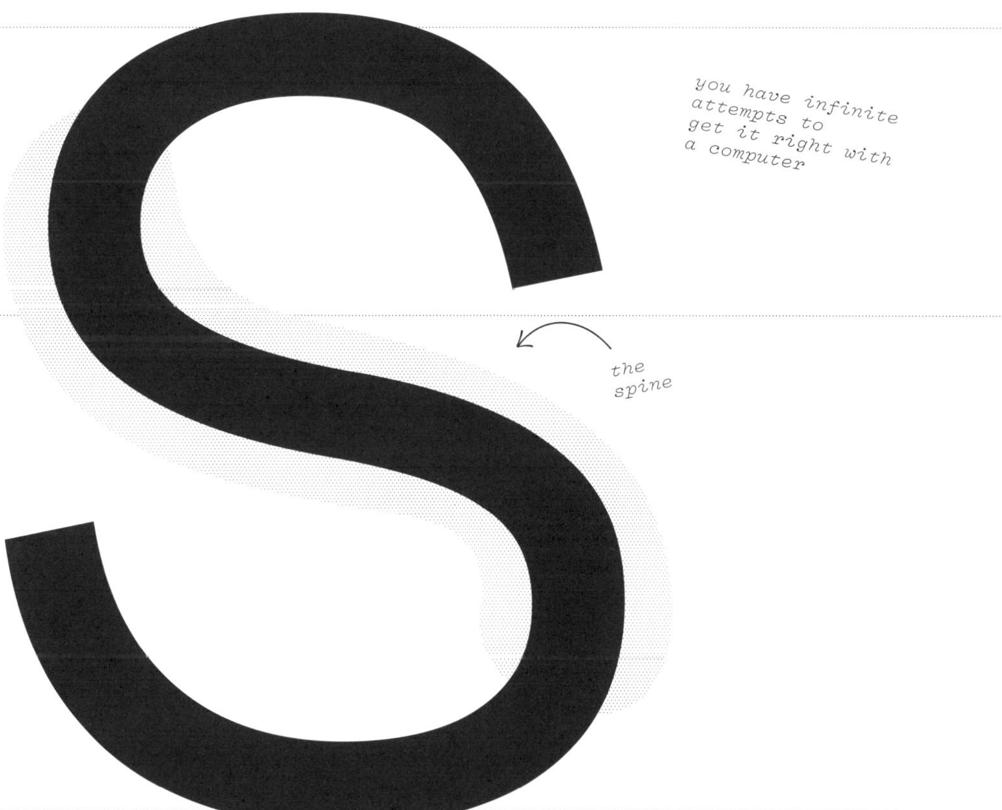

It has been said that a sign painter might only really nail one or two Ss in their entire career. That's why I wholeheartedly prefer the extremely low-risk, low-stakes, and low-fumes world of type!

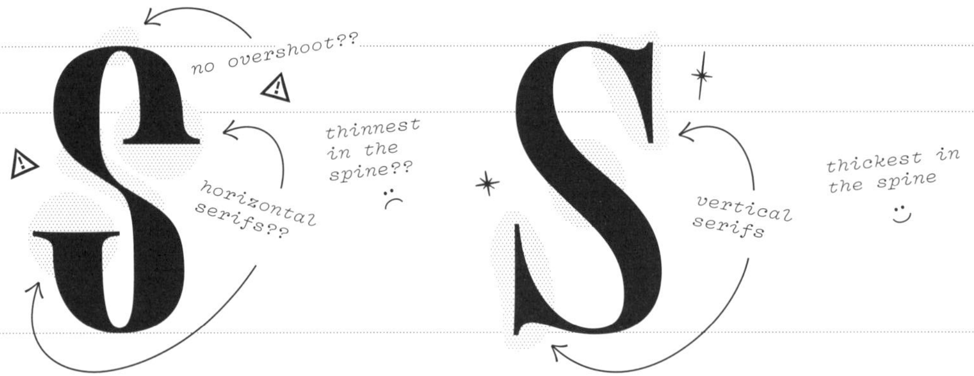

Here's an S that is *really* blowing it.

And now here's that same S with those issues resolved.

Here are two rule-breaking Ss with a thin spine. They get away with it because they are *reverse contrast*.

scge

CGScagesyª
23569?$£€¢§

two options for terminals in Obviously

scge

CGScagesyª
23569?$£€¢§

As we've previously mentioned, S's terminals echo through many of the letters.

And now that I think about it, it's a feature that goes way beyond just that.

When drawing the s, make sure you flip it backward, upside down, and back again, while you measure and evaluate in context.

Lots of times, especially in italics, the lowercase s has different terminals than the uppercase. I could talk all day about S/s, but that's good for now.

REVIEW

- S and s are almost always thickest in the middle of the spine.
- Flip an S/s in every direction while you draw.
- My dream car is a 2013 Toyota Sienna with under 50,000 on the odometer.

T is another letter like A, V, Y, and L where legibility depends on huge pockets of negative space on the outsides of the shape.

This is particularly problematic when trying to achieve tight spacing, for instance in a super bold design.

"difficult combinations should be treated as the rule, not as the exception."

—Erik van Blokland

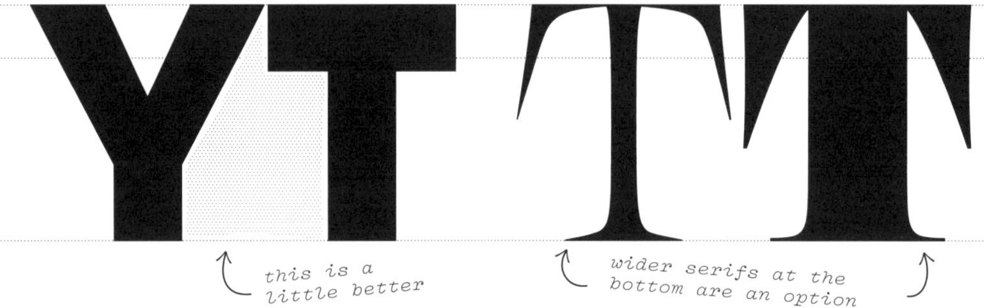

All we can do is make T a little narrower. The above quote from Erik van Blokland blew my mind when I heard it, and it is some of the best and most succinct advice on spacing out there.

For the serifed T, you can make those top vertical serifs quite big. They do a good job of filling in space!

Now it's time to address one of the most common mistakes among all students of type and lettering.

bht

this looks like a small deal, but it matters a lot

seriously.

no joking!

The top of t isn't a normal ascender; it is much shorter.

ta

crossbar

in some sans styles you can get away with the "jesus t"

ttt

serif *script* *sans*

The serifed version of t doesn't even have serifs! And look how short it can be. Wow, that's short.

In almost every style, the *crossbar* hangs from the top of the *x-height*.

Here's a big idea: Whenever you're not sure about the conventions in a particular contrast model, just *check out some references*. You aren't stealing — you're building upon hundreds of years of history.

REVIEW

- **Tricky pairs are the rule, not the exception to the rule.**
- **t is shorter and has no serif up on top.**
- **I always try to cover each letter in seven diagrams, and it always takes nine.**

U is so simple, what could possibly go wrong?

I don't have to even tell you the most common mistake found on U. It rears its ugly head on hand-lettered sandwich boards the world over.

?

?

verticals are thick, U has two verticals, so they're both thick, right?

The notorious double-thick U. It is as prevalent as it is hideous. It will never die—only regenerate in a slightly different form.

Hundreds of years of tradition say that (in typefaces with normal contrast) the right side of U is treated as a thin.

a true g!

Respecting that tradition aids in legibility, as most folks have been reading Us with contrast their whole lives.

In some classical designs, uppercase U takes a form very similar to the lowercase. We even see this on the Trajan Column.

this one's crazy!

In sans land, the u is just an upside-down n. Isn't that crazy?

these shapes relate

But in the serif form, we see that u is no longer an upside-down n.

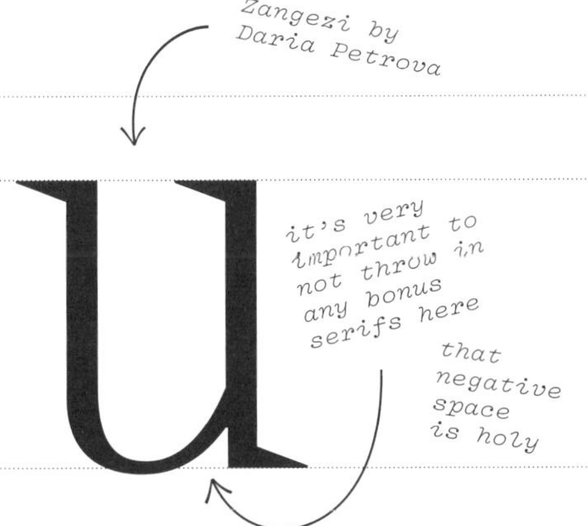

That's all I feel compelled to say about u. It is a humble little creature. Respect it, and it will respect u.

REVIEW

- **Uppercase U is usually thick on the left and thin on the right.**
- **u is an upside-down n in sans, but slightly different in serifs.**
- **Loretta was obsessed with *Frozen*, then *Frozen 2*, then *Coco*, and now *Trolls*. I think all four are fantastic cinematic achievements.**

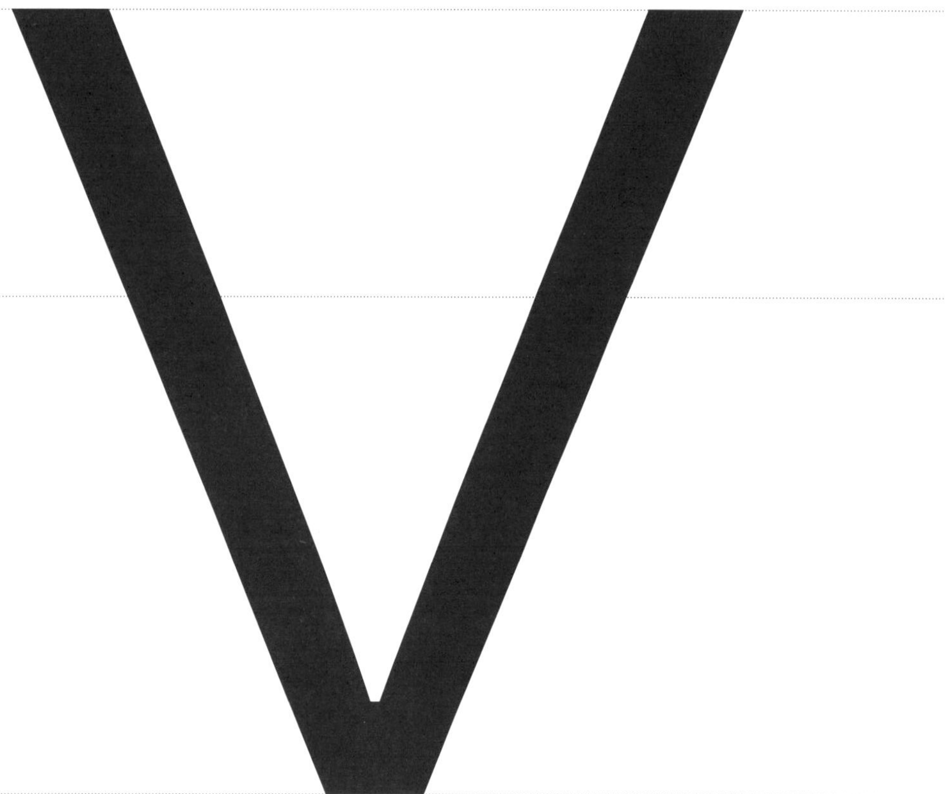

What could we say about an upside-down A without a crossbar?

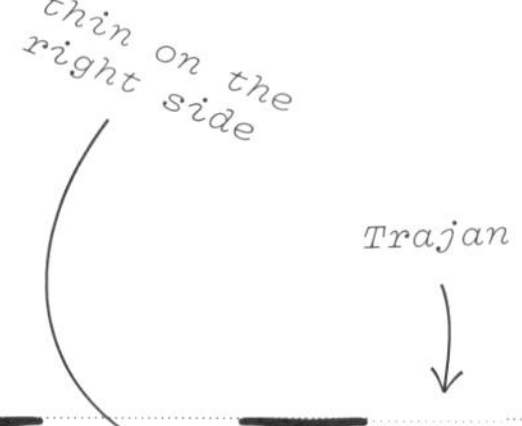

Well, it's not always an upside-down A. V doesn't have serifs on the bottom, or *vertex*.

Historically, V had some large exterior serifs, and the interior ones were a bit smaller. Trajan lets these shapes overlap. I say why not?!

I can get carried away with the opposite strategy: making the interior serifs huge and the exterior serifs tiny. This allows for tighter spacing while maintaining *drama*.

ooo fancy!

For the script V, the entry stroke relates to the one used in a lot of other places.

The lowercase v is a scaled-down version. So easy.

REVIEW

- **V has no serif on the bottom.**
- **The script V uses some existing anatomy: copy/paste!**
- **In five years of teaching workshops and classes, there have been almost zero jerks. People who want to learn about type and lettering are 99.9% chill.**

there is a V in the background for comparison

Let's face it, the W should be called a "double-V." That's what it looks like, and that's how it is built.

At its most basic form, we see even in a serif (in this case slab) version, the form is made up of two *narrow* Vs.

Sometimes the two Vs overlap in a more dramatic fashion.

When you need to make the most narrow W possible (for instance, in a monospace), you can make the apex quite short.

Messer by Inga Plönnigs

why no overshoot? probably because the serifs here are closer together, thus clearly defining the x-height

more vertical
more angle
more angle
more vertical

If any part of the W is pointy, overshoots help to maintain optical alignment.

In order to make W/w space a little nicer, we can make the outside strokes a bit more vertical, and the inside strokes at more of an angle.

And if all else fails, just throw your I into the blender and see what happens!

REVIEW

- **The W is two Vs.**
- **There are lots of options, but none of them includes serifs at the bottom.**
- **Today I bought my dream car. Do you remember what it is?**

Sometimes, the simplest things can be the most complicated.

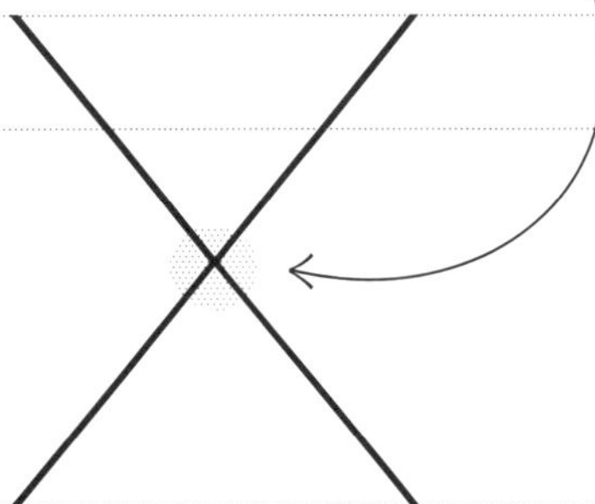

One would expect that X is constructed from two intersecting diagonals.

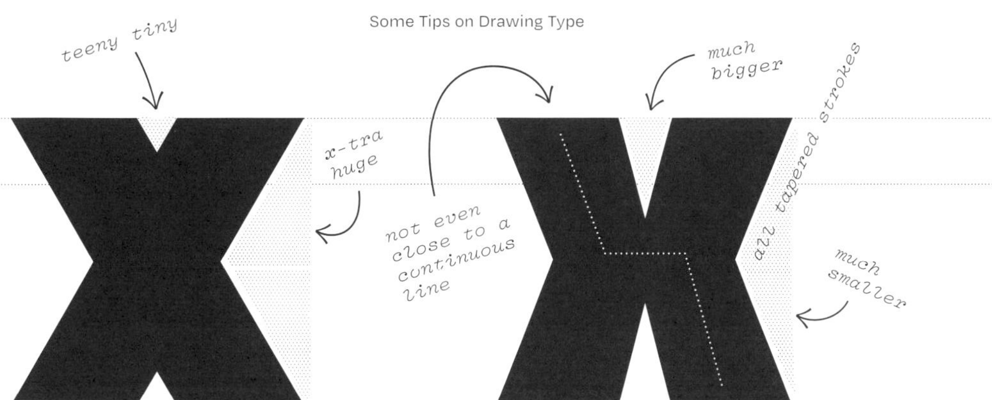

But if that's our only move, a bold X begins to look fugly very quickly.

Call it "cheating," "trickery," "black magic," or "witchcraft." The point is we have to do some interesting moves to balance the sizes of the *top/bottom* and *left/right* negative spaces.

all these moves are in the name of equalizing the four negative spaces in X

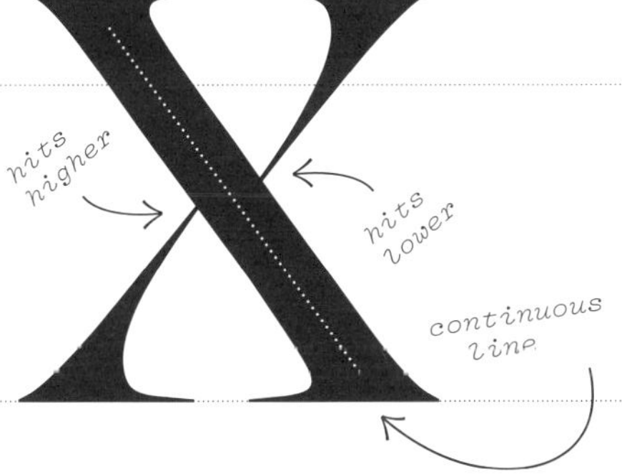

In high-contrast designs, the main diagonal might need a continuous throughline, but in that case, we can offset the other diagonals.

Whenever drawing really bold slab shapes, I just draw the serifs first and worry about how they'll all connect later. This is especially helpful on X.

Lucky for us, lowercase x is just a scaled-down version of the capital.

The *translation* x can have top right and bottom left terminals that relate to the r and s, etc.

Eames Century Modern
by Erik van Blokland

xrs

This is also true for *expansion*, but the italic expansion *x* can take one of the coolest forms out there and remain perfectly legible.

REVIEW

- X is only as simple as two lines intersecting each other in really light styles.
- Cheating, or bending the rules of geometry in favor of optical harmony, is the name of the game.
- I can't stop watching my CNC cut things, which negates all the time saved by having a robot do the work.

Y is simply a V that hopped on top of an I in some sort of typography-based cheerleading scenario.

When the joint (or crotch? sorry) of Y hits right in the middle, the letter appears a little high-waisted.

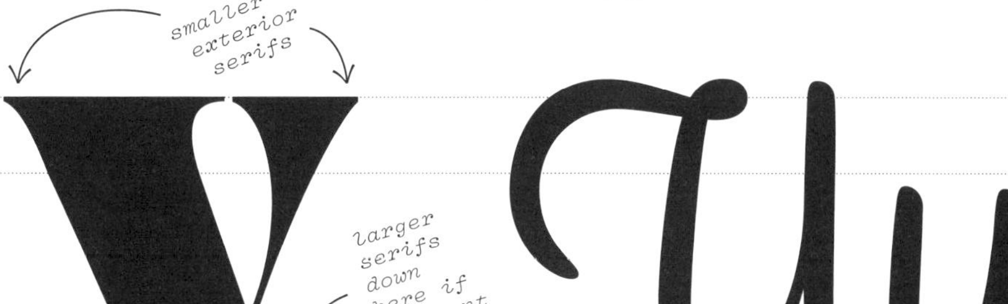

When we get very bold, we can drop that joint even lower! In fact, we have no choice.

For the script Y, the form relates to the lowercase italic form.

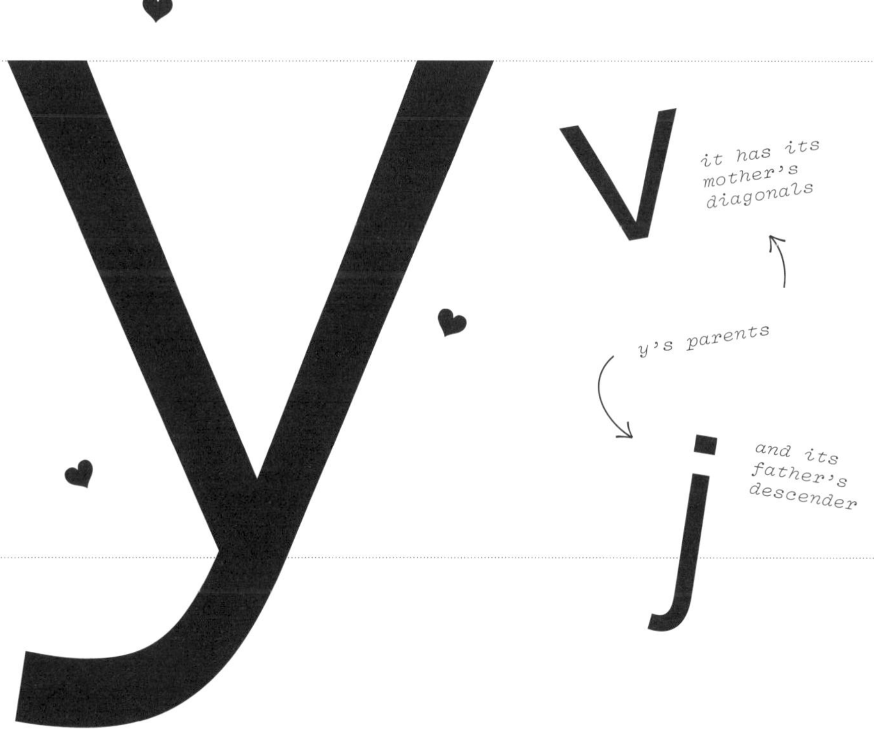

Lowercase is a bit like a v and a j made sweet, sweet love, conceived, and gave birth to a y.

this part doesn't have to hit the baseline!

But often, for italics, lowercase y is more like u and j.

Actually, italic y takes all sorts of crazy forms. Cooper Black Italic relates a lot to what Garamond does. This is type design in a nutshell—an understanding of the classics gives you a framework to play a new game on top of it.

REVIEW

- **Y is similar to a V and I, and y is similar to a v and j, or u and j.**
- **Referencing classics is always a nice idea, even for the crazy new things that might appear to be unrelated.**

getting the weight of this diagonal right takes time

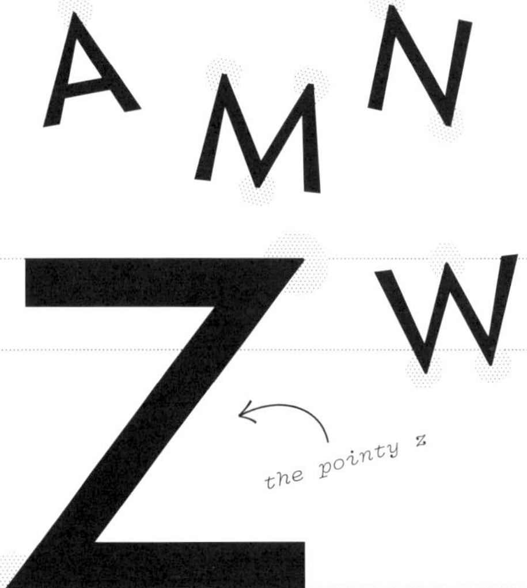

Z is last in the alphabet, and it's also the letter I usually design last—perhaps because diagonals are tricky and annoying.

In some geometric and certain humanist designs, the Z can get pointy. It would probably match some other points, and we don't usually see this in grotesque sans.

The serif Z has perfect pockets of negative space for the serifs to grow to extreme, dastardly lengths. These space fillers help especially in bold designs.

But don't let my bias toward hefty serifs sway your personal taste. Just look at these little chunkers by Graham. They fit perfectly with the rest of the players and are quite cute.

In sans designs, the lowercase z is just a scaled-down version of the capital.

Messer by
Inga Plönnigs

heavy
horizontals

light
diagonal

Eames Century Modern
by Erik van Blokland

This part is crazy: The lowercase z occasionally takes an unexpected reverse-contrast form. This is actually closer to what the pen creates naturally.

But the italic z for expansion serifs gets one of the most delightful forms in the entire alphabet. We can see how it relates to the bottom of 2.

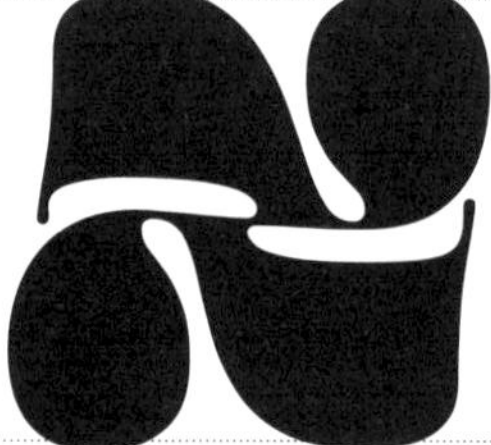

Often I get the question "What's your favorite letter to design?" That's tricky to answer. Roman or italic? Bold or light? Expansion or translation? At this point, the person who asked is no longer remotely interested.

Next time, I'll just say "lowercase italic z." That's probably a nerdy and verbose response, but it's truly an awesome form, fun to draw, and challenging to solve. Uppercase still sucks tho.

REVIEW

- **Take your time when figuring out the weight of the diagonal of Z.**
- **Lowercase z has many more interesting options than you might think.**
- **I sharted on the first day of high school.**

CONGRATS! YOU MADE IT

You have survived 26 letters, about 200 diagrams, and even more stupid jokes. I'll get around to the numbers and punctuation (accented glyphs? dingbats?) someday, but for now, maybe it's nice to do a quick review of the whole thing.

HAVE SOME REFERENCE

With hundreds of years of type history to rely on, there are probably some typefaces that are both well-drawn by a legit type designer and similar enough to your design that you can steal some ideas in a healthy way.

ATTEMPT MULTIPLE VERSIONS

For every successful glyph, there are at least a few iterations that weren't quite as successful. Testing out variations in context is the only way to declare a real winner.

HAVE A GOOD TIME

If you're ever hating the *initial* sketching and drawing of a typeface, maybe a little soul-searching is in order. Do you have a solid concept? Or are there too many good ideas floating around? The beginning should be fun. If you're hating the last 10-50% of *finishing* a typeface, good! You're supposed to!

Acknowledgments

Sadie. Your unwavering love and support mean the world to me. Everything that I've been able to do with Ohno has been because of you. You are the greatest partner and mother to our children that I could ever ask for. I love you more every day.

Mom and Pop. It might have been an accident, but you gave me exactly what I needed to grow up: huge pockets of uninterrupted time. Thank you for the LEGO sets, musical instruments, home-cooked meals, and five remarkable brothers. The debt we owe our parents we pay to our children. Hope you're cool with that!

Mark. I always say that you are my finance brother. But the truth is, you've taught me more about the value of time than anything else. I'm forever grateful for your kindness and generosity. But I'm even more grateful for Monique's babysitting.

Paul. You gave me my first design job and paid for a huge portion of art school. I can never thank you enough for that. You've inspired me to take risks and work hard. I forgive you for all the times you tricked me into looking for a hole in your pants.

Alex. When I was nineteen, you offered me a room in San Francisco for a very generous (to you) rate. I loved that time because I got to know you as an adult and friend, not just an older brother. I have always admired your writing, sense of humor, and over-the-top aesthetic sensibilities. Thank you for being you!

Cameron. There are too many things to thank you for. All of the Christmas presents where you stoked me out beyond belief. The encouragement to explore any and every creative field. To be your producer so you could be the ideas man. I am beyond grateful to be your brother, and even if I wasn't, I'd still be your friend for life.

Georgie. You died two years ago this week. I think about you all the time. Thank you for always making me feel like all I needed was to be more like myself. You were one of a kind. It's not your fault the world wasn't suited for you.

My Family. Monique, Robin, Lauren, Audrey, Tracy, Mom (Telly), Auntie Baby, Lauren, Lou, Allen, Wowie, Choy, Auntie Vian, Uncle Andy. Nephews and nieces Georgia, Julia, Lila, William, Lauren, Clark, Simone, Kira, Alina, Jonah, Cece, Kaleb, Gwen, Koda, Ollie, and Marlowe.

Ohno Team. Infinite gratitude to Jamie Otelsberg, Lynn Barber, and Colin Ford. You have ushered us into the next era, and I'm so happy to be a hard-ass boss!

KABK. Teachers Erik van Blokland, Paul van der Laan, Peter Verheul, Peter Biľak, Françoise Berserik, Jan Willem Stas (RIP). Classmates Mark Frömberg, Hugo Marucco, David Chmela, Sláva Jevčinová (aka Slavie Slaverson), Mark De Winne, and Nina Stössinger.

CCA. Rod Cavazos, Bob Aufuldish, Christopher Simmons, Brett MacFadden, Scott Thorpe, Angie Wang (!), Mark Fox, Michael Vanderbyl, Dennis Crowe, Backwards Man (RIP), Steven Skov Holt (RIP), Mara Skov Holt, Emily McVarish, Jon Sueda, and Eric Heiman.

Friends. Marty Grasser, Jim Parkinson, Nick Sherman, Eric Duke, Connor Davis, Ricky Odbert, Old Skool Rob, Dana Moore, Matt Kingstreet, Juanito Olivarria, Ian Webb, Matt Cantrell, Erik Marinovich, Kel Troughton, Tommi Sharp, Tad Wagner, Tânia Raposo, Frank Grießhammer, Nina Stössinger, Indra Kupferschmid, Rob Stenson, Jack Stratton, Christian Schwartz, Jeremy Mickel, Ken Barber, Travis Kochel, Lizy Gershenzon, Gen Ramírez, Zrinka Buljabasič, Sandrine Nugue, Julien Priez, Jérémy Landes, Corinne Ang, Ari Remoundakis, Camille Sibucao, Christopher Slye, Sam Berlow, Debi Sementelli, Ondrej Jób, David Jonathan Ross, Ben Kiel, Gustavo Ferreira, Frederik Berlaen, Loïc Sander, Maria Doreuli, and Tal Leming.

Finally, thank you to everyone who has bought a license for our fonts, told a friend about us, reshared the stuff we post on social media, or supported us in any way. I am forever grateful.

James Edmondson
San Jose, California
September 2024

James Edmondson studied graphic design at California College of the Arts and type design at the Royal Academy of Arts in The Hague, Netherlands. With his comrades at OH no Type Co., he creates custom and retail typefaces. In 2018, James cofounded Future Fonts, a platform for distributing fonts in progress. James has taught type design programs all over the world and resides with his family in San Jose, California, aka the Valley of Heart's Delight. @ohnotypeco